The Creative Epiphany

Visit www.booksurge.com to order additional copies.

JO ANN BROWN-SCOTT

THE CREATIVE EPIPHANY

GIFTED MINDS, GRAND REALIZATIONS

2008

The Creative Epiphany

TABLE OF CONTENTS

Following that realization he reveals the ways he has reinvented himself, making sense of the pieces of his life's puzzle while following his bliss.

This Book Is Dedicated
To
Tom, Kelly And Jason

There Is A Fountain Of Youth:
It Is Your Mind, Your Talents,
The Creativity You Bring To Your Life
And The Lives Of People You Love.
When You Learn To Tap This Source,
You Will Truly Have Defeated Age.
Sophia Loren

INTRODUCTION

After compiling the first book, *Epiphany and Her Friends—Intuitive Realizations That Have Changed Women's Lives*, it occurred to me immediately that one book about epiphanies was not enough. I had leftover questions that still needed investigating. Most of my own epiphanies have been related to my continual questioning about what my purpose is on this earth. Perhaps you have felt the same...has your life purpose been revealed to you? Was it delivered to you in a startling epiphany? How receptive were you to that profound information?

An epiphany can come to anyone at any time, regardless of your age, IQ, emotional intelligence, education, religious beliefs or financial circumstances—intuitive breakthroughs and discoveries do not discriminate. If you have received an epiphany of any kind, you are listening to your inner voice and you understand the advantages of having that dedicated guide because it has provided you with valuable information in living your life. An epiphany is always without distraction, without fail, on *your* side. Its wisdom is focused upon you; its truth is your truth.

This voice has probably been in touch with you from time to time affirming the ways in which you are gifted and creative—and *everyone* is gifted and creative in some ways, and at different things. (Few people are gifted and creative at most things or in most categories.) Creativity's various manifestations have always fascinated me. I have experienced epiphanies related to my creativity that have opened my mind to possibilities I had never considered until the candle was lit in the deep recesses of my being. And I am certainly not alone. Down through history, remarkable achievements have been born in the minds of people during the moment of having a brilliant creative epiphany.

A creative epiphany brings discovery, illumination or new understanding to your creative endeavors. It often provides a tidbit of vital information or an intuitive realization, delivered with a high degree of life-changing power and strength that enables you to more clearly define and utilize your special gifts of creativity. It is a knowing. It is a message from your most pure and noble inner voice—your soul—your higher self. This soul voice has no agenda other than your well-being and balance. If you have received an epiphany of the creative sort—the kind that brings a joyous leap forward for you in your creative goals—you are one of epiphany's creative friends. If you are yet to receive some pivotal information and guidance and would like to know just exactly what to listen for, read on and you will learn to recognize an epiphany when it happens.

You creative ones vibrate with excitement at the birth of a new idea. You are the vehicles who facilitate the initial breath of the unexpressed; the few who see possibilities, while others dwell unconsciously in the blinding glare of the obvious, closed off to their potential. You know Creativity very well—you walk with her, you talk with her and you dwell with her—you are the few among many who understand her strength and magnetism. You might be creative in many directions, you might be especially creative in just one or two areas, or you might be creative in simply making life choices that bring spectacular results. But you know with certitude that you and your creativity are an inseparable, winning combination.

You are, in fact, Creativity personified, without whom risk would have no companion. But the risks are worth the rewards.

Creativity finds solutions, she improves, she invents, she re-invents herself; she does not resist the paradigm shift. She shocks; she awes. Creativity keeps close company with Epiphany, Inspiration, Imagination, Eccentricity, Expression, Awareness, Beauty, Passion and Honesty. Unfortunately, Loneliness, Self-doubt, and Criticism try to get their six big feet in Creativity's door to spoil the party of the joyful spirits. And Depression hides outside in the shadows.

Epiphany, however, will always be Creativity's best friend, her illumination, her guardian angel, her candle in the darkness. Epiphany always brings news. Creativity must keep an open mind for Epiphany's message—so she lives in the now, receptive and eager for that special visitor. She listens for her, she watches for her, she can feel the vibration of her impending arrival whether by a thunderous, earthquake shifting of thought or as subtle information, delivered like the slightest flutter of a butterfly's wing, discernable amid worldly chaos. When Epiphany arrives, you know it. She has no substitute—she is never mistaken for anyone but herself. All the other crazy voices in your head step aside to facilitate her entrance. She brings full body chills to Creativity.

Creativity dwells in our soul and travels through our hearts and our minds. She enters from the open door of the universe carrying free samples of *Inspiration*. She gets you out of bed in the morning; she calls for your attention. She sings the music of ideas. She chants mantras of encouragement. She meditates while performing humble rituals. She is the reason for wondering. She challenges you to do more—to continue at your work, your hobby, your garden, your learning, your love of life—and to discover your authentic calling.

Imagination differs from Creativity. He—Imagination—is a bit elusive and arrives in daydreams and wishes. Past a certain age he visits less frequently and never stays long. On the other hand, you can detect Creativity in an infant's widened eyes and once she establishes herself in that fresh new soul, you know she is there for the long haul. She shows up early and stays late. Creativity is a force to be reckoned with—moody, impulsive, invigorating, inspiring, stunningly beautiful and hard to channel in just one direction. She is hungry for constant stimulation, but well worth the effort of cultivation. Imagination, though enigmatic and whimsical, is a little on the lazy side by comparison.

A certain aura of multi-colored *Eccentricity* swirls around Creativity, like an enchanted, inseparable lover who compliments and enhances Creativity's every move. Because of their romantic symbiosis, Creativity performs better and has learned to dress fancifully just for the amusement of her lover, Eccentricity—one long striped sock, one short solid. Orange upon aubergine, texture over texture, pattern paired with plaid. The turquoise jewelry and alligator cowboy boots combined defiantly with a gray, three-piece pin-striped suit worn by the rumple-haired artist at his one-man show. The gifted star-athlete who designs his own line of fabulous and affordable shoes. The three-year-old ballerina who prefers to wear her sequined tutu upside down, fluff pointing skyward. Intricate, flowery embroidery on a pure white, immaculately pressed Mexican wedding shirt worn by the sun-tanned, chiseled man with the cerulean blue eyes who is finding good homes for puppies frolicking in the back of his van. Hats of every conceivable style. Hair that is hardly ever tamed the same way twice in one week. Tattoos not just on rock stars but proudly displayed on skinny arms of elegant women who lunch at The Palm; the parade of indigenous tribal patterns in the robes worn by Ethiopian women. These are clues of the presence of Creativity and the love of her life, Eccentricity (who also answers to the nicknames Incongruity, Contrast and Contradiction).

Creativity weaves her conversation with bright red ribbons of slang, silver Baroque description, yellow mixed-metaphor, black primal simplicity and home-made hot pink words of her own invention. She loves the sound of the spoken word and the sung lyric. The final arrangement of printed words on paper is thrilling to her. Creativity travels on the back of *Expression.* Printer's ink, paint and pencil, Adobe Photo Shop, music, silk thread, bronze and clay, glass and stone and wood and film and theater and food. The designer of software that changes an industry, the producer of special effects, the dancer who analyzes architectural plans in her day job and mountain bikes on weekends, the Indiana Jones global adventurer who documents his climbs with technical drawings of places where no man has climbed before and writes stories of his hair-raising experiences, the handsome Harley rider who appreciates fine linen, wine and the pleasures of a long walk in the woods, the teacher who performs five live shows a day in her classroom, the fishing guide who knows the waters, the salesperson who closes the deal with a flourish and a drop dead smile, and the carefully nurtured children of a free-spirited expressive mother are just a few of Creativity's expressive media.

Creativity is often lost in depths of thought as she calculates her next surprise. Creativity prides herself on *Awareness* and yet she is nearly run down by cars, close to walking off piers, as she contemplates the play of color, light and sound displayed in the distance before her. Perhaps she finds herself sitting alone at the gate to her flight, everyone else on board and the door closed, while she has been absorbed in a thought or a book or a person across the terminal whose body language she finds fascinating to watch. Many of Creativity's ideas hide in rumination before they are revealed to the waiting world. They hibernate. She is aware of the potential shock value in releasing them. But she is also aware of perfect timing, and when she believes the ideas are fully formed, Creativity knows the sweaty labor of birthing them one after another in litters, without benefit of midwifery or painkillers. Then she feels the anxiety of waiting for the reviews of her unique offspring. She agonizes; she hopes for acceptance and applause, but if the reviews are dismal she rationalizes that she has been misunderstood and that she must be ahead of her time. She knows that her time will come; Creativity is one gutsy broad; she perseveres.

Creativity is on constant sensory over-load. She believes life is full of *Beauty*, but Beauty is highly subjective and Creativity finds it in unconventional places. What turns others off might attract Creativity. She defines Beauty for herself. She gulps in the beautiful stimuli of life from first breath, mentally sorting them into categories for later use—the eloquent, over-heard conversation she will use in her novel, the certain shade of bittersweet observed in a fruit that is perfect for the half-finished painting, the tune some passerby is humming that sparks a breakthrough in a song being composed, the arrangement of shapes in a window display that inspires the architectural drawing. Every sight and sound and smell and thought is beautiful in its own way, including faces and places others might never choose to photograph or paint.

Creativity is wildly, deeply *Passionate*—she is easily bored; impatient with the "norm." But at the same time it is difficult to be bored because life is too full to completely comprehend, and even thinly sliced nuances of mind-numbing "normality" are put to use somehow in the creation of some freshly approached "thing" about to explode from its creative confinement. Creativity has learned how to milk even the boredom and put it to work for her. Creativity builds "Ellen DeGeneres" types of comedic monologues around the most mundane, neurotic observations, and people fall out of their chairs laughing. Artists paint nothing but pebbles and suddenly you are re-fascinated with them.

But because Creativity is so Passionate in her beliefs and her interests, she is stunned to silent disbelief by people who can't name their favorite color, flower, book, food, film, charity or trip. She wakes up passionate. She loves to tell stories. She dances alone in her kitchen. She will still savor the smell of new crayons when she is sixty-five…well, probably even eighty-five. She has a passion for people of character—she sees it in a well-weathered face—where wisdom can be read, line by line. Her idea of ugliness is the unbending mind that cannot be enlightened, the greedy hand, the violent act and the ungrateful takers. She adopts causes—she champions what she believes in. She sides with the oppressed. The days of her life are never long enough for the doing.

Close on the heels of Passion is *Honesty*. Creativity is brutally honest—she is sometimes blunt to the point of being rude. She values truth. She will not be denied. She calls it as she sees it, and she is hardest on herself, because in addition to being honest with other people she must be honest with herself and true to her talent. Creativity will not be suppressed without a fight. She cannot fake life—she must do what she must do without substitution. The actor at heart who has been told to put a lid on it and do something practical will always wish he had acted. The closet adventurer who stays home and just watches TV, the writer who will not find time to write, the musician who denies his classical gift and decides to write advertising jingles instead, the career Banker who yearns to own a winery—all represent creativity denied. And when she is denied her finest endeavor—her greatest calling—her authentic, shining moment in time—Creativity has a fit. A full-blown temper tantrum. Heads roll. It can be loud and rebellious or quiet, profound depression, but frustration takes its toll on Creativity. That being said, Creativity herself is sometimes at fault by not being entirely candid about her own worth; too humble for her own good and in denial of her fine full potential. During denial is when epiphany is most likely to appear.

Creativity does have a down-side. After all, she is only human, isn't she? She has ongoing relationship issues with *Loneliness, Self-Doubt and Criticism.* You have heard the expression, "There goes an egomaniac with an inferiority complex." Bingo. She does not always play well with others. She has problems fitting in. In spite of her flamboyant, life-of-the-party behavior, she can be quite shy. She sometimes leads a solitary life, fleeting in and out of thought incessantly at odd hours of the day and night and then disappearing for months at a time, completely off the radar. Creativity finds it painful to be taken for granted and does not ever come when she is sternly summoned. Even being labeled "creative" is a heavy load to carry through life. People expect a lot of Creativity. And she tires easily. Sometimes she burns herself up in a colorful flame-out. Then there is *Depression*...circling around Creativity's camp like a hyena waiting for pieces of flesh, steadfastly marking his territory. Creativity is sometimes deeply fearful. She is plagued with insecurity. She has foot-stomping anger management issues. She hates criticism and feels tricked when it is called "creative criticism." She is easily offended. But after a dry spell she appears again, rested and giving, ready for some fresh endeavor because she says, smiling, that she was missing you. To make up for her absence and undependability, Creativity takes you on serendipitous journeys you had never dreamed of taking. She shows you the world in one blink of her exotic eye.

***

Does the definition of Creativity imply a certain degree of neurotic behavior? Who decides what is weird and what is creative? Are they one and the same?

Have you ever wanted to drop everything, run off and join the circus? Seriously now, perhaps even leave for a deserted island, taking care to pack your plein air portable paint box and your cell phone but allowing time to stop at the bead shop for wire and clasps on your way to the airport? Have you considered joining the Peace Corps, against all advice from those who know you well and think that idea incongruous with your life of excess? Are you still inclined to wear your lucky jeans (the ones you wore for five solid days in the mud at Woodstock, and are now so old that they are nearly rotted) at times when you might need them? Do you fail to see the value in EVER acting your age? Have you felt like not just a square peg trying to fit in a round hole but the one person who could invent a much better game than putting pegs in holes? Is your idea of pure torture getting up early every morning to drag your body to a nine to five job to work in a nine to five cubicle, wearing your nine to five cubicle dress-code clothes that do not allow for high-top sneakers? Do you have a difficult time finding the perfect card in the greeting card aisle so you buy two and put the front of one with the inside of another? Is it nearly impossible for you to follow a recipe without adding a twist or three of your own? Do you have a business card for each of your hobbies so that perhaps a couple of them will miraculously become profitable pursuits?

Do you sometimes feel that the crazy way you see things is truly a sickness? Do you sometimes wish you could dial it down a bit and look at the world in simpler terms, so your mind can get a rest? Do you sometimes wish you could turn off your constant *need* to paint? Or your *need* to write about every observation you have about life every single day all the time? Or your *need* to constantly re-invent and search for a new system or software or gizmo or better way of doing every single little thing? Or that you could *stop* searching for new physical challenges or places to see in the world? Or that you could *switch off* the re-decorate-house-button in your mind so you can get some sleep?

Or maybe you are so severely demented that you just need to stop doing all of the above *concurrently*…in your forty-eight hours of free time on the weekends or during the brief vacation time you have saved up from your dreary day job in your cubicle of life.

But no...you don't really want to stop any of this "sickness" because it is what makes you breathe deeply and want to live long. You gulp it in. You are a creative genius. Everyone knows you are a gifted person. So at your dreary day job, when the committee gets bogged down and can no longer find direction, when too many cooks spoil the broth, when the planners and the movers and the shakers are all slumped deep into their leather chairs from a lack of inspiration, they send someone out the door to find you and your rolodex of brilliant solutions. You have a reputation for being "a bit of an oddball" who could turn out to "be somebody" if you would only "apply yourself and focus." But that does not necessarily mean you want to rise to the top of the corporate ladder—you might rather go home and paint.

But then what if you have dumped the day job and chosen to do *only* what you love and the money has not necessarily followed? In your life's journey, looking for the niche where you might fit, have you discovered that your niche does not yet exist? Have you found that you must have a back-up occupation so you can support yourself while you take the leftover hours of your life to invent your own damn niche since no one else has ever figured it out for you in any of the aptitude tests you have completed over the years? Has any aptitude test ever encouraged you to continue painting or singing or writing or dancing or making jewelry?

As we navigate life there are many opportunities that smack us squarely in the face and some that barely brush against us while we are distracted and busy squeezing along with the zillion other grains of sand through the hourglass of our days and nights. But creative people pay more attention to that subtle brush against our minds—that first bud of an idea—that hidden potential in the smallest situation. They see possibility in nearly everything, and it can be daunting and it can be exhausting for them and those around them. Their imaginations constantly running away from them with gleeful abandon at breakneck speed, waving prayer flags of exotic colors in seventeen directions at once. The upside is that seeing so many possibilities in fresh perspective every day is indeed invigorating and often does provide a selection of innovative, life-changing ideas that excel and rise to the top like pure cream, just by the law of averages. Selecting those creamy, worthy ideas to follow outside the shuffle of the idea crowd is the challenge. Having an abundance of ideas is never a bad thing; choosing the best ones to pursue is the trick.

"For every nine people who denounce innovation, only one will encourage it...For every nine people who do things the way they have always been done, only one will ever wonder if there is a better way. For every nine people who stand in line in front of a locked building, only one will ever come around and check the back door. Our progress as a species rests squarely on the shoulders of that tenth person. The nine are satisfied with things they are told are valuable. Person ten determines for himself what has value." Za Rinpoche and Ashley Nebelsieck, in *The Backdoor To Enlightenment, Eight Steps To Living Your Dreams and Changing Your World*

Being the tenth person is a heavy load. Gifted and creative people often have a difficult time acknowledging, living peacefully with and trusting their own uniquely inherited talents. They are usually multi-talented, with dozens of ideas streaming across the "high-def" screen of their minds in a moving sort of neon, pulsating display of enticing, seemingly impractical options for making contributions to humanity. Creative people are intelligent and driven—they *must* fulfill their compulsive need for expression because the world needs them. But to focus on just one aspect of their talent is like being less than a whole person. They see ways of tweaking their creative choices. Then they see the tweaked alternatives as offering newer, more complex possibilities and soon the entire exercise in career selection or life direction has become so out of the real world that it seems impossible to take even one step forward. It is so limiting to have to choose just one or two plain-vanilla avenues toward success. That seems too simple, too lazy and not enough.

How does the creative person keep the craziness at bay? How does one still the rattle of the different drumbeats that we supposedly march to in order to hear the quiet rhythm that matters? Stilling the creative mind for brief times is critical to hearing the one inner voice that offers honest direction. Clearing the mind of clutter is everything—it is the only thing that invites epiphany. Even in the midst of a chaotic situation, epiphany must find a still path to be heard. Nurturing a peaceful time of quiet nothingness on a regular basis is the best way to listen to your higher self, your soul, and receive a focused message of epiphany. A clean mind-canvas is the foundation that allows creativity to find its path and make its first brave mark of color that begins a life composition. Becoming practiced at clearing your mind and hearing your inner stirrings in these incubation times is the key.

Personally I find that the phenomenon called creativity steels into my mind most easily in the blackness of night, riding on the strength of a good night's sleep, and opens my eyes in the morning to the confetti colors of life all fresh and new with possibility, and I am seeing wakefulness again but as if for the first time. It was an epiphany for me to realize that my particular brand of creativity does not thrive on chaos and sleepless anxiety. It thrives on a healthy life-style and a foundation of order and calm. Let us be honest about what is effective for us and what is not. Let us not get caught up in traditional hype—let us disprove the notion that we are addicts and drunks and that we live lives of sloth except for one or two accidental, fleeting but brilliant moments when we create.

Some would argue that our greatest creative minds have been weak of character; dysfunctional, flawed personality types who use and abuse. Yet Michelangelo and Van Gogh were tortured souls who created masterpieces in spite of extreme personal discomfort and during historically chaotic times. Does this demonstrate little regard for the guidance of the inner voice? Or does it actually demonstrate a laser-like focus on the creative effort supported by the steadfast guidance of a higher self? These creative geniuses were in constant battle with the negative influences and agonizing realities of life literally doing laps around them. Still they managed to rise above the madness, with assistance from their unwavering inner conviction that their work was on a higher plane and perhaps even divinely inspired. The strength of that inner voice was certainly tapped into, guiding the artist past enormous earthly noise. This ability to follow an illuminating inner compass allowed the genius soul of the artist to triumph over distraction and live on forever through work that was aligned perfectly with the purpose of that artist and his universe during his particularly shining, rarified point in history.

You, whatever type of creative being that you are, have perhaps had the experience of feeling uncomfortable accepting all the credit and praise for your own fine achievements. Quite honestly, you might feel you were a mere vehicle for the expression of your greatest creative ideas—you were just the means for giving them life. They happened *to you* rather than *by you*. You feel that some of your finest work and your most original ideas were effortless and not entirely of your own mind—so "involuntarily" accomplished that they seemed to flow through you from somewhere above you as if your actions were being orchestrated by some far more gifted conductor. You felt like a puppet channeling gifts from beyond, strings attached, arms flying in all the right directions.

If you are an artist who can tap into this "flow" of creativity it is more a surprise to you than anyone else that your best work is born through the strokes of your own paintbrush. In fact, it is difficult for you to remember how the process unfolded, because initially this experience was beyond common understanding and unlike anything that had ever happened to you, the creative person, when it first occurred. It was of course your work, it was your style, it was your time and effort; it was your paint and your canvas and it was done in your studio space, but the inspiration was so obviously not of this world and the result so much better than your own mere earthly thoughts could have planned to achieve. When this happens, as the work is progressing, the hours fly by, energy does not wane, the steps taken toward completion are automatic and effortless; this level of inspired work is achieved in far less time than other paintings labored over for weeks. And yet it results in your most inspired work; it is the work of your soul in sync with the universe.

Ken Robinson, in his brilliant book about creativity titled *Out Of Our Minds, Learning To Be Creative*, says on page 154:

"Creative processes draw from all areas of human consciousness. They are not strictly logical nor are they wholly emotional. The reason why creativity often proceeds by intuitive leaps is precisely that it draws from areas of mind and consciousness that are not wholly regulated by rational thought."

On page 155 he continues:

"The term 'flow' has been used to describe peak performances. These are times when we are immersed in something that completely engages our creative capabilities and draws equally from our knowledge, feelings and intuitive powers. These peak performances typically occur when someone is working in their element at the peak of their performance. In this respect, creativity involves particular attitudes and being able to access deep personal resources. There is a further factor, which is difficult to describe. Perhaps the best word for this is passion."

This magic happens in other creative endeavors besides art—musicians such as Sting speak about having no remembrance of how a particularly brilliant song was written or truly understanding the profound meaning of his own lyrics until years later...inventors suddenly *know* what must be adjusted for the efficiency of their revolutionary new whiz-bang idea.

An epiphany can arrive in a sudden shudder of realization, or a slow unfolding of obscure information that forms a finished puzzle as it reveals itself in your mind. It can arrive via an inner voice from your soul that is most assuredly audible in your mind's ear as it offers you instant advice or a fast solution to a problem just when you need it. Something seemingly unrelated, unsophisticated and of humble origin might trigger the breakthrough of epiphany required for your missing solution to be heard. Epiphanies come in many costumes. They are not proud; whatever type of energy carries them along is just fine for their purposes. Because whether they arrive in elegant style with pomp and circumstance or in the most common of events, they always bring discovery and illumination, as if a light bulb was suddenly turned on, clearing the shadows of our mind. Epiphany is always offering a previously over-looked solution or a startling jolt of new information or a missing ingredient essential to your creative process thereby clarifying your understanding about something you urgently needed to know. Epiphany always knows what information to bring to you if you will listen.

I believe this alignment with the universe, when a brilliant message of creative realization is received and then executed by an aware mind, is a CREATIVE EPIPHANY.

Being in tune with your creativity and your universe and being present in the moment is the key to having an experience where the epiphany discovery is channeled through you into your creation. Your creation might *simply be a creative way of living your life in general that feels divinely directed through a series of eye-opening epiphanies.* An epiphany is an "other-worldly," magical, spiritual experience where a message of truth and discovery from the universe is delivered directly to you. It can and does happen repeatedly. It must have happened to Michelangelo on a sustained basis when he painted the Sistine Chapel. He lived totally in the moment and was constantly, miraculously provided with solutions to each of his creative problems just when he needed them most and was at the point when his mind was open to receive them. He knew how to dwell in the now; he waited faithfully for the information to be provided to him when he required it, instead of leaping ahead and worrying about the future before he was ready for it. So much can happen in an hour—a day—a week. I believe that the truth will be revealed when you need it most. It will find you.

Most assuredly a creative epiphany can happen to any person who realizes that creativity flows first from the soul of the intuitive human being before it is indicated in any tangible worldly achievement. You do not have to be traditionally religious. You need only believe that we each have an individual place in the universe where we can be an integral part of the greater good and make a positive contribution. Your calling will come to you.

"A calling is a deep sense that your very being is implicated in what you do. You feel that you fit into the scheme of things when you do this work. You have a sense of purpose and completion in the work. It defines you and gives you an essential tranquility. The work that provides such a deep reward may change over time, and you may go through several periods in your life defined by a different work. Toward the end of your life you may see all the jobs you have done as fateful, composing your life work and answering your calling." Thomas Moore in *A Life At Work: The Joy Of Discovering What You Were Born To Do.*

***

We will begin by talking about initial indications of giftedness and creative genius and what we can do to foster its further development in our children and grandchildren. Then let us tell you some stories of how creative epiphanies have enlightened a selection of extraordinarily gifted men and women. Waking up to your purpose in life is the challenge of every human being on the planet. The decision you must make in order to align yourself with the energy you require for fulfillment; and the confidence you need to achieve the success of being a positive force in the universe, is deceptively simple:

You must sincerely engage yourself in the life direction that is true to your soul.

Spiritual teacher and enlightened author of the transformative book, *A New Earth—Awakening To Your Life's Purpose*, Eckhart Tolle, tells us that rather than asking ourselves what our life purpose will be, we should ask life itself what purpose it has for us.

Often this knowing, this revealing, this intuitive realization comes to us in a life-changing *series* of epiphanies. The challenge is to be listening.

The answers you are given when you are offered an epiphany will show you direction—solutions—purpose—clues about where to begin to discover your best creative life. How will you know an epiphany when you hear it? How will it stand out in your consciousness, apart from all the other routine noise in your head?

This epiphany might be percolated to you over a period of time in perfectly timed quiet illuminations. If at first you choose to ignore the whispered epiphany—rejecting the message, ignoring the challenge—this instruction from your soul will present itself more frequently with a louder voice, a brighter color, a stronger suggestion that eventually cannot be ignored. The whispers will become shouts, commanding your attention. Still, some people will struggle to ignore the realization, maintaining a wall of denial and a concentrated blockage of fear between the noble voice from their soul and the negative voice in their head; never seeming to understand or accept that a voice from within the stillness of their being might make a difference in the life they choose to live.

For the fearless and the creatively gifted, the mission is to live our lives in acceptance of the enlightened suggestions of this voice. The result of your acceptance of your inner voice's wisdom will simply be to become the person you are authentically meant to be on this planet in this life. In accomplishing that, you will reach your finest potential and make the best difference for the greater good while you reside here. How very creative that is.

The memoirs we have chosen to include in this second book in the Epiphany Series are authored by men and women who have written sincerely and authentically, from their own unique perspectives, about what has happened specifically to them. Our stories have not been embellished or fictionalized and are true to the recollections of the authors. We know that you will enjoy them because they contain universal themes that inform us all about the mysteries of life and why we are here.

For additional information on all of our contributing writers, and how we define the epiphany experience please visit our website at: www.epiphanysfriends.com

CHAPTER ONE

GIFTS FOR THE GIFTED
Kristin Leigh

Children almost always are capable of much more than we expect of them and regularly say things that surprise us. One winter morning, I pulled open the blinds and exclaimed, "Oh, it snowed!" My newly three-year-old son said, in an eye-rolling tone, "Well, mommy, there was just water in the air, and it froze." I was surprised by his logical explanation, but I shouldn't have been. Children absorb so much more than adults realize and are capable of great imaginings, explorations and discoveries. Within this group of remarkable humans is a subset of children labeled as "gifted." There are many views of giftedness and many manifestations. Though there are several characteristics linked to giftedness, it is important to realize that giftedness is not necessarily linked to general intelligence. Children can be gifted in one area and have average skills, or even learning disabilities, in another. Still, I hope to describe some characteristics of gifted children that are important to recognize, and to suggest a few "gifts" that caring adults can give these children to nurture them and help them develop to their potential.

Gifted children seem to make early, rapid progress in a specific content area. They are intrinsically motivated to make sense of this area and do so without much help from adults. They tend to show great persistence and concentration when interested, and these interests can often become obsessive. Gifted children often march to their own drummer.[1] Frequently, they want to do things their own way; they are nonconformists. Often, adults see this independence as argumentative, willful or difficult. These children can be highly sensitive, often with advanced, yet unevenly developed, moral reasoning, which can lead to an acute sense of justice. As a teacher of the gifted, I remember frequently having to smooth things over between Tim*, an exceptional student that I enjoyed immensely, and several other adults at the school. Tim was passionate about all kinds of ethical and political issues. Many were played out during the school day. For example, one day Tim was livid, upset to the point that he was unable to work, because the adults staffing the lunchroom that day had decided it was to be a "silent lunch." This was punishment for a previously noisy lunch period, but Tim was incensed that the students' one chance to "get their ya-yas out" had been removed. He saw this punishment as contributing further to the problem, not as a solution. Without a chance to relax and visit with friends, the students would be only louder and more out-of-control for their teachers upon return to class. This argument was unappreciated by the lunchroom staff.

Gifted children sometimes are not especially good at being child-like. They often prefer solitary play or play with older children, though the older children don't always want to play with them. Extremely gifted children sometimes become socially isolated, which can have emotional repercussions. In addition to these sometimes socially awkward children is the more rare child whose area of giftedness is that of a highly developed sense of others, of treating other people with dignity, grace, sensitivity and goodwill.

Living with gifted children, like living with any child, is an adventure. In addition to loving them and keeping them safe, there are things caring adults can do to nurture the child's gift, and these are the same things that help all children learn and develop. These are "gifts" that can be given to help the child grow and develop, and, like any gifts, these should be given freely. They should be intentional and personal, prepared thoughtfully. The three gifts I suggest here include the gift of experiences, the gift of a collaborative partner, and the gift of trust.

Areas of giftedness don't just spring, fully-formed, from the minds of children. Their sources are more complex. These children may progress rapidly in a content area, but content is a consequence of experience. The gift of experiences, both individual and communal, is one of the most important things an adult can give children to support their learning and growth. Opportunities for experiences with content are usually provided by an adult, sometimes intentionally with thorough preparation, sometimes by stepping back or through "neglect," and sometimes through artifacts or accumulated habits of culture. In an interview on the BBC, scientist Richard Feynman described an early childhood experience provided by his father. He said:

"When I was just a little kid, very small in a high chair, he had brought home a lot of tiles, little bathroom tiles—seconds, of different colors, that he'd brought home. We played with them, setting them out like dominoes, I mean vertically, on my high chair—so they tell me this anyway—and when we'd got them all set up I would push one end so that they would all go down. Then after a while I'd help to set them up and pretty soon we were setting them up in a more complicated way—two white tiles and a blue tile, two white tiles and a blue tile and so on."[2]

Experiences can be simple—looking at a pile of rocks, finding patterns at the grocery store, observing animals at the zoo, getting covered in paint or clay—but it is the relationship between actions and consequences that give the experiences meaning.

John Dewey wrote:

"An experience has pattern and structure, because it is not just doing and undergoing in alternation, but consists of them in relationship. To put one's hand in the fire that consumes it is not necessarily to have an experience. The action and its consequence must be joined in perception. This relationship is what gives meaning; to grasp it is the objective of all intelligence. The scope and content of the relations measure the significant content of an experience."[3]

Children flourish with the resources given to them by their culture and by some creative or loving adult who creates access to those resources. Part of this gift of experience and access to resources includes providing children the opportunity and the encouragement to slow down, observe, and notice things. In Feynman's interview he described how his father did this for him:

"One day when I was playing with what we call an 'express wagon'...it had a ball in it, I remember this, it had a ball in it—and I pulled the wagon and I noticed something about the way the ball moved. So I went to my father and I said, 'Say, Pop, I noticed something. When I pull the wagon, the ball rolls to the back of the wagon; it rushes to the back of the wagon. And when I'm pulling it along and I suddenly stop, the ball rolls to the front of the wagon,' and I say 'Why is that?' And he said that, he says nobody knows. He said, 'The general principle is that things that are moving try to keep on moving and things that are standing still tend to stand still unless you push on them hard.' And he says this tendency is called inertia, but nobody knows why it's true. Now that's a deep understanding. He doesn't give me a name. He knew the difference between knowing the name of something and knowing something, which I learned very early."[4]

This issue of opportunities for noticing and experiencing and of access to resources explains why the same giftedness may express itself differently in different cultures.

Another gift adults can give children is the one of being a collaborative partner. Vera John-Steiner describes the gift of confidence as an important gift on which people can lean during periods of self-doubt and rejection.[5] As the stories in this book show, life devoted to creative work can be especially insecure. A collaborative partner who uses constructive criticism effectively can be a crucial support system for the child. In addition, a supportive partner provides legitimization of the new language that is part of the creative breakthrough. Children need the opportunity to share their ideas and discoveries and to clarify their ideas during this sharing process. Caleb*, a student I worked with, had great anxiety about writing fiction. It didn't seem to fit into his mastery of the literal world. He was extremely hard on himself and overly critical of his writing. However, I found that if I listened to Caleb work through his ideas, I could give him honest feedback that helped overcome his anxiety. I respected his criticisms, but pointed out when they were unwarranted. This collaborative process improved the writing, but the larger benefit was Caleb learning when he was being unnecessarily hard on himself.

A third gift adults can give children is trust. Children need to feel mutual respect and trust with the adults in their lives, and they need acknowledgment that they are their own people. Gifted children may feel this need to be acknowledged as an independent person intensely. Adults can acknowledge this independence by providing children with opportunities to show ownership of their activities and learning and to have control of interactions. This can be as simple as allowing children the freedom to choose their own clothing in the morning, even if it's unconventional, or the freedom to investigate more complex matters, like religion. Activities with many decision-making opportunities and with multiple entry points and possible outcomes should be provided. For example, instead of providing children with specific instructions for an activity, where a certain result is expected, try providing a set of materials that allow many variables to be manipulated and that encourage several possible outcomes and discoveries. In this way ownership of the activity shifts to the child, who can feel a sense of independence and control of his or her own learning.

Another way adults can show gifted children that they are trusted is to appreciate the idealized moral reasoning described earlier, often shown as intense feelings about what is right and wrong or about political and ethical issues. Often, the child who exhibits these concerns is seen as stubborn, willful, or difficult, like Tim in my early example. Another example is Kyle*, who felt strongly at a young age that he wanted to be a vegetarian. He saw no way around the idea that killing living creatures is wrong; it was intensely black and white for him, despite his parents' attempts to get him to eat what the family was eating. Similarly intense feelings were felt by Jessica*, a gifted fourth grader, who became highly emotional during a science lesson on light. The teacher was discussing with the class the results of an experiment where light was shone through a container of milky water, making the water appear bluish. She conveyed this phenomenon as a reason why the sky is blue. Jessica became very argumentative, because she felt so passionately that the sky was blue because God made it that way. It wasn't religious belief that made this story remarkable, it was the intensity of moral reasoning and argument that Jessica displayed. Though their conviction is admirable and adult-like in some respects, what gifted children lack is the life experience to go along with this reasoning, and this lack of experience is not something that the children will recognize or appreciate. Dewey described it this way:

"A child's experience may be intense, but, because of lack of background from past experience, relations between undergoing and doing are slightly grasped, and the experience does not have great depth or breadth. No one ever arrives at such maturity that he perceives all the connections that are involved."

Adult caregivers should appreciate the children's concerns, while helping them to understand when a situation represents real injustice and when it's "just life."

Gifted children are interesting, beautiful little creatures, but they are challenging and exhausting. They need the respect and support of caring adults, even though the children may think otherwise. When loved and cared for and given the gifts described above, these children will grow into creative adults, capable of having and inspiring great epiphanies and of contributing their own special gifts to this life we share.

*Names used in this chapter are not the names of the actual children.

ENDNOTES

1. Ellen Winner, *Gifted Children* (New York: Basic Books, Perseus Books Group, 1996), 3-4.

2. Richard Feynman, produced by Christopher Syckes, *Horizon: The Pleasure of Finding Things Out*, BBC, November 23, 1981.

3. John Dewey, *Art as Experience* (New York: Capricorn, G.P. Putnam's Sons, 1958), 44.

4. Richard Feynman, produced by Christopher Syckes, *Horizon: The Pleasure of Finding Things Out*, BBC, November 23, 1981.

5. Vera John-Steiner, *Creative Collaboration* (New York: Oxford University Press, 2000), 128.

6. John Dewey, *Art as Experience* (New York: Capricorn, G.P. Putnam's Sons, 1958), 44.

BIOGRAPHY

KRISTIN LEIGH

Kristin Leigh began her career in education teaching fourth grade in Arizona. For five years she taught elementary school, ending that period of time as the teacher for the gifted program. Most of what she discovered about how children learn came from this time in the trenches; however, she also earned a Master's Degree in Curriculum and Instruction, Science Education at Arizona State University. Seven years ago, Kristin and her family moved to Albuquerque, New Mexico, where she ultimately became the Educational Services Director at Explora, an innovative science education institution with over two hundred experiential classroom programs and two hundred and fifty exhibit activities in science, technology and art.

When not working at Explora, Kristin is surrounded by creatively gifted people at home. Her husband, David, is an artist, curator and writer, and together they're raising three-year-old Grant, who surprises them every day with brilliant songs, drawings, observations and discoveries. "He is an exhausting, beautiful little creature," Kristin says.

CHAPTER TWO

BATTLING WITH ENTITLEMENT
Adam R. Hand

The phrase "starving artist" drives me crazy. These two words, used together, have caused my resentment toward anyone who wields them. Maybe consciously people think the notion is romantic, but the subtext *I hear* people insinuating is, "Who are you to think you're so special? You think you are better than the rest of us? You think you don't have to "work" like the rest of us and be a part of the system? You don't even deserve the basic amenities of those around you. Nay, you deserve poverty. You deserve to starve."

Admittedly, life is not easy for most of us. All one has to do to see the struggles of life is get in the car and go for a drive downtown, and as revealing as that may be of bad luck and poor choices, it does nothing to account for the sacrifice and hard work of those who appear outwardly successful. Although life is tough, as they say, I think many people with exceptional talent face a very peculiar sort of adversity: the insidious impetus to create, and the fear of losing the ability to do so.

The majority of people do not have a talent that makes them stand out or feel different even when they are very young, so they are free to make simpler decisions based on self-interest and what is best for their future. I have many friends who say they love their jobs. What they usually mean is that they enjoy the work they do or the environment, but as in any loving relationship, to love something means you'd go through the ringer with it, or at least you are willing to. I have had many jobs, and honestly I have not been able to say that I enjoyed a single one of them more than I enjoy making art. I love making art. I am willing to fight with it and have quarrels, and yes, sometimes my mind wanders toward other callings in life, but it always comes back to the art. It might be this thing inside me called art that prevents me from enjoying a job for what it is, because deep down, I feel that my time is being wasted and I am being robbed of my destiny. Employers pick up on this. Sometimes, sending me on my way, they haven't even said, "You're fired!" but have actually said, "Go make your art..."

Maybe it is because there is a common belief that art has an intrinsic reward separate from survival, and I concede that to become an artist in order to survive is an absurd notion. But for those of us who must create, the notion of working a forty or sixty hour week for twenty or forty years to secure a retirement is far more absurd and insidious than doing what we love, even if we fail in other areas.

What is it that makes me an artist? My personal story is that I am naturally gifted. I can draw things others cannot. I can see things others cannot. It's almost as if I never had a say in the matter of whether I was to become an artist, whereas for some, I am sure it is something they are drawn to over time. I personally could not have been anything else. Without trying, I was the kid in first grade who won every poster and drawing contest. In an alternate universe, had I become a doctor or a banker, although I have the intelligence and capability, my natural aptitude for making material objects would be in the way. On top of that, I am addicted to paint, color, line, form, rhythm, composition and the idea of ideas. I think people with the natural talent become addicted to these and other things. We are able to create our own universes with skill and relative ease and people want to see our unique ability. Our inner workings become a tangible manifest reality, unlike the machinations of a mathematician's mind, the work of a gifted astronomer, or the secret work of a CIA agent. What though is the value of our work? Is it useful? Does it matter? Is it selfish and self-centered? Do we give our lives and minds to it so much so that we miss the point of it all? These and other questions must pass through many an artist's head, for besides natural talent, the other great ingredient in an artist's make-up is obsession—some more than others.

As a child and into my early twenties I heard too many times from people that they must hold on to this or that little sketch I had created because one day I would be famous and it would be worth something. I never really knew what people meant, but it did make me feel special. I felt different, and maybe I am as much different as I am the same. For so long I just painted or drew because it was something to do, and it was enjoyable; then people became interested in "my work." I had to explain myself and my pictures. I had to answer for what I had done. There had to be reason behind it. As soon as this was happening it was about time to go to college, and I had to decide what to do with the rest of my life. I had never really thought about it before, but there it was, in my face, staring me down like a heavy battleship. In any situation I had ever been in, I had been "The Artist." It was fairly obvious what to do with my life, but it was scary to pronounce to the world and to myself that I was going to go on a path that led to obscurity and madness and poverty. In sports we were always told how few athletes make it to the major leagues and how the odds were stacked against us. I was suddenly aware that the odds of becoming a successful artist were probably more heavily weighted against me than if I wanted to play football. At least athletes can take steroids. I knew about performance enhancing drugs for artists, but I think they are more effective when the audience takes them. I decided if I were to go down this path without a fall-back plan—which was the only way to do it as far as I could see—that I had to fully commit to it. There was no more Adam who played football and guitar and liked to swim, there was only Adam the artist. I would dedicate myself twice over to improving my skills as an artist and to being an artist, whatever that meant. Not only did I feel different now, but I had committed myself to being so. I really did not know what I was in for, because all the things people had said to me...I was beginning to believe.

Life, however, was not great. I was a mess. I could not have cared less about my emotional health and well-being. My number one priority, even ahead of taking care of myself was becoming a great artist. This took its hold on me on many levels. I would spend countless hours working on paintings and sketches, attending all of my college courses (the ones in the studio at least), and I would do this for several weeks at a very high intensity, never giving myself a break or taking anytime to *live*. The end result was that I would be tattered and manic, or depressive and crashed out, ignoring everything for the next week.

So much can happen in a week.

When I would talk to my girlfriend it was an endless regurgitation of my obsessions, which I thought impressed her. At the end of such a push I was prone to impulsive and reckless behavior, and would indulge in wine and laziness, or go out into the world and try to show people how outside of the box I was. But I was really just disassociated from the rest of the world. I was off so far into the world I had conjured that I couldn't relate to anyone with a level head.

This continued for many years, and what's worse, my talent carried me through much of it. I was self-important and thus a born salesman. I was the only person in art school that was making ends meet with painting. I worried about my future less and less, because the evidence continually stacked in favor of its brightness. By the time I graduated college with my BFA in painting, which took six years to complete, I had forgotten what it was like to hold a job. My track record as a young artist was fairly impressive, but as a contributing member of society it was not. In fact I had become quite good at taking from society. I saw selling paintings as a hustle rather than as a way to make people happy. I would spend a lot of that money at bars. I was often in need of loans, or would sell my artwork for nothing. My relationships with people were always on edge. Many of these were relationships I knew only really existed because people thought I had a very special talent and were always curious to see what would happen with it. I can blame some of it on not being understood. When an artist goes deep into his world there aren't many people to communicate with about it. I can blame some of it on the unconventional lifestyle I had, but what had really happened is that over the years my ego had eaten away at me like a cancer and I viewed myself as exempt from life because I believed I was destined for greatness. Entitled.

I had an instructor for my Painting II course whom I did not like before we ever met because we were not allowed to use oil paints in his class. The things he said to me, however, stick with me more than any of my other instructors. He had immense respect for my talent and yet he picked on me in class because of that. His classes were morning classes, and I was not a morning person. (I know, no excuse.) I was absent quite often, and he would lecture me about how my talent wouldn't do all the work for me. I knew he was right, but my ego told me that because I completed all the work, and to a higher standard than the rest of the students, I ought to be exempt from following his rules. During the final critique of my first class with him he decided to single me out and unfairly accused me of not fulfilling the requirements of the assignment. I disagreed with him strongly, and the rest of the class stood behind my argument. He ended up looking bad in front of his students. He approached me in the halls afterward to both apologize for and justify singling me out, and I did a little bit more than give him the cold shoulder. I was afraid he would fail me after that.

Two years later in order to graduate I was forced to enroll in another class he taught. I went to the dean and begged her to make an exception for me. She told me that the year before when I had taken that first class from him his wife had died from cancer with almost no warning. It had happened in several weeks. That semester he failed every single one of his students and was put on leave. That first class I had with him was the first class he taught after coming back from that leave. It was sad for both of us. He cared about me. He was trying to teach me what I wasn't learning anywhere else.

Upon graduating with my degree in painting I won the Graduate Painter award, further confirmation that I was an exception. There were two big awards for graduating seniors at my university; the Graduate Painter Award and the Studio Painter Award. I misread the application for the Studio Painter Award and showed up to the viewing with my artwork several hours late. This was a typical missed opportunity. One of my favorite professors told me in confidence after graduation that when the vote was made for the other major award, the Graduate Painter Award, that that particular professor was the only one who voted against me. He expressly argued that I was irresponsible. He was right. Because my art was at a higher level than most, I was looked at by many other students to be an example. Though I freely offered them help with techniques in painting, geometry problems, and honest criticism, it was sheer arrogance of me to show up late or not come at all. I acted as though some of the professors had nothing to offer me.

Inwardly my intentions were not to be so conceited. It was sometimes difficult to show up to a class full of students who were not as serious as I. It was silly that there was no way for me to get any credit for all of the extracurricular time I put into my craft. It was frustrating that in class as I painted I had to listen to some of the trite conversations about where best to eat lunch if you were a bored and wealthy divorcé. I was unaware of who I was. I was pushing myself as hard as I could. My last semester I was given a security pass to get into the studios after hours and was referred to by the janitors as "The Ghost," because there wasn't a time during the day or night when I wasn't in the art building painting.

I had a studio set up in my backyard as well, and if a young girl were to come pick me up to go out, she would often have to wait for me to shower once she got there, because I would not stop painting until the moment she arrived. To relax I would read art theory at the coffee shop. I was immersing myself as though I were the chosen one, put on a strict regimen of brush exercise and a mental diet of Mondrian, Motherwell, and Medardo Rosso.

(Contrast this with the year I committed to doing awful paintings; just as I would commit to doing great paintings. I realized that they were not awful paintings at all, probably due to the level of dedication I had to them.)

One day in class my favorite professor asked me if I was okay. I told him that I thought I was losing my mind. I was so over-committed to my artwork that it controlled me. I did not control it. It was having its way with me. I was its rag doll; its slave. I was in bondage and I did not have a problem being in bondage to something I believed in so much, but I was truly worried that I was going to lose my mind; that the world would turn into paint. It sounds absurd, and it was absurd to be as frightened as I was.

My professor reassured me that I would be okay and told me that what I was going through was a sort of "growing pains" time for an artist. Relief was to come though. It was going to be the fruit of all my hard work, and it would come in several stages. *An epiphany of the educational variety.* The first thing that occurred happened in my life drawing class. I had taken six or seven of these classes whereas most students take three to graduate. I was bored in class, bored with life-like representations and verisimilitude. My paintings had become modern. I would try to make things interesting in the class, working with different mediums like pen and ink when everyone else used their charcoal and crayons. I might try doing one hundred drawings in one class, or make my renderings cartoons. I am lucky my instructor wasn't a rigid classicist, but a Frisbee-golf playing stoner. I am sure I gave him something to look forward to when he came into class. At the root of what bothered me was that life drawing classes were extremely competitive. They were full of students who were angry at themselves and frustrated. The human figure is an extremely complex subject, and yet we know it better than anything. It is a well balanced machine, a piece of architecture beyond compare. When drawn it must appear as though it works. A hundred lifetimes could be devoted to the verisimilitude of the human figure in drawing. Any artist who has tried to capture the beauty of another human being in this way can understand the frustration. The great American portrait artist, John Singer Sargent, was said to paint and then scrape off a face thirty or forty times before he got it right.

I had the chance to see an exhibit at the Getty while on a trip to Los Angeles. I had never been to the Getty before and was happy to see a number of things they had on display; Van Gogh's *Irises*, a Francois Bougeraux, Corot, an unexpected Pontormo; but especially their exhibit in the basement, "The Drawings of Sculptors."

It was a drawing by Bernini that took my fancy. Its economy was impressive. He would suggest a plane with two or three crosshatch marks that swerved with the contour of the face. The end result was so much more than the parts. I found it far more interesting than a drawing with the final purpose of being just a drawing. What it really was were instructions for a sculptor, but it was very modern as a drawing. I placed it next to a Manet in my mental style-files. It was very revealing of a calm mental character that did not struggle, but chose well instead. It was the *selection* of what to include in a drawing and how to include it, characteristic of a very calm and decisive mind, free from worry. I wanted to be like Bernini. I didn't want to feel the competition in those life drawing classes anymore, and I didn't need to.

I remember when I discovered the secret of pretending I was someone else. I used to pretend I was Pablo Picasso when I was struggling with painting, to boost my confidence. This time it would be Bernini. I had studied him too. He was a great business man and an excellent manager of people. His studio had thirty or so sculptors working in it, some who specialized in one part of the carving such as plant foliage or hands. I hate it when people criticize Andy Warhol for having others do his work. Any artist as prolific as he was has done it—with maybe the exception of Van Gogh and Picasso. *Who was Bernini* to do a drawing like that one at the Getty? It was probably a luxury for him to find time in his schedule to actually draw. He probably walked into a studio on a beautiful day after dining with royalty. An assistant had set up his easel and supplies. He had a casual conversation with whatever royalty it was that was sitting for their bust to be carved. He sat them down almost as a formality. He had drawn them in his mind scores of times already. He picked out the essential information and set it down on paper—simple and effective like a great business strategy. It has been said that we get 80% of our results from 20% of our work. It is called the eighty-twenty principle. I might argue that it's more like 95% to 5%. I think he knew which 5% of what he did was effective.

Anyway, that day in life drawing class I walked in and sat down. While the other students set up immediately and started frantically drawing as though an impending natural disaster were about to happen any minute, I studied the model for the essential information I needed. When I had what I needed I calmly got out my materials, set up a nice piece of paper and carved a bit of wood off to freshen up my pencil. My professor was very curious and didn't say a word. He knew I had been working on something new again, but because he couldn't see what I was doing right away he was in suspense. I drew slowly and methodically, but although what I had done had been done slowly, I was finished with the first drawing in almost no time at all, and what's more, it was the type of drawing that one might work many years to achieve. I did another one that day, and for the rest of the semester that must have been my favorite class to attend. The reason students get so frantic is because they think they are making a beautiful drawing. All I was doing was recording the information that was put before me. An obsession had been lifted. I no longer thought that there was any extra effort I could make to do better work. I realized that what I had to do was work smarter, not focusing on what I was doing, but focusing on those essential qualities of my subject. It is sheer ego to believe that the more work I put into something the better it is. Great artists make it look easy because for them it is. I didn't have to struggle anymore.

A similar realization happened for me while working on a commission for one of my most generous benefactors. This realization took the pressure not off of my skills, but off of my creativity. I was working on a geometrical abstract and the under-drawing had been done. I was using color theory to make the decisions I had to make about color. I was trying to play games with color to make it harmonize in ways it wasn't necessarily supposed to. I was relying on my knowledge of color theory and had to think about this game though, and with every color I added it became more difficult to choose the next. Then something took over inside me and showed me what color to use. There was only one choice now and I didn't have to make it, all I had to do was mix the paint and put the paint on the canvas. It was such a relief and it kept happening. Ever since that time I haven't had to make any decisions or try to be creative. *All I need to do is start doing and I am given instruction. I am not even an artist anymore, I am a conduit.*

Maybe it is something greater than myself; maybe it is my subconscious. But whatever it is, all that pressure I had been putting on myself, the pressure that I was worried constantly about that was driving me mad, is now gone.

All of this isn't to say that my life got any better, because it didn't, but the pressure I put on myself to be a genius all the time was gone. What did happen with my life was what happened to everyone else's. September 11, 2001 I woke up and my roommates were glued to the television. When I saw what happened I thought of a documentary I had seen that said the World Trade Center had its own zip code, and that two hundred thousand people were in and out of there every day. I thought of the numbers and became sick. Thank God there were so few fatalities compared to what could have happened.

I do not know anyone who was in the Towers that day, and of course I was profoundly saddened by the losses, but it did end up directly affecting my life also. Because it had such an instant effect on the economy I could not sell a painting at a fair price to save my life. My prices got cut to one-third, and my profit margin got cut to one-sixth. For the next year I got tight with my money and was able to postpone getting a real job until I graduated from college.

I decided I was going to move to Hollywood, California. I had a slew of friends who had been migrating there and I knew that the number of people with a disposable income was much greater than existed in Tempe, Arizona. When I graduated I had an art show at my parent's house and made about four thousand dollars. I took this as an omen that I would do well in Hollywood. I put my paintings in a U-haul and hit the road. Before I even returned my U-haul I had found two places to hang my artwork; a coffee shop on Melrose Avenue and an antique furniture store on Sunset Boulevard. The names of these streets are famous, and I felt great about being able to hang my work up right away instead of putting it in storage until I found a place to live. Later that week I went to a coffee shop on Melrose and saw David Hockney having tea. I was sketching naked ladies on my napkins and as he exited the shop he walked by and said, "Nice." I was in heaven. This was the beginning of the rest of my life, and I wasn't going to have a thing to worry about as far as I was concerned. Unfortunately the world wasn't on the same wavelength as I was.

It took me two months to find my first job, and I knew I was being exploited. I was designing a line of jewelry for a millionaire jeweler who gave me forty bucks a day and brought me his leftovers from the expensive Italian restaurants where he picked up women every night. It wasn't covering the exorbitant rent I was paying for the one bedroom I was sharing or the materials it took to build a wall to make a bedroom out of half the living room so that I didn't have to listen to the car crashes and gunshots and screams constantly emitted from the television set my roommate watched all day and night while he wasn't on tour with this or that band as a guitar tech. All things considered, I was not the success I had relied on being. I was a nothing. Proof of it was the money I kept spending at the bars, convinced that I would run into my first Angelino benefactor and seal a stipend agreement over shots of tequila at this or that dive bar. I did meet a few famous people and drank with some, but they weren't interested in my dream. In the end all I had left were credit card bills I didn't anticipate having to pay and a rapidly declining self-esteem. *I was in the process of becoming humble.*

I went through a number of jobs in Los Angeles and each one of them was a learning experience. They were especially hard to land, however, because I had no job history and nepotism is out of control (as is racism of all kinds) in Los Angeles, and there weren't too many white people working at McDonald's, or Burger King, or any other places where just my degree in painting qualified me to work. I saw my application thrown in the trash can immediately after walking out of a Pizza Hut that had a Help Wanted sign in the window. I guess white boys weren't what they had in mind. I finally got a job as a personal assistant to a Hollywood producer, and the pay was okay, so I held onto the position even though the woman I worked for had a penchant for verbally abusive managerial techniques. This was her way of pressuring me to be a creative problem solver rather than just a wage laborer who follows good instructions. My adjustment to this involved some turbulence. She thought of herself as a do-gooder, and she rescued cats off the street. She had six of them. Two were blind. The cats had a room in her house the size of my apartment, and there were three litter boxes which I had to clean twice daily. The entire time I worked for her I resented the cats. She bought them whole roasted chickens to eat and had an elaborate process of boiling them and then refrigerating them to harvest their gelatin. The cats were eating better than I was, their room was bigger, and they had someone to clean up after them and cook for them. The entire situation was a sort of distilled irony that was the epitome of my existence in Los Angeles. There were an enormous amount of things I loved about being there, the museums and parks for instance, but the mental and emotional rigors of daily life in the viscous city were an endless bargaining I hadn't the patience for.

In the course of eight months I had managed to drink and drive away all my friends and all I had left were my two lackey jobs and my insanity. Hollywood once looked like the land of opportunity, and it was beautiful, but from my perspective it was looking more and more like a deathtrap. After eight months of struggle and confusion I decided to go home to Arizona. I moved in with my parents and things only got worse because we began to fight about what I was going to do with my life and I had no answers. My parents were consistently supportive of my artistic talent, but not impressed with my drinking; although greatly curbed because of living with them, it still must have been a miserable thing to watch. On the job front I was lucky that a friend of my mother's had been waiting since I was a child to commission me to do some artwork. In addition to enjoying painting again (rather than taking on the angry TV producer's grunt work) the job paid well and I was able to finish quickly. This, however, only proved to be more trouble. My ego was puffed up again from doing what I was good at and I now had a fair sum of money in my pocket; both just more fuel for the fire of entitlement.

Typical of my new living situation, my mother came home from work and we began to fight. This was a daily routine we had that never resulted in anything good. She was doing what she thought she had to do as a mother; getting on my case about not living a virtuous life in addition to my painting. I didn't know how to solve the problem. My high hopes for myself had been dashed, and I had no viable work experience to be anything other than an artist. I felt doomed, and the disapproval from my mother did not inspire me, but rather dismantled any feeling of self-worth I had managed to hold on to during my stay in the city of angels. Since I had arrived home I hadn't had the freedom to drink that I wanted, because I didn't want my parents to see it.

One day in particular after fighting with my mother I decided I would have to get seriously drunk. It turned out it would be my last night of drinking, and I am lucky to have lived through it. I woke up the next day in five-point restraints; hand-cuffed, ankle-cuffed, and with my head strapped down to a gurney in a hospital and nearly a hundred stitches in my arms. A nurse, noticing I had awakened, quickly leaned over me and informed me that I was lucky to be alive and that I needed help with my alcohol problem. My blood alcohol level had been high enough to kill anyone who hadn't spent years developing a tolerance, and on top of that I had lost nearly enough blood to have bled to death as well. At this point they did not even know my identity, because my wallet had been stolen. She informed me that I had to tell them who I was and give them the name and phone number of an immediate family member who could care for me or I would be admitted to their mental health facility for psychological evaluation for the next month. I reluctantly gave them the name and number of my parents who came and got me without saying a word. It took me a week to find my car. When I found it, it was clear that I had driven on the rims for quite a distance. There wasn't a shred of rubber left on the wheels.

After a few days of physical recovery, remorse and self-pity, I climbed out of bed, pulled a phonebook out and found the number for a twelve-step program to help me deal with my alcoholism. This was the beginning of a major change in my life. Like most change, it did not occur overnight. But, it did commence immediately. I was unfamiliar with what the twelve steps were, and I found out over time they were designed to get us in touch with "a higher power of our own understanding." Several of the twelve steps even had the word "God" in them. As far as God went, I was a firm non-believer. But, I was getting better at life, and hence getting better at making adjustments.

For a higher power I first chose my cat because he had the stone-cold façade of Buddha. The unfortunate thing was that my cat's health had deteriorated so much that he was put to sleep within a month of being appointed my "higher power." I was worthless at this point, and doing not much of anything was even getting old. I was able to read and dress myself, and the other thing I could do was paint. I didn't want the pressure that painting had been to me before, but for some reason I chose painting to be my new "higher power," and I would pray to it an hour each day. I remembered that the strongest time I had ever felt a direct contact with a power greater than myself was when I had been working on paintings that sort of seemed to paint themselves. I had to do the work; stretch the canvas, mix the colors, put them on the canvas with my brush, but something else was giving me instruction to follow, and this something else knew what it was doing more than I did. I would now work on paintings for the sake of the act and so that I could communicate with the guiding force I had been introduced to. It would be my time to commune with that elusive higher power.

Although it was during these painting sessions in the early stages of recovery from alcoholism that I discovered the foundation of a new spirituality in my life, I also discovered that much of spirituality, the kind I had been lacking, was not about communing with nature or seeing visions or even feeling the "touch of God" in the creative work I was doing. The kind of spirituality I learned about was what most people call common sense. It had never occurred to me that spirituality could be practical, that it could be a part of everyday life, even the most mundane parts of it like ordering food and doing my finances. *Concerning my art, I had a major epiphany that was a part of my newfound spiritual sensibilities that has allowed me to be a much happier and more productive person: I could not depend on art as a way to make a living!*

As much sense as this probably makes to most non-artists, or artists who have a much more realistic perspective than I, for me it was a groundbreaking revelation that meant I was free. I was freed from my special and unique talent, my entitlement, and I was free to use all of the other qualities I had as a human being to whatever effect and result I chose. I probably could manage to make paintings and make enough money to survive as I had, but would that make me an artist? *Profiting from our creations ought to be the last thing that we use to justify to ourselves just what we are.* In fact, I believe that many people who make money doing one thing or another really aren't that great at what they do, but are just good at selling it. The more I made paintings for money, the less I personally felt like an artist. Many of the paintings I have sold have been what other people wanted me to paint, or wanted *me* to want to paint. I don't know how many times I went out on a job and sat down with a potential client who I expected to get a commission from and heard something to the effect of, "wouldn't it be cool if you could paint..." and then they would throw out some frivolous sentimental idea that I was totally disinterested in. I resorted to playing games with myself to make it interesting or I would rationalize, "at least I am painting," but that didn't mean I was doing what I loved. I always had the skill to put their ideas onto canvas, and I had also become quite good at mind-reading, or visualizing what someone else was visualizing. I turned communication about the visual into an art form. Certainly it often brought me joy to make other people happy, and it was great to be able to work on my skills, but ultimately it was not helping me be who I wanted to be or helping me make the art *I wanted* to make. So the challenge became less and less about how to paint something someone else wanted and more and more in painting what I wanted. If I could just separate in my mind who I was from what I did to make money, I would have been so much better off, and my work and ideas as an artist probably would have been further along as well. The truth is that after years of this I came back full-circle to what I had been in high school when I was faced with that choice of what path I was going to follow. I had an enormous amount of talent and skill, and just wasn't sure what I wanted to do with it. I had become lost.

Honestly, I must say that it is still very much a question for me: what do I want to paint? I have ideas of what kind of art I would like to make and why. Any of my ideas would cost a great deal of money or require an enormous amount of time, and that is actually good reason to have the ability to make money in other ways. I personally have learned how to do various types of construction because it is enjoyable and profitable work for me. There is a romantic notion that many people have that an artist must be compelled to make something at any cost, whether it be financial, emotional, physical or spiritual—that "starving artist" concept. Today I do not need to live out in my life the romantic notions that others have for me. What I actually believe I am supposed to do with my life probably goes against everything we are supposed to believe according to all of the new-fangled books that tell us how to properly manage our time and be effective people who manifest their own destinies through focused efforts and smart work. John Lennon wrote a song that I can relate to quite a bit; the lyrics of which are, "People say I'm crazy—people say I'm wasting time." To make great art is not always to be in constant action, planning out and executing every last whim and fancy of the intellect. Sometimes making great art *is* about "watching the wheels spin round and round" rather than ceaseless and tireless creation. Pablo Picasso very much considered himself an entertainer, as did Bob Dylan. Very seldom was it that they were disclosing profound realizations through their artwork. More often it was just that they were exhibiting their virtuosity and mastery of a craft and simply entertaining people. Not to discredit entertainment or the exhibition of a person's unique ability, especially that of a master, and not to say that art must always be profound, but my God! What pressure there would be if that were the case—that to be art it must be profound. We would have no artists! This might be the reason that artists of importance in the Twentieth Century were not required to make breakthrough after breakthrough; one was enough. Marcel Duchamp and all of his work will always be considered important because he understood this, and he brought us the found object which forever revolutionized art. Jackson Pollock searched an entire career for the breakthrough in painting that his drip paintings finally were, and continued to work in that style the rest of his life. I keep working on my art, and sometimes I don't think it's great. Sometimes it just is what it is and that is enough to reassure me that I am alive.

Along with the intellectual pressure I was relieved of, not waking up every morning and having to be a genius, I was also relieved of feeling like I had no "outs"—that I either had to make it as an artist or I was a failure. I should have known this however; I have read many biographies on artists and I am grateful for having done so. It has taught me that art is a lifelong pursuit and to be wary of so-called overnight sensations. One day I hope to be an overnight sensation after years of hard work. Many of my favorite artists were not successful until later in their lives. Vincent Van Gogh never experienced financial success or recognition for his passion and his art, but I am quite sure that he felt successful almost every time he completed a painting, of which there were many. My aunt who is a true artist herself told me once that whenever anyone asks me how long it took me to paint something, to say, "My whole life." And I have already lived a lifetime.

I still very much want to make art for a living, for the wisest of men do what they love in order to support themselves, and I very much am a lover of making art. But now that I am not putting so much pressure on myself to make my art make money, I can make artwork that I believe in, even if no one else does. Hopefully at some point people will see in my work what it is that I am seeing, and they can enjoy it as much as I do. *They can have an epiphany.* Instead of asking me, insultingly, out of thin air, why a person like me who could draw or paint just about anything in the world of my imagination chooses to paint what I paint, they will just think to themselves, "Wow! That is really beautiful." (I never complain when I look at a Corot.)

Here are two things I learned along the way that helped me get back the joy:

Take instruction.

Relax.

Epiphany.

BIOGRAPHY

ADAM R. HAND

Adam Hand was born in Phoenix, Arizona November 23, 1977 and moved to Colorado two months later, returning to Phoenix at age thirteen. Naturally gifted as an artist, Adam won many awards throughout his education in the public schools including three consecutive "Best in Shows" at the Arizona State Fair, and he was chosen as one of six finalists in Sister Cities International, a competition including sixty countries.

During the last few years of high school Adam was given a job as an assistant to Jerry Cox, a prominent local figurative bronze sculptor, where he learned much about the process of making large bronzes and doing patinas.

After graduating high school Adam attended the New York School of Visual Arts on partial scholarship. While in New York, Adam worked as an assistant to a professional artist named Ira Sapir, and worked on Ira's S2 project.

After returning home to Arizona and graduating from Arizona State University he won the 2002 Graduate Painter Award at ASU. Adam immediately went to Los Angeles after graduating college where he held various positions including jewelry design, furniture building, set design, and was the lead assistant to a television producer. Unhappy with his prospects as an artist in Los Angeles, he returned to Scottsdale, AZ where people had already been investing in his work for many years.

Adam has shown his artwork in numerous group shows, furniture stores and restaurants, as well as briefly working with galleries. Adam has also curated shows for other artists in Phoenix and Los Angeles. Primarily, Adam's work has been sold on a commission basis and through word of mouth. Bypassing the gallery system, in 2007 Adam opened his own gallery, Portal Gallery in Scottsdale showing just one of his several styles of work.

Adam Hand is known for his large abstract work which is a throwback to abstract expressionism but using techniques he has developed himself over the years which he calls "organic expressionism." Adam has also worked as a portrait artist, both for individual clients and for The Autograph Company, a subsidiary of Topps baseball cards. At thirty years old, his career is relatively young compared to his skill and vision. Adam has many other talents, including artisan style construction and eco-friendly design which he has recently pursued in the remodeling of a loft-style condo as well as his gallery. It will be exciting to see what the future holds for this gifted young artist.

CHAPTER THREE

JUST ANOTHER WORD
Kathy Park

Freedom's just another word for nothing left to lose. Kris Kristofferson and Fred Foster

She was a slight woman. When hurricane winds scoured her native Puerto Rico, a couple of robust aunties must have tethered her to the ground or else she'd have flown off like a yellow kite. Yet her slender frame had no bearing at all on the force and weight of what she was telling me. I stared into her steady brown eyes across the circle from me while her words gusted through my head. She waited for me, the calm eye of a storm. The other women sat silent and still, watching us. All I could think of was the irony, the irony.

We were sitting cross-legged on the carpet in a small room in the middle of a large compound of brick buildings inside a ten-foot tall double fence topped with loops of concertina wire sharp with razor blades. Federal Correctional Institution (FCI), Dublin, California, 1993. I was leading a stress management group for long-term inmates, twenty vivacious sassy women locked up for all kinds of crimes, most already imprisoned for over ten years and counting, some clinging to only a slight chance of parole far in the future.

Across from me sat the Puerto Rican Independinistas, a savvy and articulate group who had fought underground in the 1970's for Puerto Rico's freedom from the U.S. Ironically, however, one man's freedom fighter is always another's political terrorist. They were quickly put on the FBI's most wanted list and captured soon thereafter. I didn't even know Puerto Rico's freedom was an issue. On my left was a militant African American woman who was convicted of hijacking a commercial airliner. The way she told it, her volatile boyfriend had announced his plans to reroute the plane to Cuba by pulling out a gun and showing it to her thirty-thousand feet above the earth. She, pregnant and with a toddler on her lap, felt sure he would botch the job with unnecessary violence to the plane's passengers. So she decided to help him. Next to her squirmed a blonde Soviet spy who had used her seductive skills during the Cold War to garner state secrets for her homeland. A stout woman who had run the Columbian cocaine cartel that predated the infamous Medellin cartel yawned next to her. The rest of the women were mostly "mules" from South or Central America who knowingly or unknowingly had delivered packages of drugs stateside only to be sniffed out by the drug-detecting dogs. A colorful group of women from different countries, speaking different languages, and shaped by different experiences, all unwillingly connected by doing time in prison. Now they were choosing to explore that connection, humanize it, possibly deepen it by sitting together in this stress management group, the cornerstone of the holistic health program for inmates and staff I had founded three years before.

The average man does not want to be free. He simply wants to be safe. H.L. Mencken.

I never planned on working in a prison nor did I ever consider a career in corrections. At that time in my life, I'd never set foot in a prison and frankly didn't care if I ever did. Not that I wasn't aware of injustice in the justice system; it's just that, like many of us, I was content with merely paying lip service to a liberal point of view. That was about to change.

One evening when I was practicing at the Aikido dojo I belonged to, I trained with a slight curly-haired woman, fast and strong, but high-strung like a hummingbird. As we were folding our uniforms after class, she introduced herself as the Medical Director of FCI, Dublin—the head doctor for the entire prison. Knowing that I was a trained bodywork therapist, she asked me if I'd be willing to teach two stress management groups to a group of long-term inmates. "Yes" popped out of my mouth before I had a chance to think. Apparently it was time to walk my talk.

Besides spouting a comfortably liberal view, just what, exactly, was my talk?

I have known since I was very young that I am an artist. I have also known, more painfully, that that blessing makes me substantially different than most people. Lucky for me, my family was used to having a few oddball artists in almost every generation, and they encouraged my art. Perhaps they also encouraged it because they were used to being identified as outsiders, oddballs and out of the norm themselves. That's because the constellation of my family revolved around physical disabilities.

After serving in World War II in the South Pacific, my athletic and virile father came home to his young family of three with an unknown stowaway gestating in his nervous system: the polio virus. Suddenly stricken in his upper body, he was shipped off to the hospital in Warm Springs, Georgia (the same place Franklin Delano Roosevelt recovered from his polio). My father spent six weeks in an iron lung that forced him to breath. He emerged from this cold cocoon with an emaciated upper body and a bitter heart. Gone was his upper body strength, and with it, his faith in a fair world. I never knew there could be such a thing as a devout atheist, but if such a thing exists, my dad was a member of the congregation. No loving or fair God would have so eroded his life.

I am the fourth child, born after my father's polio during what must have been a difficult sex life for my parents. Five years later, my sister was born with a severe birth defect called spina bifita. At the base of her spine was a soft sack of nerves and spinal fluid that never made it where it was supposed to go—not to her legs, not to her bladder, not to her rectum. Mary's chances of survival were slim to nothing. My mother was not advised to fall in love with her. As if that were possible. But my infant sister survived a urostomy so she could pee into a bag strapped to her stomach, her first major surgery at ten days old. And then she survived sixteen more.

If my father had felt bitterness toward the whims of a dispassionate God, imagine how steely he felt now. At least he had experienced the joys of an athletic life. My sister would never have the chance. If my mother had had her hands full with a five-year-old, three teens, and a disabled husband, imagine how burdened she felt now.

Everyone was so focused on Mary's huge and compelling needs, some of us were lost in the shuffle. I'm sure my older siblings couldn't wait to leave the nest. But until I was old enough to leave too, I became the sturdy little workhorse of the family: Mary's protector and legs, my Dad's arms and strong back, my overwhelmed Mother's confidant and solace. I was healthy and tough and without special needs. Or so it must have seemed to everyone at the time.

About the only place I got to throw off the harness was through art. Through art I was free to flourish. I could envision and create the kind of world *I* wanted to live in. And I could escape into that world. As a young girl, I drew and painted and worked with clay, first on the wheel and later in terra cotta sculptures of strong, massive women. Later when I moved away from home, I learned to carve wood and stone with a hammer and chisel, chip by chip. Perhaps not surprisingly, I was involved with figurative work: how we shape ourselves in our bodies. I became interested in the martial arts, especially the non-violent art of Aikido. I wanted to experience the body as capable of expanded awareness, graceful power, and sharp focus. I got involved with yoga, meditation, and many forms of therapeutic bodywork. I wanted to experience the inner cellular life, how memories are stored in the body, how fine-tuned awareness could help transform and heal. I wanted to feel freedom inside my own body.

All my sojourns into body-centered wisdom have informed my art. Making art was and still is the center of my life. Even so, I know that on the day when I said "Yes" to coming into a prison, I had no idea how much working in the prison would influence my art, my life.

I remember the first day I came through the prison gate. My volunteer paperwork, urine analysis, and FBI background check had all been cleared. Inside the guardhouse, one guard put my belongings in a locker while another wanded me with a hand-held metal detector. Their stiff and humorless faces seemed like cold plaster masks and I shivered. The heavyset woman behind the desk looked me up and down, her lips a thin line and her eyes gunmetal gray. I wondered if her professional game face got stuck over time, or did it soften when she went home to her spouse and children?

I was glad to see the doctor's birdlike smiling face meeting me at the guardhouse. I followed her through a corridor with locked doors at each end and stepped inside the prison, the heavy doors clanging shut behind me. I felt a jolt of adrenalin as I remembered what I'd learned during the mandatory prison volunteer orientation two weeks before.

"Don't get any closer than four feet from any inmate," the burly guard with a shaved head had advised as he paced back and forth at the front of the class, coffee mug in hand, the other hand fingering his key chain, pacing like a caged leopard. "And remember, we have a 'no hostage' policy here. What that means is if you're taken hostage for any reason, we are not, I repeat, NOT coming in after you. You gotta understand that you're going into this prison by your own volition, voluntarily, of your own free will. Once you're inside that gate, you're on your own."

My heart had thrummed like a demented drummer. What on earth had I agreed to?

Now, looking over the doctor's curly head, my first glimpse of the prison compound was deceiving. The tight claustrophobia I expected to feel did not gnaw at my insides. Instead I felt the earth underneath, the sky overhead, a slight breeze ruffling my hair. Spread before us were green lawns and winding concrete paths connecting low brick buildings edged with flowerbeds—more like a college campus than the only west coast federal prison for women.

I remember seeing the women themselves, most dressed unflatteringly in men's khaki pants and shirts. Some bent over rakes and hoes as they tended the grounds. Some walked the paths to and from their housing units. Some headed to work in the kitchen or for UNICOR, the Federal Prison Industries that employs most prisoners while they do time. When the women spotted the doctor beside me, their faces opened in smiles. But they tightened as they shifted their eyes onto me. They were scanning me with invisible bullshit detectors. Was I another empty-headed liberal do-gooder? A Christian missionary looking for converts? Could I be easily conned? Would I last or would I wash out?

I took off my sunglasses and tried my best to look into their eyes. I knew I needed to show myself in the raw so they could really see me, see that I was not hiding some secret agenda. Yet their stark appraisals made me nervous and amped up my self-consciousness, especially around my eyes.

My eyes, my strange lopsided eyes. One lazily closed as if in another world only I can see. The other valiantly open, too open, doing the work for both, straining in the glare. I wondered what the women saw. I wondered if they could see past what I looked like. I wanted badly to put my sunglasses back on, but I hoped they would see my honesty. Vulnerability. Pain. We could at least have that in common.

I breathed into my belly and remembered that looking goes both directions. Even though I was uncomfortable being looked at, scrutinized, sized up, I could look back at them. As I shifted my focus, I had the first of many epiphanies that were to come from working inside the prison. *These women were not that different from me.*

That may seem like an odd thing to say. The doctor and I are Anglo. Most of the women prisoners were Black or Latino—not surprising, since most US prisoners are Black or Latino. The similarity I saw wasn't about ethnicity or color or nationality. It was something else. Something familiar. Something of myself.

Like a fog of déjà-vu, I couldn't place the feeling of recognition. Was this a reunion of some ancient tribe of Amazons? Uppity Women United? Were we a group of misfits and social outsiders suddenly connected because we were inside a prison? Or was it simply that I realized I had done things in my own past, smoked and swallowed things, that with a couple of different twists and turns could easily have fast-tracked me to this very prison? Haven't we all done something stupid or illegal (or both) at least once? Haven't we all, against our better judgment, hung out with some dubious characters and tried our best not to admit that they were up to no good? Haven't we all made some lousy decisions we lived to regret?

I couldn't figure out why the women seemed so familiar. All I knew was that I could be one of them, and any one of them could be me. We could change places in a heartbeat.

Years ago I recognized my kinship with all living things, and I made up my mind that I was not one bit better than the meanest on the earth. I said then and I say now, that while there is a lower class, I am in it; while there is a criminal element, I am of it; while there is a soul in prison, I am not free. Eugene V. Debs

As the doctor and I continued touring the prison, she told me about the multiple stressors the women must bear while doing time: unremitting confinement, lack of privacy and overcrowding (often three to a small room with an open toilet and sink), bureaucratic red tape, limited medical services, lack of creative outlets, and lack of training in "real life" skills for when they are released. No wonder recidivism rates are so high. Add to these stressors ubiquitous racism and violence, and constant difficulty communicating with family and friends on the outside. These multiple stressors lead to chronic health problems such as over-dependence on medication, substance abuse, nicotine addiction, depression, obesity, insomnia, high blood pressure, on-the-job injuries, and injuries due to fighting. I was stunned to learn that most incarcerated women are mothers having to endure the worst stress of all: the bitter frustration of having to parent their children from a distance.

The doctor pointed out that prison staff also suffers from being in a prison environment. Despite the job security of the corrections industry—prisons are considered a growth industry in this country because we incarcerate far more people per capita than any other country in the world—the stress of working in a prison often leads to poor physical and mental health. Short tempers, substance abuse, on-the-job injuries, broken marriages, and dysfunctional behavior, which are taken home to their families.

Urged by the long-term inmates under her care, the doctor wanted to try a more holistic approach to physical and mental health. She hoped such an approach would benefit not only those working in prison, but also those who had to live in it. As she described her vision, I realized I must have passed the first of many tests the women put me through in their ongoing and thorough calculation of my character. By the time we ended our tour, the prison grapevine outpaced us; the women were not only smiling at the doctor, but also giving me shy smiles as well.

As the doctor led me to the chapel, she briefed me on the group of twenty long-term inmates waiting inside. They'd been convicted of white-collar crimes, drug running, political terrorism, hijacking, espionage, and murder. They were all maximum security.

I stopped at the door and gulped a breath. The doctor smiled, "Oh, and there's a waiting list too."

Those first two stress management groups were such a big success that the women informed me I was not done coming to prison. They were positive I was coming back. While I laughed at their certainty, I could feel something growing inside me, something I hadn't quite banked on. These women weren't just a captive audience politely indulging my liberal volunteerism. They were unusually attentive students, eager and grateful to learn anything that would make their time more meaningful. In many ways they were better students than the often times jaded people I taught in the "free" world. These women's approach to learning was open, fresh and genuine, as if they knew they had nothing to lose. I was falling in love with them.

When I got back into my car, I swallowed hard. Finding more time to work in the prison would require nothing less than a complete overhaul of my life. Yet I had to agree. The women were right: I wasn't done coming to prison. Captive audience or not, there was something incredible happening here with these hungry, welcoming women; something to really give; something to really learn. The Prison Integrated Health Program was born.

Those first two "stress groups," as I came to call them, turned into four years of volunteering in prison, writing and winning two privately funded grants, directing and administering the program, enlisting a co-director, and training a small army of volunteers which eventually included even my husband Henry.

Our program of comprehensive holistic health was unique to the prison system, and still is, as far as I know. In its heyday from 1990-1994, the program filled three full days a week with classes in yoga, meditation, conflict resolution, arts and crafts, stress management, and parenting. Special workshops for prisoners included voice and theater, drumming, creative writing, multicultural issues, storytelling, dream work, and a special journal-writing workshop for incest survivors. Special classes for prison staff included relaxation techniques, conflict resolution, meditation, team building, parenting, and preventive health care. Despite prohibitions on touch and the burly guard's admonition about getting closer than four feet to an inmate, we also offered therapeutic bodywork and massage to prisoners and staff alike. We even managed to produce a day of Women's Spirituality and a weekend Multicultural Festival, events that required many volunteers and extensive cooperation from the prison staff; events that would be unheard of today.

Within a few months, the program's success was undeniable. Women in the stress group were able to stop smoking, a very difficult accomplishment because smoking is everywhere in prison. Some broke through debilitating depression or gained control over eating disorders. Overuse and over-dependence on medication for chronic pain was curbed. Relaxation techniques helped an insomniac sleep, a woman with high blood pressure to get back into the normal range, and another with chronic migraines to recognize the preliminary symptoms and ward off the headache before it had a chance to clamp down.

Because the program was independent from the prison administration, we were able to earn the trust of the women more easily. They felt safer in confiding in us without fear that their trust would be betrayed. The stress groups became safe havens, a place to let down, speak the truth, listen from the heart, even risk letting go into tears. With the reduction of stress, many women were able to open up into creative expression, a possibility they previously didn't think possible. Henry's arts and crafts class was a favorite every week. Women drew and painted the most intricate work; the longer it took, the better. When a presentation of the famous "Names Quilt" commemorating AIDS victims came to prison, we were able to help the women add two large sections, one depicting incarcerated women with AIDS, the other the epidemic's orphaned children.

Over time, the women who participated in the program not only improved their own physical and mental health, but also improved their relationships with fellow prisoners and loved ones on the outside. Old grudges were reconciled, festered wounds bathed with words of forgiveness.

The holistic health program did not just benefit the women prisoners and their families. Prison staff was able to reduce internal conflicts and tensions, making the prison a safer and (slightly) more agreeable environment in which to work. Volunteers like me who had never been inside a prison before brought outside to the larger community the story of the program's success, which inspired other volunteers to come inside. Consciousness of the plight of women in prison—an unsung story despite the fact that women constitute one of the fastest growing prison populations today—was carried home outside those razor-wire walls.

There is a wonderful mythical law of nature that the three things we crave most in life—happiness, freedom, and peace of mind—are always attained by giving them to someone else. Peyton Conray March.

Yet, despite evidence of both anecdotal and medically documented improvement in health among participants, the Prison Integrated Health Program was to enjoy only a brief moment in time. The punishment model, epitomized by "three strikes and you're out," edged out the more compassionate rehabilitation model. The door swung shut.

But I'm getting ahead of my story. How could I know that day, sitting in the stress group across from the small Puerto Rican woman who had just spoken to me, what the program's ultimate fate would be? All I knew was the cumulative weariness and discouragement I shouldered in that moment. My neck muscles felt like piano wires and I couldn't escape the dull red headache I'd had all morning. My lazy eye was cutting out even more than usual and my hyper-vigilant eye ached with the effort of compensation. I took a deep breath and tried to pull up energy from the ground. Nothing doing.

"Kathy," the small woman began again with a slight lisp. "You're tired, dragged down, depressed. You say you never sleep well the night before coming here. You have to get up at, what, 4:30 to get here by 7:30? It's getting to you. You're burdened by it, burdened by lack of funding and collecting rejection letters from those foundations. It may not be obvious to you, but it's obvious to all of us."

Several women nodded. I took in a breath to protest, but the little woman stopped me with her little gap-toothed smile. "Kathy, you say you're throwing bones at your art. You told us that dream you keep having about the horses, the horses you forget to feed or water? I think you're burning out. It's like running this program has become a prison for you, an emotional prison. In comparison, we're enduring our imprisonment easier than you are enduring yours, in the 'free world.'"

I looked at her, stunned, my sleepy eye flickering. She held me with her gentle brown eyes.

"Kathy," she said softly, like an ocean breeze at dawn. "You need to get out of here. You need to set your release date. You're no good to us if you're burnt out. Go. Make your art. Follow your dreams. That's what you're always telling us, right?"

None are so hopelessly enslaved as those who falsely believe they are free. Goethe

I felt like I was spinning. That strange vertigo when what you think you know is turned on its head, and you realize you don't know anything at all. An epiphany coming down the birth canal.

She was right. I felt trapped by the work in the prison. Gone were the early optimistic days where anything seemed possible, the high of our success carrying us all forward like the seventh wave of the seventh set. Gone were the days when the women could throw a fortieth birthday party for me, serve me contraband cake and chicken enchiladas they cooked with an iron. Gone was that heady sense that we were creating a new model, one other prisons might even envy and copy.

Now in our third year it was hard. If the women sat in a circle, suspicious staff thought we were a witch's coven. If a woman painted spiral shapes and the moon, she must be part of a pagan cult. Even my co-director thought bringing in twenty conga drums so the women could drum together was going too far. "We shouldn't encourage too much expression. What the women need to survive being in prison," she said, "is the ability to contain themselves."

As if the walls weren't doing that already.

As it turned out, I never did agree with my co-director on this point. While she saw the need for more of an "anger management" style of teaching so the women could control and contain their negative outbursts through meditation, I thought their understandable outbursts of frustration and rage could be better redirected into positive expression. Perhaps I argued in favor of expression over containment because I saw the imprisoned women through my own biased eyes, my faith in the power of creativity. But my argument was strengthened by the fact that the women seemed to bloom when their creativity was nourished. Their faces relaxed. A light turned on in their eyes. They could afford to be friendlier. Some even told me that if they had had access to creative expression before being in prison, they probably wouldn't have committed the crime they were imprisoned for in the first place.

Another clue that the women needed more opportunities for expression, not less, was that they didn't want their creative experiences to stop. They consistently picked the longest method to create something, the most detailed pencil or brush work, the tightest and tiniest plaits when they were allowed to braid each other's hair, as if by doing so they could prolong the creative moment and its sweet promise of freedom. Freedom of the soul to envision new worlds, freedom of the spirit to actually create those worlds, the kind of freedom that can't ever be stopped by a wall.

Unfortunately, however, most prison administrators agreed in principle with my co-director, not me. Increasingly, access to creative outlets inside prison is drying up, a refreshing spring seared under a hot sun.

I pulled myself back from my musings, back into the small room. I squirmed and shifted my position. Freedom of expression or not, the truth was that I felt driven by the prison work. Obsessed and burdened by it. When neither Henry nor I slept well, we called it a prison night. A night of grinding teeth and endless lists. A night of worrying about funding and how we were going to pay rent. A night of dreaming my recurring nightmare about forgetting to feed and water my horses. A night of gnashing about prison politics, the program's politics, the larger political climate. Many in society didn't want to hear about incarcerated women having time to do yoga or to eat from a heart-healthy menu (another accomplishment of our program). Prisoners should be suffering for the crimes they committed, shouldn't they? We mustn't be soft on crime. We should lock them up and throw away the key. I was obviously conflicted.

Sensing a door beginning to close, I felt as if my life were narrowing into a long cramped tunnel. Even the small woman sitting across from me could see it. All the tight places in my body resonated with the tender truth of her words.

I sat in the safety and silence of the group. I was no longer their teacher. I was just another woman, not all that different from them, trying to sort out the truth in a world clogged with deception. They did not push me. They did what I had taught them to do: they breathed; they stayed present; they waited.

I remembered a walk Henry and I had taken in Colorado the summer before. A long walk down a dirt road through a sea of sage to the Rio Grande gorge. Walking and talking about our lives. Summers were our time to recharge from the prison work, keep the embers of our own dream of making art full-time alive. As I walked, even then in summer's glow, I realized that most of the time I felt driven. Almost all my sentences began with "I have to, I've got to…." or, as Henry was quick to point out, "We have to…" Hardly any of them began with "I want to…"

Why was that? Was it my nature, some immutable warrior gene in my chemistry? Was it the dregs of 1960's idealism when we thought we really could save the world? Did it come from growing up in a family marked by disabilities? My father's emaciated upper body? My younger sister's stunted lower body? My mother, her own needs unclaimed and unfilled, with her hands full? My own vision problem overlooked because I was counted on to be the helper, the one who didn't have special needs?

I squinted against the lowering sun and sighed. I adjusted the patch I was wearing over my strong eye so the lazy eye could get a workout. Here I was, the supposedly healthy one, developing my own disability. Having at last to lay claim to my own needs. How ironic.

What did I need right now? Did I really need to feel burdened, driven insane by the world's problems and my puny and laughable attempts to help solve them? What would I do if I didn't HAVE to do anything? What's the worst that could happen? Would I turn into a slug? Would the world get any worse?

Suddenly, a small epiphany. Hot tears as I claimed it. I turned to my sweet husband, pulled him down on the warm ground beside me. "I want to be happy doing whatever it is I do," I told him. He smiled, nodded, held me close, tasted the tears on my cheeks.

"Even if you do nothing?" he asked gently.

"Hey, don't push it," I replied. "This is a big step for me."

"I know, I know."

I felt so seen, so understood by Henry in that moment. So thankful that I had at last found a man with whom I felt free to be exactly who I am.

As I felt now, in this small room inside a prison, in this circle of women and the resonating irony of gentle words of truth. I looked across the circle. There, sitting across from me was a young, passionate, articulate woman, imprisoned for many years and looking at the probability of many more because she acted on her beliefs. Here she was telling me that *she and her incarcerated sisters understood freedom in a way that I, living outside the prison in the free world, did not yet grasp.*

I chuckled. Wasn't freedom about having choices? Mobility? The freedom to jump in your car and boogie down the road? The freedom to sleep-in if you felt like it, be irresponsible, go out drinking, watch movies all day and all night? The freedom to not even vote? To thumb our nose at troubles in the rest of the world, as if we had an edge on freedom?

If we are such a free people living in a free country, how come we aren't free in our minds, spirits, bodies? How come we have to keep fighting for the freedoms our Constitution guarantees? How is it that we can feel trapped, burdened, oppressed, imprisoned by our jobs and responsibilities, living our lives as if we have no choice, no spirit, no freedom? And why do we construct prisons of concrete and razor wire? Why do we construct prisons in our souls? Does one reflect the other? How is it that a small, brown-eyed woman locked up in a high-security prison can feel more free than me? What is the secret she knows?

The questions generated that day inside a prison still live in me.

They move me, pinch me awake when I've grown too complacent. They help me catch myself becoming my own jailor, entering down some long narrowing tunnel as if I had no other choice, becoming resentful and bitter under my burdens—not realizing that the constriction I'm suffering from is self-imposed. They help me shake myself loose and remember.

Remember to catch the updraft, soar on the warbling flight of creativity.

Remember the gift of freedom.

What have any of us got to lose?

Freedom is what you do with what's been done to you. Jean-Paul Sartre.

BIOGRAPHY

KATHY PARK
aka Kathy Park Woolbert

I'm an artist, writer, Aikido black belt, gardener, and wife to my best friend Henry, who is also an artist. This year is our twenty-fifth wedding anniversary, quite an accomplishment in this whacked out world. You can see our work on our website www.dreampowerartworks.com. Most recently we've been collaborating on making masks together. Way fun to trust each other's artistic sensibilities after all these years.

I just graduated from college at age fifty-seven, something I never thought I'd do, and now I'm headed for graduate school, going after an MFA in creative writing so I can teach at the college level and maybe even be able to afford health insurance! That's the plan anyway. Guess we'll see what life says about that. Meanwhile, my husband and I live in a tiny village of artists, ranchers, and farmers in Colorado's vast San Luis Valley just about half a mile from New Mexico. Us artists are known locally as "artesians," which I guess is a combination of artist and Martian. When we go outside at night, Mars winks back at us.

We keep a greenhouse and grow a big garden so we can eat food year round that actually tastes good, and so we can trade and sell veggies with our neighbors. There's a lot of that around here, the old fashioned barter economy. Living in a poor, tiny, rural place, you kind of have some idea of what life will be like after the shit hits the fan, because in many ways, it's already happening here. Besides, we know what to do with shit.

When I'm not teaching Aikido, hoeing in the garden, shaping a mask, painting a watercolor, or tapping on the keyboard, I hope I'm out carving on a big block of marble. I've got one positioned on my worktable right outside the kitchen so I can look at it while I wash dishes. It's starting to talk to me.

My chapter says a lot more about who I am and what I've done in the world. Hope you enjoy it.

CHAPTER FOUR

I AM THE APPLAUSE
Christine Mahree Fowler

You could say that to the creative spirit, I am the ultimate groupie. I am the applause, the cheer from the balcony, and thrower of panties upon the stage. My heart soars at the sight of a great painting, the sound of a perfect melody, the flawless performance or the record-setting achievement. I am the ever-grateful, awe-struck fan. I bow before creation and yet I have not dared to call myself "artist." I am humbled at the mere thought.

Surrounding me are an eccentric collection of brave souls who courageously wear the crown of creation, sometimes golden, often thorny, while I cheer them onward and upward from my shadowed seat in the audience. Oh and I have been among some of the greats. Physically embraced by world-renowned artists, kissed on the hand by Andy Warhol, smacked right on the lips by the distinguished Sir Laurence Olivier and locked in conversation on a bar stool until the wee hours of the morning with my favorite Rolling Stone. My brushes with greatness have indeed been grand. But can I see myself as an artist? Where do my masterpieces lie? What is my contribution beyond that of adoring fan, cheerleader or perhaps muse?

As I have continued to ponder this question, I am taken back to a moment of awakening, the definite *breath of epiphany,* on a cold rainy afternoon some years ago. It was the saddest of days, a funeral of someone so very dear to me and my grieving soul was stripped down, naked and exposed. I had been asked to speak at the service and I had written as best I could from my heart but it seemed not nearly honorable enough, good enough, or real enough. Standing at the gravesite, I was surrounded by many people who seemed vaguely familiar yet still unrecognizable to me. Many were from childhood; people whom I had not seen in perhaps some twenty-odd years.

I looked up to see a small, frail, gray-haired woman walking carefully through the grass toward me. She wore a tiny, black pillbox hat and a mischievous, nearly bursting little smile as if she were about to laugh. She, I recognized instantly, had been my fourth grade teacher. She took me in her arms, firmly squeezing me right back into elementary school. Looking lovingly into my eyes, she said, "You know I've always played a little game with myself when I think of my students going off into the world. I think of them and I imagine what they are, what they have become in life. And do you know that I am almost always right?"

My eyes widened and I listened on, a little fearfully as she continued, "I have thought of you so often and do you know what I always imagined you are doing?" Shaking my head, I couldn't begin to imagine. "Showbiz, honey, showbiz! Am I right?" I replied as honestly as I could, "Well kinda! You know you are very close..." "Yep," she replied, I just knew it." And then she toddled away.

I was always putting on a show; writing school plays, acting in them, directing them, and even making the props. When I wasn't in school, plays were created and performed in the garage. I'd write the play, dress up my brother like a dog, or whatever I could get him to be. Yes, I was born to produce a show and I clearly continue to do so to this day.

In that moment of epiphany, it became clear to me that everything I do, the very way I have lived life, is lit by an electrical current of a "show bizzy" kind of creativity. I have plugged into it and have been blessed with the ability to act my way through the most amazing, challenging roles. If performed upon the stage or screen, I am certain they would qualify as award-winning performances. I have used this energy and spirit to create ways to encourage and even feed my young children when no viable resources were in sight. I am extremely resourceful and inventive. This gift of creativity has also given me the ability to tap dance and jump my way onto center stage in order to see and experience people and places that have all contributed to who I am. Once, in a time of great need, I was able to walk into a very exclusive art gallery, with paintings costing upwards of one hundred thousand dollars, wearing a sad little dress from the Salvation Army, to inquire about employment. I had no experience but was in such character that I walked out with one of the best jobs of my career. It was a grand and convincing performance.

Several years later I found myself the owner of a million-dollar gallery, much to my own surprise, as a result of a series of events and a situation I "fell into" through sheer hard work accompanied by innocence, naivety, eternal optimism and my trusting nature. The experience of owning this particular gallery was not a successful one in the long term in any sense other than it taught me to be less gullible and more hesitant about persuasive, glassy-eyed, "born-again" people who are so very anxious...so very desperate...to unload their financial burdens onto the shoulders of the less experienced. At that historic moment in time, on the heels of 9/11, nothing short of divine intervention would have saved that business, and *HE* was pre-occupied with greater needs than mine.

I was not the first, of course, to lose a battle involving art and the economy and unscrupulous individuals. The fine art and musical culture in which I have dwelled through the years is the land of broken dreams and tarnished golden opportunities. Artists, musicians, writers and their other creative friends and lovers are the most melancholy, funny, warm-hearted and emotionally wounded people on earth. Sit down with a group of them and their stories will kill you with sadness, and you will hear about the "takers" that are sprinkled into their colorful world who will grab any opportunity to take what is not of their own creation and corrupt it some way, somehow. Bad contracts are signed, or good ones never manage to get signed—images and words are copied and used without being accredited to the proper owners—promises of fame, notoriety and fortune are made and never fulfilled—lives are used and abused. For every successful artist or musician there are hundreds equally as gifted who simply did not get the proper exposure or who were never in the right place at the right time—the less fortunate ones who are far more gifted at creativity than self-promotion. Many gifted ones are too trusting, poor judges of character and place their futures in the sweaty palms of the wrong people. You can read about them in the papers and the magazines—along with the names of their predators who have robbed these creative few of their spirit and their future. If any creative soul has a price or a weakness, pond-scumming people will discover it. Some of these leaches are doing time in white-collar prisons as we speak, but most never pay for their crimes of the heart.

What is it about us that tends to make us victims? Without refusing all responsibility for our bad decisions, and having known many creative people, I would venture to say that it is our childlike innocence. We are the stuff that dreams are made of—we do actually "dwell in possibility," as the saying goes. Our imagination is our fuel, our belief in the basic goodness of life is our inspiration and our dreams are what keep us going. We see things that others miss. We know things that others do not. We take instruction from our souls. We want to heal the world. We hold onto the eternal hope that someday people will hear our message and grasp our intention and learn from our vision. In our complex and creative view of the universe, we are often simple and child-like at heart. We refuse to grow up, in many ways. Our refreshing optimism leaves us vulnerable. We trust too easily.

I have been the victim of predators myself, but always I have been the genuine facilitator of dreams for others—I have prepared the stage for many of my artistic friends; the ones I adore, the ones I applaud. I am the one who rolls out the red carpet at the gallery show, I am the hostess of the invitation-only private event and I am the curator of the museum quality African Artifacts exhibit. Many people sell art; I can sell art like a champion because I truly love and understand the artists—whether they are up and coming talent, experienced mature artists or indigenous African people trading ancient relics. I feel their passion and their compassion because I know both sides of this creative fence. I understand the force of creativity and I am able to communicate the message in the art to the potential buyer in a language that speaks to their soul; I have a talent for tapping into the creative voice of both the artist and the gallery visitor. I have come to realize that we do indeed share the creative fire that enlightens us, warms our souls, and burns in and around us. Yes, I am a dedicated fan; but in addition to that I am more often on the selling and marketing side of the creative process—the wind that has the ability to blow the creative flame into a raging fire that will ignite the passions of the collector and make the sale for the artist. If you are a collector, a student of the arts, or the creator of the art and you need motivation, I can certainly provide it. I can feed your flames. I am the great awe, the appreciation, and the boundless love for the creative spirit burning brightly within each of us.

The most powerful weapon on earth is the human soul on fire. Ferdinand Foch

My epiphany is simply that the creative gifts I see in others that I admire and love are also *within me*; they might manifest themselves in a different way under the circumstances of my particular life, but the gifts are there, nevertheless, and they are mine to claim as my own. I am creative; I am a survivor because of my unique brand of creativity and I am proud to walk the walk with the best of the best. They are my kind of people. My fourth grade teacher was correct—it is show biz, baby! We are all actors on the great stage of life and the performances never stop coming. But we are also the applause.

BIOGRAPHY

CHRISTINE MAHREE FOWLER
aka Christine Mahree Hier Fowler

Born in Denver, I was the first child in the sixth generation of a family native to Colorado. They had long settled in the ranch lands south of the city where they raised me in an idyllic setting on wide-open plains with mountains stretching endlessly to the west. I grew up with horses, cats, dogs, chickens, ducks and as much land as I could explore. Here my love of nature and wildlife took root.

At the age of twelve, I was taken to South Africa, just for a visit, but the journey was to have such an impact on me that I would continue to travel back many more times. First falling in love with the incredible vast array of wildlife, next with the people, I also developed a deep fascination with the culture and art of the continent. I eventually purchased land there with the plan to spend my final days on that great and mysterious continent.

Many people come from broken homes; mine was one of the shattered and early on I learned to survive on my own. I left home at the age of sixteen to live in a remote cabin in the mountains of the Sangre de Cristo. There was no running water, no electricity, and no heat with the exception of a wood burning stove. I learned to chop wood, cook over a fire and survive somewhat brutal conditions while embracing some of the most beautiful country I have ever seen.

Eventually, knowing I needed to finish my education I left my home in the mountains and attended college in Fort Collins, Colorado. Here was where I fell in love with literature and art while simultaneously falling in love with a man, getting married and having a son at the age of twenty.

After college, I traveled west to Beverly Hills to work in some of the finest art galleries in the country. I found great success and had amazing experiences working with extraordinary talents from around the world. My career thrived and my love and knowledge of art grew even stronger.

It was during that time, in a hospital on Sunset Blvd. that I would give birth to my second child, a baby girl.

With two children to raise, the pull of Colorado was strong and I eventually made the decision to move my children out of L.A. and back to the small town where I had grown up. My first marriage ended and within a month after moving, I would meet my second husband. I continued working in the art business while raising the children, although it was always more challenging and tumultuous than in Los Angeles. I have now sold art, represented artists, imported artifacts, managed and owned galleries for over twenty years. My life has been enriched by the arts in every way.

I continued to travel to Africa and other parts of the world but Africa would become my passion, my love. I imported African artifacts for a short time with my dearest friend, the author of this book, and I continue to collect African art to this day.

My son and daughter have grown into beautiful adults now; one has developed my love of nature and the other my love of art. I am currently working with my brother selling real estate; mostly land, which I never imagined myself doing. But this has completed a circle for me, bringing me back to my best friend from childhood and making a family whole again. And, after all, selling land is like selling a great work of art, by the greatest artist there is. I continue to dabble in art dealing and it is never far off my radar. It is a passion that I will carry with me throughout the remainder of my days.

I see myself eventually in my Africa, where I feel most at home and more myself even than in Colorado. I feel that it too is where I belong and it is where I will return one day.

CHAPTER FIVE

MY MAGENTA RETURN
Randy Pijoan

This is a story of one man's voyage from pessimism to optimism; from Cadmium Dark Red to Pale Magenta Hue; from the textures of gravel and broken glass to the supple fluff of a room full of white down comforters.

Often times I have referred to the "PHASES" in my life—my word for transition, I guess. There have been many phases for me, and often I find myself in the *actual process of phasing or transitioning.* Just for my own purposes I have labeled the two primary phases in my life as BC and AD. These are abbreviations which I have loosely and subjectively re-defined from their traditional meaning of major markers in time to my own labels, specifically as in "Before Marriage" and "After Divorce." I should have just called them "Before Jaded" and "After Jaded," as in the pure virgin mind and emotional body and its newly broken and jaded spirit. But this is no time for me to get cynical; in fact I have to rise out of this by a few years and find another moment in my life where I really understood my function in being "*dis*-functional" and my "*dis*" as in being *dissed,* by the overly active AD chapter in my life.

I do have to make you aware of how many times I've been "phased;" in my personal vocabulary, the times I've been jaded to the point of being phased out of or into new realizations. It's not really bragging rights I'm after here, but the result of these times comes close to that thing we call PTSD (post-traumatic stress disorder) or the ever-clever, all so common moment when men stand around showing each other their scars. I always have to show the ones on my knuckles from all the fights I had in junior high. "See that one there," I chime in, "that's from when I punched Jason in the teeth." I can trace the number of times I hit the poor bastard from the crooked pattern that his front teeth left across my knuckles.

The Phasing events in my life may not seem a lot to those of you who have experienced major trauma, but mine number at about eight in total, and in all honesty most of them were mainly due to my pursuit of some female and the quest for the perfect relationship. You see I have made a lot of bad choices and stumbled into situations that were way past my educational background, and despite all my *known* faults I always seemed to discover new ones—new aspects of who I am. But it made a better artist of me.

The first-ranked heartbreak of all my heartbreaks that I have experienced was the "Mount Kilimanjaro" of heartbreaks. This was the point at which I fell hard for the first time, totally unaware and unprepared for the difficult trek I was undertaking. After the break-up was when the climb became the most rigorous of climbs; meaning the challenge of *getting over it.*

I also think of this time as my Fall more so than *fell.* Like the changing of a season; Spring, Summer and Fall. Because it was followed by the longest Winter of my life. But that Winter needed to happen in order to freeze and kill whatever germs I had previously held to be the truth. The path I was on seemed to be one of search and destroy, rebuild, refocus and then being set back on track like a squeaky toy train by some big hand from above. I believe the purpose was to see if I had learned anything from the previous derailment disaster.

This mountain of an event delineated that BC from the AD time in my life, and little did I know in my washed out, colorless world of the BC that all the art I had painted up to that point was flaccid, sallow and lacking contrast.

My First Phasing

We'll call it "The Fake and the Furious." Sounds like a bad movie about some Las Vegas stripper who nights as a vengeful vigilante, but in fact it took place in the mountains of Colorado. Co-starring an artist and a scientist, both of whom were young, in love, and fooling each other into the "simplicity" of their marital plunge into an intended happy lifetime in sickness and in health, so on and so forth. Please note, I know the commonality of this theme but really you've got to hear where this plot takes our desperate character (me), so don't worry, I'll speed up this tangle so it seems less broken than it really was.

In January of that year I had moved out to the mountains seeking some refuge from the town that reminded me of everything I had lost—and I had lost a lot from that divorce. I moved into a remote cabin that became a retreat for me—my personal healing space, so that I could search out the answers to what the hell went wrong. I didn't realize that this would be the Winter straight out of the history books; blizzards, wind storms, creepy animals, broken cars and poverty. The latter of which was almost a running gag due to the one meal a day, no running water, and a pellet stove that heated my studio whenever I had money to go out and buy the three dollar and fifty cent bags of pellets. Otherwise I slept on the floor in my sleeping bag trying to keep the mice from finding warmth in the same bag. I *was* the proverbial "starving artist," picking mouse turds out of my rice and painting into the night just to distract myself from my hunger pains, never knowing what deep and powerful painting would emerge at 2am. I could only pull energy and inspiration from my emotional self, because nothing was beautiful to me anymore. I began to see the despair in what I was feeling, wondering just how far the bottom was from where I was at that point in time, and if I would ever feel the joys of love again. I know—pathetic—like certifiably psycho and pathetic. But the thought of suicide was very close to actuality.

Every now and then the man that had given me this space to work in would come over. He'd come bursting through the door followed by an avalanche of golden retrievers, wagging and barreling through the studio after him and his trail of cigar smoke, like a speeding locomotive arriving at the station. "Randy, how's it going!?" he'd yell, while making himself at home, as he should since he owned the place. "Fine," was my wimpy reply from a messy head-space. He would walk over to the large easel and say "What are you working on? Hmmm, interesting," as he puffed proudly on his soggy cigar.

He was a fan of my work and supported my efforts to rebuild my life. I would explain that I was actually discovering what the artistic piece meant as I painted along with it, and that I thought maybe it was a depiction of my death and demise.

"You know," puffing and explaining, "I see a lot of Hope in this piece; I see your freedom and your plight as being a way out of your current straits."

And he was right, but I sure didn't feel that way at the time. Over the next few months I reached bottom, the real bottom, and that was just as hard to reach as ascending to the highest peak of the climb. It reminded me of Switzerland, when I was there years earlier visiting my great-grandmother. I noticed how the peaks were like the valleys but inverted, both coming to perfect points; and I had indeed reached the bottom point, in an epic moment.

Shortly after, my business partner had handed me one of two little blue mushrooms and said, "Here, these are the last two and I think you need one. Cheers!" as we thumped their tiny blue crowns together and swallowed them like multi-vitamins. "Thanks," I said as though I had been given a prized possession and off I went to my bedroom. I wasn't afraid of the drug because I had never done anything like them before, and because my friend had been eating these things for years and it had never seemed to bother him. But that was the big surprise in all of this. Even he had not been exposed to one of this type before, and I on the other hand was about ready to ride the fast train to the bottom of my soul.

Hours had gone by without any effect, and then suddenly as I lay on my back hardly sleeping, the room started to unfold into a multitude of fanciful membranes. Like layers of an onion, my physical world was fast becoming a sewn and sinewed kaleidoscope of living tissue. I was intrigued but bewildered at the connectedness of all that is and all that isn't, and from an artistic standpoint I was wondering if this world was really made up of this stuff, but I was fast becoming air-sick. I was wondering how much longer that this wavy airplane ride was going to continue; (and it wasn't minutes at all, but days) when it became forty-eight hours of my little blue friend showing me just how delusional my life really was. Then the pain of my spinning, out-of-control mind screaming "Help Me! Help Me! I Can't Live Any More!"

So after three sleepless days and nights my tired body put me out of commission and into a deep dream state; quiet, peaceful, to the point that I thought "I may be dead."

As soon as I woke up, ten pounds lighter, I tried to shake off the bad memories, bad hair, and even worse that bad taste in my mouth. I immediately headed over to my business associate's studio and calmly asked, "What in the #!%&**#$ WAS THAT ALL ABOUT!?" I wanted to avenge my damaged mind. But to my joyful surprise, like a breath of fresh air, I was finally in and out of the "bottom lands" and on my way toward the only direction left for me—up. And oh yes, my kind and giving business associate also had three days of psychedelic hell, if it's any consolation.

It was around this time that I started dating heavily again, and I wasn't without my flash-backs or jaded cynicism towards life, and the ladies, but I did start to see for the first time in my life the effects this whole thing had on my creative work. I had a new way of, let us say, painting the shadows darker and richer than ever before, and not only that, but my ideas had even gotten bigger, and a more important emotional content had entered into the visual concepts. It seemed that a fresh, brave palette and a new depth had infused my spirit and my art.

Following this up I found that my spirituality had turned a corner as well, and increasingly my world was filling up with positive events that I couldn't explain away, and if I could they were quickly chased by another event and another. It seemed to be connected to the healing of my emotional self. Like once I was on the floor of my studio in a piled up mess, gripping my stomach, writhing and praying for something good to happen, when the phone rang. "Hello, Randy Pijoan's Studio," I answered confidently. (I would answer that way just to convince myself of my professional status.) This time it was a phone call from a man who knew Dr. Michael Pijoan, and wanted to know if I had any relation to that person. I told him that he was my grandfather. "Who was your grandmother?" he asked. I explained that I was the grandson of Susan Axon and knew them both very well of course. He went on saying that he had been with my granddad in Nevada during the years that Michael was going through a divorce with my grandmother. At that time this stranger who called me was just a teenager working on an Indian reservation in northern Nevada, helping my grandfather with a multitude of medical needs, all of which could keep my grandfather occupied during the duration allotted for a legal divorce. Nevada seemed to be the place in the thirties for men seeking a "quick as possible" separation, and after a brief conversation about this man's experience with my granddad and his situation with his ailing wife it sounded like a rush visit to his house, one hundred and twenty miles away, was in order.

All of this, and the experiences that ensued at his suburban home, snapped me further out of my funk, and once again I had time to visit the past with my late grandfather's memories. Remembering him as the one that showed me how to fly fish, (he was a very well known fly man, and had written books on the subject) and more importantly his starting me off, when I was just three, on my way to being an artist with my first oil painting lessons. Now it was as if he was reaching out to me from beyond this earthly life to help me find what was really important, especially since nobody in the family had any clue as to his activities during those missing years. So just like that, a two-year period in his complicated life had finally fallen into place. And there I was with this stranger, happy again and finding my own story in my granddad's, and flipping through a photo album of carefully collected moments of those mysterious years. As fast as it had all started, one moment I was copying the black and white photos there in the guy's cozy dining room and the next I was back on the road home, closely guarding my newly found good mood. I was content and eager to get back and use that same magical phone to call my family with this exciting news.

Sampling the air around me, I wondered just how thin is this veil between our world and the next? Why was there such an obvious ripple effect from a single stone thrown from my emotions? Being cast into the blank pool that I thought was just the space in front of me. What is this matter? This water? That transferred my energy to the other side and then back to me again? My only answer was the effect of the funny little blue mushroom, "all its membranes sew together with live webs made by the depths of our connections," besides the feeling of wanting to throw up of course. Now I was truly on the AD side of my phasing and all the art I made after that was much more real and relevant. In fact even to this day I look back at that body of my work and wonder—did I even know I was painting *that well* at that time? And I sometimes get jealous of the person that I was then.

Phasing Two—The Epiphany

Now that I have given my introduction to the Phasing process I think it's time for me to explain the arrival of the Real Epiphany. Maybe for all intents and purposes it's a smiley little face, appearing at my door nine years later as a remnant from Phase One, give or take a month. But it came after a brimmed full nine years of cause and effect, fight and flight, and any other limbic crushes you could think of. In fact this

Epiphany, brazen with confidence, would be the one to answer all of those deep and meaningful questions. Little things like *what is the meaning of life, why do things come around that go around, how do I paint car headlights so they look like they're on, what is better than money, when is it appropriate for us guys to use pink in a landscape painting, and just how thin is that veil between our world and the next?* Oh yes, you're right, those are not all epiphanies, but if you have a Grand Epiphany you need to have a notebook ready to write down everything you've learned, a camera for the before and after photos and in my case, lots and lots of canvas to paint on.

I, like many young boys, have nine lives, and I have found myself in a continuous series of bad judgment calls that have led me straight to the brink of major calamity. Don't worry. You've heard most of these scenarios before, such as driving too fast with your peers egging you on while nearly going off a steep cliff or the classics of getting too close to fire or lighting a brick of firecrackers with a fuse that is shorter than a chihuahua's hair. But really what I'm about to tell you about that has happened to me goes even beyond what you might believe to be improbable.

The list is as follows:

1. Nearly drowning twice, once as a baby in my mother's amniotic fluid, and again as a mischievous five-year-old in my grandfather's swimming pool outside of Santa Fe. On that occasion my sister informed my mother that I was floating face down in the swimming pool, and my mother, an RN, jumped in and resuscitated me back from my peaceful float.

2. I have been struck by lightning twice in my life "that I remember" and both times my hair was the only thing missing from random spots on my head. I've always wondered if the third time will be a charm but I'm sure I'll live through that as well.

3. Rock climbing has served its share of mishaps, and as you can imagine in that spot there is little room for error, so a few too many times without proper equipment and incorrect assumptions brought me close many a time to the End of Randy Days. A well placed tree or rock ledge always seemed to be my saving grace.

4. Canoeing, or other mountain adventures that make up the outdoor sporting list, and some that may have been beyond my skill level, could have been seen as my last voyage on a number of occasions. My nerve was always bigger than my common sense.

But on one totally unrelated occasion I was getting some acupuncture work done on me and the doctor explained that I was lucky to be alive. "What do you mean?" I asked full well knowing the truth of his remark. "Well...," he explained, "after all you've told me about your mountaineering and intense rescues I'm surprised that you haven't died of an Aortic Dissection."

"Okay," I said with some hesitation, "what the hell are you talking about?"

Because I knew there had been plenty of "non-aortic" circumstances that might have had me in the cross-hairs but thankfully nothing had happened. I do know how Chinese medicine has helped millions of Chinese but where was he getting this diagnosis from, the color of my tongue or the spots in my eyes? Chinese medicine has always helped me but this just seemed too far out there, but since my doctor has never been wrong before I listened with intense curiosity.

"You have Mitrovalve Prolapse, and from the sounds from inside your chest and other symptoms I suspect that Marfans might run in your family."

Silence found my lips for the first time, a target never before missed by my busy brain, but now I was silent. Marfans?!

"Actually it does run in the family, but why do you say I'm lucky to be alive based upon this?"

He then put his hand on my shoulder and began to explain it in laymen's terms. I won't bore you with this part, but he basically told me that I should be careful because I could die of an aortic dissection due to my rigorous adventures. Let's just say that I didn't think I would ever be a victim of any of this; so the words bounced off of my twenty-nine-year-old indestructible body. In fact I knew my mother and sister had this Marfans, but I was pretty sure it had missed me or at least I had healed myself of it. No really, I believed this. The entire "victim thing," I always felt, could be controlled from my head, and this Marfans syndrome was not worth it because I was saving myself for much bigger tragedy, something a little more heroic. I could live in fear for the rest of my life, and it always seemed like just a huge waste of energy spent on worrying, fretting and the possibility of dying and other things that may never happen. That mysterious event is going to happen and you may never know when or where; and by the time it does, the inflictions and/or inflictors will have moved on. It is what it is, so now is the time to either ignore it or fix it. But Mafans? What is the enemy here? And I didn't even know if he was right. Chinese medicine, for the first time, seemed to me like it needed more proof to back it up. Where are the MRI's, CAT scans, X-rays and blood tests? For me, after the one day I gave myself to think about it, it was back to life as usual and time to move on with a shout of full speed ahead readiness.

In the back of my mind the Marfans faded into a bad history lesson, retreating fast into the rearview mirror of mist left from my high speed car cursing ahead in the rainy commute to my new Chicago studio. I had just met the new love of my life, a young artist, a sweetheart candy pack with an eye for adventure. She and I had a plan to move to Southern Colorado and remodel a straw-bale, off-the-grid, out-of-the-way ranch. We were both set for the task but as all things go you really don't know what you're in for until you've been doing it for a year, and by that point you may or may not be up for the long haul.

Once there, she found another love interest who was a friend of mine who came complete with her ticket out of the tiny remote border town. Leaving me alone with my wild-west tumbleweed landscape, and an inner scene that closely resembled one of my minimal expansive paintings. I was heartbroken like I had been many times before, and it was getting easier but in degrees only I could find obvious; to the outside world I was in desperate need of healing my wounds. I found myself going to my studio a lot, and after the twenty minute drive to my new studio in a drafty sculptor's shop located in the oldest town in Colorado I was finally ready to paint. My friend the sculptor, by his own right a famous artist, had given me a new start under his wing. Finally I was being productive and doing my best work ever; I was preparing for a big show in the early spring with my best gallery in ten years. A show I could count on to always bring home the bacon, especially important in the year following 9/11, a time in which all the artists I knew were hustling to regain the nineties' momentum. My new studio in San Luis was perfect for me; I could meet the locals and visit the coffee shop daily with my new-found sculptor friend, talk shop and remember the good ole'days. But I was very lonely and longing for companionship. I would never have moved out there to such a remote location if I had thought I would have been up against those elements alone.

One of the best ways to fight the loneliness was to just start exploring the "land of the ladies." I had always believed that I was meant to be with the right person, and after a life of meeting dozens of interesting gals I knew that I wasn't going to find her sitting around my studio pouting, and would you believe on my first outing from that lonely ranch in months I went to the nearest city and found her at an art opening. It was the entire movie cliché, with our eyes meeting from across the room, as I leaned towards my friend next to me.

"*Who* is *she?*" I panted. I felt like I had known her in my mind before ever laying eyes on her, and with an introduction that night, and two months of disciplined pursuit I had my first date with "the glowing gal from Minnesota." After a few weeks of having fun together, even if it was from a distance, I soon had her over to my house in the country. I seemed ready at that time to take the dating to the next level but she used the visit to tell me that it was over, and she wanted us to be just friends. Right; within moments I realized that I had not gotten over "The Chicago girl," and soon I would be back to my windy landscape of coyotes, sagebrush and dark nights packed with clusters of stars on steroids. Alone again.

It was winter now and the firewood was stacked to dry in the Southwest winds and my cats were up to their normal catch and release torture tactics of finding mice coming into the house from the cold winter nights. In the morning I would often find little blood spots on the adobe oxblood floors from the be-headings of the night, and those chilly sunrises were full of small rituals. Lighting the fire in the woodstove and filling the tea kettle, and sometimes the occasional hot shower to waken from my slumber.

This Monday morning didn't seem much different. I awoke from a night out on the town with collectors, celebrating, with great fanfare, the purchase of their new painting. It was a piece I had painted years before and had held onto due to its importance. A piece that launched a new body of work called the "Light Bulb Series," and they had somehow convinced me to sell it to them. I may have been upset, groggy and disappointed from the break-up from Minnesota's girl the day before, but I was going to attack the day with gusto. Sliding out of bed in my boxers, stretching into the sun's light pouring in through the large east windows, I coughed; you know, like the kind of morning cough that clears your throat. That's when I felt it; a tearing sensation in my back just between my shoulders. "What the Hell!" I coughed again and that's when I felt even a stranger sensation of pain. Grabbing for the counter in the kitchen I stumbled toward the phone. There I was alone and losing consciousness while pressing the redial on the phone, having no idea who the person was I had previously called.

Luckily, my neighbor Henry answered quickly "Hello."

"Henry," I barked. "I'm dying, please come fast." I was in pain and quickly blacking out on my way back to the bedroom to lie down again, and I thought I had made it but found myself floating away from my collapsed body half under the bed and twisted into convulsing spasms.

I saw myself with new eyes, unafraid and without a care of the old body; floating weightless towards the corner of my room, up in the vigas and latias of the north corner above my bed. I continued out of the house able to see from all angles at once; the top, bottom and sides, all part of one wide sight; and sound was an energy felt but not heard. This was bliss without any question. I thought it and it happened, I felt it all and it was all good. So without a moment's decision I found myself over my favorite spot on the cliffs overlooking the Rio Grande. Gravity was an illusion of the Earth that I was not even concerned with; plainly I had to make the next move to jump off—to leave, and that's when I felt the sounds of my neighbor's voice.

"Randy, come back, we're here...." The female voice was like a magnet, I knew it was me they were calling for, and within that thought I was moving fast back to my house on the prairie. I got within inches of myself and saw the suffering and twitching of my body—the cold hard reality of me on the mud floor curled in Henry's wife's arms.

"No, not for me," too uncomfortable and harsh, and the river pulled me back like an opposing magnet.

"Randy, wherever you are, take a deep breath in and bring it back with you," she repeated. I was being given a choice between suffering, or total and utter bliss. Inexplicably I chose SUFFERING, and with the sucking in from the bliss world back into the physical world I realized that I had made the choice. Suffering is often under-rated, and from the first inhale I could sense the denseness of this reality; thick inhauls of air felt like I was trying to breath in chunks of soupy water. Shaking and coming into full focus of my new situation, with paramedics standing over me now, their annoying voices sounding like a cement room full of angry dogs barking and fighting to see who could be the loudest. When would this all end? How would this all end? And by God could someone tell these people that I don't really want to be here answering their stupid questions.

The long ambulance ride ended in the nearest emergency room fifty miles away, and from the genius of the doctor at hand the diagnosis an hour later was that I was barely alive from a 99.9% Aortic Dissection, and an airplane was on its way to pick me up and take me to Denver for my first surgery ever. Yikes, now was not the time for me to *joke* and declare my life's work as a success. I reached toward my sculptor friend in one of my few serious moments behind the ER curtains.

"Huberto," who was standing close enough to hear me. "You know those paintings in my studio? They are the best thing I have ever painted, and please know that I don't mind going out at this time."

Huberto leaned in to say something comforting like "Oh, you'll be back to do more and better," but I interrupted explaining, "No you don't get it; Huberto, you have to promise yourself that everything you do from now on must be created like it's your last piece!"

I could tell that the doctor was getting impatient and wanted the people in the room to leave.

"Seriously Huberto, I have no regrets. I've done everything in my life that I set out to do; no regrets; do your best work like your history depends on it."

On that note the doctor had whisked my company away, putting me under a drug-induced sleep and I was quickly on my night flight to Denver. After the landing and hopping onto a vibrating helicopter, my eyes caught glimpses of the busy highways below, almost as cold and lifeless to me as my body on the floor of my house just hours before. This city seemed foreign for the first time; I felt uncomfortable with this detachment since I had loved the city before.

The surgeon greeted me with my family priest and my father.

"Randy, you have had an Aortic Dissection and we must operate now; we give you less than a five percent chance of making it here tonight!" he explained as the automatic doors of the roof-top ER closed out the sound of the thumping helicopter.

My father's face looked on with hope, "Son…,"

I interrupted, hoping to give him some strength, "Dad it's so good to see you.....I was planning on coming up to see you and Mom soon, but not this soon."

"Son, I love you...," as I went to fade the jumble of frantic voices fell away into nothingness.

Next thing I remember was waking up as the nurses tugged on one of the many hoses and tubes coming out of places on my body I had never even paid attention to, and that's when I saw, through blurred eyes, the huge bandages and wounds for the first time. Science and technology were hanging out of my ass like cosmic tethers from an astronaut's orbital life-suit. Cables and wires were connected to just about every beeping box and monitor in the room, leaving little room for a nurse to carefully navigate around. I was in for a real harsh, aggravatingly painful ride; the story of success, learning to walk talk and eat, like a clichéd athlete's story of coming back from all negative odds. But it was actually simpler than that; in fact my lovely sister and a couple of well-intentioned friends lifted my spirits towards a speedy recovering. Normally this is the point where I would pay homage to all of those friends and family who visited and brought flowers, and gave unconditionally to my well being. But this story is about my Mega Epiphany.

Remember Minnesota Gal? Well she came back to rescue me from my post-surgery depression. That's right, I did hate the fact that I had come back to so much heavy misery as a prize for just surviving, but my "Great Escape" from this cumbersome body was not seeming like a long enough vacation. However there I was, with Sarah, and as she pushed my wheel chair down to the end of the Cardiac ward, I realized the power of her feminine grace. She was getting me to a better view of the mountains; beyond the smog of the city you could see the sky transition from a blue-gray blend to Colorado's rugged Rocky Mountains. Sarah had no idea that this was a view of where I had spent the better half of my childhood, she just had a way to her smile that said see I knew you would like this. And damned if her intoxicating laugh didn't make me laugh uncontrollably. I think in fact if she had sneezed it would be so accurately pronounced that an entire room of deaf people would suddenly all start sneezing at once. Sarah missed her calling as a stage actress, or Broadway singer. Projecting her every emotion toward you, unabated, whether you were ready for her facial honesty or not. So there I was laughing for the first time in my new life, clutching my chest in a concerned desperation, praying that it wouldn't burst open like a zip-lock bag from staple to staple. The world somehow had turned uglier from the last time I had seen this view. But Sarah had a smile that could bloom flowers. I was back, and at least my sense of humor hadn't been scraped and bled from me.

Recovery (similar to the AA approach to the word) took a long cold Winter of healing and groaning at the pace of an eighty-year-old Banana slug. Including a month spent under the watchful eye of my mother and father at their home in Denver, and being covered by a freak snowstorm that smothered the house in forty-eight inches of snow. None of which held back the stream of truly great friends who came with gifts of hugs and laughter.

It wasn't long though until I had to be on my way back home, and after heart-felt goodbyes, a dear friend drove me back to my house in the middle of the San Luis Valley. A place that is as basically remote as you can get in Southern Colorado. A valley that channels Winter straight to you, both physically and psychologically, better than anywhere else I've ever been. I found myself back under the vastly lit midnight milky way, a shower of stars, like millions of little glowing eyes staring at me with judgment; I felt vulnerable as if being in the cross-hairs of God. My cats were also watching my every move from a dimly lit window sill as I shuffled around the stucco house. I was talking to myself like a sportscaster with Turrets syndrome, barking the plays in quick noises, but with no audience. I was alone, longing for the health I once had, and the love of life I once had before visiting the other side.

The house seemed well taken care of by my super-generous neighbors, and now with food being delivered every day I had enough to feed a family of six. How would I ever pay them back? I questioned the logic of a grown man asking for help, and I hoped this all would end soon because I was so indebted to them all. This was too much to handle; how could I ever send that many thank-you cards, a task always so daunting for my lazy system of keeping phone numbers and addresses. There were even times I found myself bringing in firewood one log at a time, panting for air, agonizing for a companion during the frigid and bitter nights. I had even written a poem about my last sleeping pill. You see I had a loving relationship with that vial of nocturnal dream machines. I fantasized about ending it with one big handful, a deep lasting swallow from the plastic brown pill jar. So a poem was in order when I got down to the last pill, one tiny pill that I decided to cherish and to this day I still have, a sign of my ability to resist addiction and handle matters from my own inner strength. If it was anything it was an example of who I really wanted to become.

Life was now coming at me with hard density, with twelve new bills from the hospital's various departments, all piling up on top of the twelve other bills I already had from living expenses. And due to the fact I didn't have any health insurance, the surgery's grand total was roughly ninety-eight thousand dollars. Made even worse by my annual Randy Pijoan Art Show at my best gallery, happening just two months after arriving home, and this time instead of the usual twenty paintings delivered I only had five. To add insult to injury the gallery sold them out, a good thing, but refused to pay me promptly and so then I either needed to get anti-depressant pills or a cause of some kind.

Remember Minnesota Girl—Sarah with an "h?" She was back in my life again. She was able (effortlessly) to make me feel like a man again, and more importantly she gave me a chance to help her out with her volunteer job at the local homeless shelter. My job was to do whatever was needed. I found myself fixing toilets, washers, dryers, doors and showers, repairing just about anything. I don't mean to simplify this part because it was the first true outward manifestation of my new "life shift." I was coming from being a self-centered, career focusing, driven madman, "my way or no way" type of guy, to a *community volunteer warrior.*

I suddenly remembered the sacrifices that my grade school teachers had made to push me on, giving me the tools and spending hours after school to help me learn the ways of art. The teachers had all done this on little if any at all real pay, and now it seemed that their energy had come full circle back to me. Had I always been meant to receive the torch from them? Or was my timeclock finally now ticking to its last season on the calendar? Was "Give Back Time" the message I was supposed to receive? I believe the answer is "Yes" to all of the above questions, and in fact I knew secretly that there was never going to be a "No" answer from now on except on the things that might take me away from my passionate cause. I was addicted to the idea of helping people just because *someone has to do it,* and the people who demand to know "what's in it for me?" are going to be out of my life whether I decide it or not.

Hell-bent, I set out on a five-year project, in fact a monumental task of construction in the middle of NoWhere, Colorado, to make sure the kids of my community would never go without education in the arts; theater, music, poetry etc. The fight was now on to save the cultural integrity and importance of teaching our next generation the value of self-expression through creative mediums. Championed by fantastic individuals, artists and politicians within the valley, a community was gathered to attach themselves to this cause, and they all, but one, volunteered on this huge task. I've always said "Take the greediest bastards you know and convince them to volunteer, and their riches will double within weeks." I mean if you truly want to get rich, I guess then give away half of what you have, and it will double without question, as long as that's not why you're doing it.

"Ventero Open Press" was born, a gallery and print shop that serves excellent coffee to its customers, and also arranges "open mic nights" and free concerts. Our organization is now the artistic watering hole for our small Hispanic town, and stands proudly as a state-wide example of a community that takes matters into its own hands, never waiting again for power-hungry suits to make the right decisions for our rural kids. Or for decisions made hundreds of miles away to be trickled down to us in sound bites and non-action. If you think you know what's best, then take it to the people and build from their instincts; only then will they support the cause that is worthy.

This is the point within my story where I will explain all of this in a nut shell. It is also the place where I will resist the urge to preach and slither out with some boasting, self-serving expletive. Instead I offer you this, *my real epiphany*:

Change that comes from within, like mine, is real; it walks, talks and breaths The Truth, and The Truth may seem too fantastic to believe for many people, or even fake. But for those of us who have been to the next life and back, and have had a very mysterious experience to try to believe all on our own, the change is absolutely genuine and The Truth is absolute. There is no possible way of faking it. After my near-death experience, even my own mother asked me if I was a "Walk in Spirit." *I just knew that I was Spirit.* That's right—for those of you atheist scientists out there, Spirit is that thing that my granddad said "Puts the fire in your furnace." It allows you to explain the emotional reasons why you do things—not for love, mind you, and not for the lovers you have had either—but for the *Passion*. Those changes from within, and the physical wounds that manifested themselves on my body, only go to show the thickness of this world. And the Art—the only Goddess I have ever known—my Muse, has kept me a living artist and not a dead one.

Maybe someday I will have these final words chiseled as my epitaph: *Passionately Laugh, Cry, Love, Educate and Die.*

Oh yeah, and don't forget to clean your brushes.

BIOGRAPHY

RANDY PIJOAN

The paintings of San Luis, Colorado artist Randy Pijoan have been establishing his roots in northern New Mexico and central Colorado for over twenty-five years. It has been only recently that his work and his home have come full circle from a journey though mind, emotion, spirit and the contemporary reality at *this* turn of the century. Randy Pijoan has become the leader and developer of the contemporary art movement known as "Phrasism," an art movement that has influenced film, theater, and all visual formats, including sculpture. Pijoan's work has been published in leading national magazines such as *American Artist Magazine, Artist Magazine, International Artist Magazine, SouthWest Art Magazine, The Santa Fean, Santa Fe Focus, American Art Collector, Chicago Tribune, Four Corners* and *Arts and Antique Magazine.*

City night-scapes became one of the latest adventures by Pijoan, and within ten years brought him national recognition as the "Premier night-scape painter in the United States." From this body of work, painted primarily in Chicago, his "Phrasist" work took on the challenges of painting crowds of people and social interactions both interior and exterior, while eliminating the all too common horizon-based composition. After writing the "Phrasist Manifesto," the first national traveling show dedicated to this movement began in 2001, and included invitations to other national artists, poets and writers selected for their cutting edge work in and around the "Phrasist" design.

Pijoan's work still continues the focus on contemporary realism of the city and rural western landscape, but since his near-death experience several years ago, Randy has been doing what he calls "Giving Back." Creating art now shares the table with teaching and opening new horizons for up and coming artists, preserving the future for his local community of artists. His non-profit organization, "Ventero Open Press" has been his focus since the time he returned home from his surgery; a focus that he believes is the most powerful and effective way to preserve the future of his community of San Luis and surrounding areas. He is giving back to the younger generations and making this non-profit the main source of humanitarian assistance for the arts and the kids of San Luis Valley.

Randy Pijoan's work can be seen at the following galleries: Peterson in Santa Fe, Blink Gallery in Boulder, Bonner David in Scottsdale, Hilligos Gallery in Chicago, Fountainside Gallery in Wilmington, N. Carolina, Ventero Open Press in San Luis, Colorado.

Visit: www.randypijoan.com

Learn more about Randy's non-profit, Ventero Open Press, located at 316 Main Street in San Luis, Colorado, 81152, at www.ventero.org

CHAPTER SIX

fireplace meditations
Kyle Moshrefi

so this is what it feels like. to be caught between mind and body. meaning brain and heart. a manual kick-start to the beat of 'where the hell did i put my keys.' i used to daydream of willow trees. and of you. and me. but that's the problem with dreaming—it's like everything else.
meaningless…unless…
lying there on the beach that night looking up at the sky and i remembered something you said. about the non-linearity of stars. and if i had go-go gadget arms i would have reached up and moved one. or two. purposefully rearranged them to fit some sort of solar plan {et.} but i didn't know back then…
i didn't know i'd be searching roadmaps of solace trying to retrace the steps of your promise. but promises aren't like the lost tokens of empty wishing wells…
this was the one
{heart}
that wasn't meant to be
broken.

my heart would tell stories if it could
oh the stories it would tell. drunk in a
sea of ache and pain it would grab you
by the shoulders and look you dead
in the eyes. i've lived lifetimes with
people who don't even know it. the most
brilliant love stories that have never
been told. never been played out
replay themselves in my mind's
heart time and again. knocking the
wind right out of me. sip. beer.
drop. tear. whirlwind adventures leaving

me on shaky ground. i've turned into all
those girls i hate. the guarded and the
jaded. the one foot out the door types
who try to sabotage anything before
it gets "too good to be true." because
i was trained and told that true...doesn't
exist in this world. good is merely
a fantasy land for those who have it
luckier than us. than me. could it be
that as good as it gets has already
come and gone. did i trade her in at a
pawn shop in exchange for that one
last glance one last chance with the
girl who didn't give a shit about me?
fuck. its just my luck. and now i've
turned into her. she taught me to
wish on shooting stars.
that our story would never
grow old. like one of your favorite
books that you turn to in times of
great comfort. the one story
that will continue to be pulled off the shelf.
but for how long. i just think i can't.
not anymore. i can't wait for
someone who isn't waiting for me.
how did i get to this place. i can't
even recognize the face that stares
back in the mirror. face. your fears.
fight through the tears of everything
broken. i'm broken. things left unspoken
building higher and higher until the
wind blows knocking us to our knees.
i wish we were three sitting up in trees.
the world so big and full of potential.
we could have been anything then.

we could have been anything we wanted to be.
just you. and me.
we would have you know.

so why didn't either one of us just say so...?

I grew up in a small middle to upper class college town. The summers were unbearably hot and smelled offensively of cow. The winters rained down on us incessantly and showered us with an array of May flowers. I suppose I had what anyone would consider a "normal" childhood. I was a happy-go-lucky kid immersed in a world of sports and innocence. It wasn't really ever anything to write home about I guess. I was blessed with supportive parents who miraculously are still together after forty years, and I was subjected to healthy torment; which came in the form of my two older brothers. It wasn't until puberty started to rear its ugly head from around the corner that my seemingly "perfect" life started to take a turn for the worse.

Accustomed to my tomboyish behaviors of rough-housing, tree-climbing, mud bathing, and juvenile egg-throwing—coupled with my tendency towards skinning my palms/elbows/knees/chin/whatever-other-bony-extremities from falling off whatever mode of transportation I was using on any particular day—the development of my Obsessive Compulsive Disorder came as a shock not only to me, but to my family as well. It had never been in my nature to worry about anything. In my juvenile opinion, stitches were cool and rubbing some dirt in them was tough. Risk taking was exciting and dangerous activities were welcomed. I had the brain of what I now call: *normal* people. If there is one thing I can consistently say I miss about my childhood it would most certainly be that; a worry-free, normal existence. At the age of twelve my life as I knew it came to a screeching halt.

The DSMV-IV defines Obsessive-Compulsive Disorder (OCD) as "a psychiatric anxiety disorder most commonly characterized by a subject's obsessive, distressing, intrusive thoughts and related compulsions (tasks or "rituals") which attempt to neutralize the obsessions."

Sounds pleasant, no? The description itself is enough to make me want to wash my hands clean of it. My own definition of OCD...well, it's an inner, silent shame.

i'm in love.
in love with the sinister sorrow of my life.
beating my fists on the locked doors and windows
of tomorrow's strife. i knew myself once and maybe
i always will. i know myself now but i suppose one

*can never truly tell. i can't tell you the time and
place of it. the day i fell. it all came so sudden
and the reality of it all comes down to two, three
or four points. it forms a circular square of mystery.
this vague miscalculated history. mislyrical
misadventures of something poetic. what is poetry
if it is not disguised with the drippings of confusion
and magical illusion.
but i'm going to "knuckle down and
be ok with this."* and my innocence is just
something i'm going to have to learn to miss.
because i'm in love. with my life. with
the beauty that was this day. even if it did
knock me on my ass in every which way.
so its ok. it's all a feigning memory anyway.
the one in the corner…
head bent, eyes down…
that's me.*

It started with an irrational fear of the sun. Of being outdoors. Of doing everything I once did that defined my childhood. I broke into emotional outbursts of confusion, frustration, and not-so-silent pain. I developed anxiety, and panic attacks became my new best friend. I replaced the wind-on-my-face with tingling sensations in my arms. Scabbed knees were replaced with loss of sensation in my legs. Dizzy spells and blurred vision superseded merry-go-rounds and running around playfully. Therapy sessions stood in for soccer practice and tennis lessons. And then the Rorschach ink-blot tests confirmed it: I must have been crazy. Right? I mean, I was ashamed. I was confused. Why else would my parents send me to therapy where doctors asked me endless questions and showed me ink-stained papers which supposedly revealed some insight into my "troubled mind?" I was a tiny little twelve-year-old girl. I had no idea what was going on. I was scared literally out-of-my-mind.

I lied to my friends. I lied to my brothers. I lied to my parents. I even tried lying to myself. None of these lies sold. I couldn't fib my way out of OCD. It is my curse…or maybe my blessing…to be a very transparent individual. I am incapable of hiding my feelings. I've been told that I have a very genuine smile, because I smile so rarely—only when I mean it. When I'm sad/mad/happy, people see it in my eyes. They see it in my posture. It's displayed all over my body. Emotions consume me. I'm merely a puppet to my emotional environment. Why couldn't I have been a Jim Henson Muppet instead? Although, I remember Kermit had some bouts of melancholy himself...what was it? It's not easy being green? Oh Kermit, I so totally understand where you're coming from. We should meet up sometime for a drink. Shed a woe-is-me tear or two into our half empty pint glasses.

My grades started slipping. Friendships became strained. My parent's frustration at times boiled over to anger, and I started to slip further and further into my shameful dis-ease.

I say dis-ease because that is essentially how it feels. I am never at ease with myself. I am never at ease in my surroundings. Years of practice have taught me to keep my symptoms to a minimum in public. Most people I encounter on any given day would have no idea what I struggle with internally. Sadly, some of my best friends today don't even know (although I tend to be oblivious to the perceptions of others). I've hid this part of me for so long and so well that I almost feel like I have split personalities. Kyle—the calm, cool and collected, versus Willie (my evil twin)—the scared, anxious, agoraphobic, angry, twitchy, introverted leprechaun that lives inside my head. A little long-winded I know, but I'm not kidding you, Willie never shuts up.

In my teen years, after my fear of the outdoors subsided (I'm fairly certain it was me and only me that kept Coppertone Sun Block alive during the nineties), soccer became my life. I used it as an escape from reality. Besides, I was good. I went from select teams to club teams, to being captain of my competitive team. My high school varsity team went undefeated every year, and I eventually earned a scholarship to an NCAA Division One university. Not to mention my few years of semi-professional experience thrown in the mix just for kicks. No pun intended...or annoyingly intended. You be the judge. But even with soccer, anxiety and OCD found a way to torture me. One of my many therapists suggested free-association writing. Maybe if I gave words to my anxieties, I would have a better time understanding and fighting them.

I gave it a shot. I went out to the nearest bookstore and bought the most "inspirational" journal I could find. You know the ones. They have motivational quotes from famous people on the bottom of every page. I figured if I could read something positive every time I went to write something negative then maybe I could change my perspective. Yeah, it didn't really work; the positive quotes nor the free-association writing. The overt "chipper-ness" of it all just made me want to vomit in my mouth. It wasn't working.

I guess I had never considered myself a good writer. I mean, I got A's in all of my English classes growing up, but I never gave it much thought or consideration. My homework of giving words to my OCD usually just frustrated me even more. I could read how ridiculous I was being. Giving words to my "insanity" only made me feel more like a crazy person. I understood that the things I was doing, and the things that were going through my mind were completely irrational, and I had no control over them. I couldn't write in a way that made me feel better. It all felt so sterile and clinical. There was no voice, no personality.

Eventually I gave up. After a soccer injury (my sophomore year of college) that left me out for an entire season, I gave up. With my sports scholarship threatened, a knee AND ankle injury that had me stationary-bike-bound, and academic probation looming over my head, I had had enough.

My roommates became worried. My teachers became worried. My academic advisor suggested I give therapy a try (little did she know I had been giving that the old college try since I was a pre-teen). And then, after one life-changing "incident" inflicted upon myself, *I* became worried. I had to leave. I had to get out of Washington and back to California. I needed to be closer to home. My anxieties had never been so bad, so I abandoned my (athletic) life as I knew it and moved back home. Yes, in my mind, I had completely given up on myself. So…I found another outlet for my frustrations.

When we are young, we make decisions that we think we know are for the best. In my case, at the age of twenty…those decisions came in the form of reckless behavior. binge drinking, pill popping, and drunk driving (yes I am ashamed of the drunk driving, and I can thankfully say I learned my lesson in the form of a DUI without hurting anyone other than myself) for example.

Having lost soccer, the one outlet that had ever worked for me, and failed suggestion after failed suggestion from my therapists, I was at a panic to grab anything to curb the anxiety and the pain I felt inside.

I needed to feel numb. My brain's idle was set at a constant speed of eighty-seven thousand, nine hundred and eighty seven thoughts per minute. It was too much for me. I was too young and I felt cheated by too many events in my life already. I had a victim's mindset of "why me?" constantly. It's ironic to me now that the substances I used to control this very out-of-control feeling that I had, were actually causing more problems for me in the long run. I can only equate it to holding AA meetings inside your own local friendly neighborhood bar. Ridiculous. Therefore, it makes sense that the spiraling feelings I have now as a young adult have worsened due to my rationalizations of "numbness" that I so over-indulged in during my early and mid-twenties.

Still, nothing was working. I was at a loss. I needed divine intervention. I needed something, anything. If the clouds could have parted and thrown some wisdom down my way I would have been grateful. And who knows, perhaps they did and I just missed the memo in some unfortunate, but not uncommon, blacked out state of mind.

Just my luck.

One night a few friends and I decided to go to a party out of town. I was excited, as I usually was, for yet another night of drunken fun. My memory from that party and that night are slightly hazy. But the key moments are clear as day. As per usual, I had drank too much which always took a turn for the worse towards the end of the evening. I would slip into thoughts of love lost, dashed hopes, and missed opportunities until eventually, I would pass out.

At this particular party, and in this particular house, there was a fireplace which had little tea-light candles glowing in place of an actual fire. I remember sitting in front of that fireplace, cross-legged, contemplating life and all of its meanings. I was mesmerized. Then I remember sitting on the couch three feet away. The next thing I remember...*slam*...a pillow to my face. One of my fellow house-party guests oh-so-kindly engaged me in a pillow fight, knocking some sense into my otherwise spiraling self.

A few days later I received an email from my pillow assaulter.

She was not a published author. She was not an award-winning novelist. What she was to me was much more than either of the two. She was a catalyst. She was, and to this day remains, one of my creative influences. She helped me realize that writing is much more than the listing of life events in a journal. Writing was itself an event of life. Up until that point it was a life that I was throwing (up) down the toilet.

I was captivated immediately by her use of language. The way her words were displayed across my screen transported me to a place I had never imagined before. Her words made me feel as though I had actually lived the events about which she wrote. I felt inspired. I started seeing words as more than just a way to communicate. Words all of a sudden had their own sounds. They had their own voices. Words came to life for me, and they came alive inside of me. For the first time in a long time, I actually felt something. I think the word for it was...hope.

At first, I felt intimidated at the thought of responding to her letter. How could I equal such a beautiful display of poetic genius? I wanted to impress her with my words, as much as she had impressed me. I wanted to inspire her, the same way she had inspired me. I wanted to give my words a language of their own. Something inside of me clicked as my eyes scanned across the paragraphs she had written. I curbed my insecurities, and responded as eloquently as I could.

A few days later, she replied, "Your writing skills are above average." That was all it took: the mere suggestion that my words had struck something inside of her. In writing for myself, my only audience was myself. But in writing to her, I found my voice. I found what I had been looking for all along.

Hello Epiphany! I've heard so much about you, and I've been waiting a long time to meet you.

"Your writing skills are above average."

I took those six words and built a passion around them. I started reading books differently. I began to notice style, and the different voices of individual authors. I wondered if I could use my words to inspire others. And more importantly...to inspire myself.

For a period of time, I found it difficult to differentiate my own style of expression from the voice of the authors I had grown to admire. However, as time went on, and as I wrote more and more, I noticed a change in my delivery. I began to notice a unique and personal form. I had developed my own style and my own voice.

I finally understood what it was that my therapists had been trying to get me to do. I had to channel and compartmentalize my own inner turmoil. I had to turn my OCD into something that was outside of me. I needed to realize that it wasn't who I was entirely. At first most of my poems were about my struggles growing up with this dis-ease. But as I started working out my issues through writing, I took it to other levels. I realized that writing was much more therapeutic for me than actual therapy. Anytime I started to feel down in any aspect of my life, I took it to paper. I used free association to purge all my negativity and pent up anger and frustration. It started to work better than soccer.

All I had to do was sit in front of the computer and my mind would shut up. My fingers took over and before I knew it I would have pages and pages filled with irrational thought pattern. I could have sat in front of the computer for hours, yet it always felt like only moments had passed by.

For awhile I never went back to read what I had written. I was afraid that reading what had been locked away in my brain for so long would just kick start some downward spiral again. I felt as though it would have been counter-productive to the task at hand. But the more I wrote, the more curious I became as to the potential I had in actually turning this dis-ease into an actual, dare I say...art. To my surprise, I was actually pretty good. My random thought patterns didn't seem so random after all. There was a pattern to my writing. It flowed. It worked itself out of my unstructured, uncontrolled brain and into some actual structured sense. I started to feel lighter.

As I gained confidence, I began reading my pieces at "open-mic" nights. I befriended local artists such as Michelle Tea and Dylan Scholinski, doing my best to integrate any advice they offered into my writing. I immersed myself in a culture full of poetry and prose. I submitted poems to local 'zines, and eventually put together my own chapbook.

I honestly believe that words feed the soul and provide the necessary link between past, present and future that encourage personal growth. The written word can live on forever, much longer than its author. I finally understood why free-association had been suggested to me—to keep alive the feelings and events that were occurring in my life. I wasn't meant to stifle or numb them out. I wasn't supposed to kill what was going on inside of me. In doing that, I would have slowly but surely succeeded in ending my own life. I was keeping myself alive by keeping my feelings alive. I was giving a place for those feelings to live outside of me. They no longer inhabited me. They belonged to me, but just as most things do when they reach a certain point, they went on to live their own lives without me.

This gift of poetry *found me*. I tripped, fell, and stumbled across it the day I received a letter from one of my best friends. I suppose it had always been hiding inside me. I suppose that all the mistakes I made in my youth were meant to be made in order for me to finally end the hide-and-go-seek game of finding my own sanity.

Don't get me wrong, I still have bad days. Bad weeks. Bad months. I am by no means "cured" of my OCD or my anxiety. Writing has not rid me of my panic attacks or my out-of-control thoughts. What it has done is provide me with a prescription of sorts. Like taking a Valium, writing takes the edge off. It provides me with some "time off" from myself. It allows me to slip into a different world…one that's filled with structure and faux control.

It's allowed me to never even think of giving up on myself ever again. And it allows me to do something constructive with thoughts of wanting to:

> *pictures haunt me smiling faces traces of a life once lived and i can't forgive this temporary occupation a sort of inoculation against my own free will my mind taken hostage at gunpoint and its come to the point of fist through walls of haunted halls of memory threatening gestures against myself i throw my past to the floor lock the door to reprieve and grieve a loss of everything i once held dear give in to fear and throw a chair through the windows of yesterday nothing will ever be the same and there's no one left to blame but the hitman locked behind the bars of my ribs rattling his tin cup against a cast-iron cage of insanity unraveling the knitted fabrics of my heart until there's nothing left i left my body years ago a prison break from my own mistakes a fugitive with nowhere to hide spotlight on an inner-fight and i haven't the will to resist the notched oval white pill in front of me taken once a day to repress…everything anything to resemble some semblance of clarity i come out waving a white flag of surrender.*
> *i give up. this…is my own now.*

This is my own now.

*Ani Difranco in *Knuckle Down*, KNUCKLE DOWN, 2005

BIOGRAPHY

KYLE MOSHREFI

A stunning contemporary poet, writing a raw, stream of consciousness poetry that gets an early grip on you and will not let go...swinging from poetry to prose and back again...revealing and insightful and true to the truth of herself.

***

I would say I'm in a transitional period of life...a quarter-life crisis if you will. At twenty-eight years old, I'm coming to realize that my life as it stands now barely resembles what it used to be.

My life had been planned out for me since the age of seven. I decided that I was going to play for the U.S. Women's National Soccer team, and if not, then at least I was going to be the athletic trainer for them. As it turns out, you can't plan out your life at the age of seven.

Currently, I work as the Documentation Coordinator for a Natural Nutrition Company in the San Francisco Bay Area. Not really my dream, just something to pay the bills for now. I grew up in Davis, California, as an athlete and devoted 110% of myself to soccer. It was my life-saver in a sea of anxiety. I went on to play semi-professional and Division One college soccer where a knee/ankle injury in my early twenties forced me into a crossroads. One path toward recovery...or another towards self-medication and reckless behavior. Unfortunately, I chose the latter.

Seven years flew by in a literal blur. Perpetually boozed up, alcohol replaced soccer as my "safe haven" away from my anxiety. I was constantly on the go, hopping from bar to club to house party to whatever distraction I could find, just to step outside of my own head.

A few close calls too many, and I sobered up. It's been a little over one year now and I find myself...lost. No soccer, no alcohol, and anxiety coming out of every pore in my body. I am once again at a crossroad in my life, only this time the roads that lay before me aren't clear. I assume if I just push through the fog, I'll eventually see what is lying before me on the other side.

Fortunately throughout it all, writing has been a very therapeutic outlet which allows me to compartmentalize whatever negative things are going on in my life. I've performed at a few "open mic" nights, have been featured in local 'zines, and with the help of a dear friend, published my own chapbook entitled "The Sort," written in the Sky Press.

I was accepted into the graduate Creative Writing program at Mills College with an emphasis in Poetry. However, I did not attend. I figured I didn't need a Master's Degree to write, and I certainly didn't need the debt.

Thankfully, I was right. Here I am writing…sans master's degree; grateful for the opportunity to be part of such an incredible book.

CHAPTER SEVEN

THE JOURNEY
Captain Fred Rossiter

Camp Buckatabon
Conover, Wisconsin—Circa 1956

The boy gingerly walked out on the dock. He was perhaps nine or ten years old and one could tell he was on a mission. He had on a dirty old T-shirt and baggy brown pants and high-topped sneakers with holes in the toes. He carried a small tackle box in one hand and a long fishing pole in the other. It wasn't just any fishing pole either. It was a bamboo fly rod with a tan fly line and a green Pflueger Automatic fly reel.

He hopped into the beaten-up green, wooden rowboat and cast off the fore and aft lines, positioned himself on the center seat and swung the big wooden oars out and into the water. The weathered boat was leaky and his shoes were soon soaked by the inch or two of water that had collected between the ribs and stays in the bottom of the boat.

He deftly rowed the boat into a position about fifty feet off the shore, stowed the oars and opened his tackle box. He selected a worn yellow popper with a green feather and tied it onto the end of the braided leader. He stood up in the boat with the fly rod and made several false casts to play the line out. Then, he sent the popper out on a long cast behind the boat where it gently lit onto the surface of the tannin waters of Lake Buckatabon. The fly sat motionless for several seconds until the boy gave the fly a gentle twitch. Nothing! Another gentle twitch. A pause. Nothing! Now, the boy gave the fly line a sharp sudden yank and the fly responded by making a loud popping noise as the concave wooden head of the fly displaced the water in front of it. Nothing! Another pause. Again, another sharp yank and another popping sound.

The male bluegill hovered over his nest on the lake bottom protecting it from intruders. The nest was a round, saucer like indentation in the sand and it contained hundreds of recently hatched fry. His exhausted mate had left him days earlier. Her job was done. Smaller fish would threaten first the eggs and then the fry and nature had decreed that the male bluegill would protect the nest and viciously attack all who ventured near it. And, periodically, the male would find it necessary to leave the nest for brief moments to eat a nearby bug or crustacean for sustenance.

It may have been the popping sound that first attracted him or the movement of the fly or the bright colors but he decided that this was a morsel he had to have and one that was worth leaving the nest for. In a swirl and a flash, he headed straight for the popper on the surface.

The bluegill hit the popper; the boy set the hook and yelled with glee. The fight was on. It was a hard-fought battle; the male bluegill was determined to return to the nest and the boy was determined to land the fish. In the end, the boy won out and the exhausted fish was brought alongside the boat. He was beautiful! He weighed about three-quarters of a pound and could cover a man's palm. His colors ran from blues on the gill plates to black with some red and gold on the belly and he had greenish fins. He had a prominent round black spot at the trailing edge of his gill plate. He would make good eating too but this day, the hook was gently removed and the boy respectfully slipped the fish back into the water and watched as he swam slowly back into the depths of the lake.

***

We Can Use The Plane Again!
Parker, Colorado—1995
I was forty-eight years old and staring out the window of my home office, day dreaming; enjoying the view of another sunny day in Parker, Colorado. My thoughts were wandering. Past events came to mind, danced around and then were replaced by more thoughts from the past. Slowly my mind began to organize these thoughts and put them into historical order. They represented the most enjoyable moments and events of my life. My wife, two daughters, camping in the Rockies, fishing trips to Alaska, Costa Rica, the sub-arctic; they were very good times to be cherished and forever remembered.

My thoughts then focused on the future and what events might transpire before I died. I envisioned a big clock in the sky...ticking away until that moment, at some unknowable point in time, when it suddenly stopped ticking. The reality of that vision brought me to an upright posture in my chair and I suddenly realized I was forty-eight years old! I had things I still wanted to do! There were sights I wanted to see and places I wanted to go to and things I wanted to own and if I was going to accomplish all that, I had better get going!

With a pen and paper I began to jot down all the things I wanted to do; go to Alaska again, catch a tarpon on a fly rod, see Africa and the Caribbean, learn to fly, build a house, live in a marine environment, buy a boat, write a book...no, I had done that. I once read that every man should father a child, plant a tree, write a book and build a house. I'd already written a simple book that was never published. It was a satisfying experience. Been there and done that. I'd planted a zillion trees and fathered two beautiful children. Build a house, Africa, the Caribbean, marine environment, boat and learning to fly were still on the list. I pondered each, winnowing the list down to build a house and learn to fly. My fishing buddies and I had fished the wilds of Alaska from a floatplane on two occasions. We had traveled the sub-arctic in a floatplane on another trip and flown throughout the Rocky Mountain West on other fishing trips. Flying was exciting. But, every time I'd considered learning to fly, it just never made economical sense. It was expensive and no matter how I played with the numbers, I just could not justify it. Scratch that.

Hey, wait! Why does it have to make sense? If it's something I really want to do before I die, I had better get going before I'm too old and it's too late. It may never make sense *but at this point in my life, time had become more valuable than money—an epiphany in itself.* That one stays on the list.

Now, building a house does make sense and I've always wanted to do that. I'm well qualified, and pushing a pen and hauling buyers and sellers around as a Realtor had become a mind-numbing experience after twenty-three years. Brain damage! My creative juices had ceased flowing years ago. I'd wrung every opportunity to be creative out of the selling and marketing process I could find and it left a huge void in my life. I needed to work with my hands, get some dirt on them, rely less on the left side of my brain and use the other side to create something three-dimensional. I'm a mechanic at heart, not a psychoanalyst.

The clock in the sky continued to tick away in my mind. I can do this. I could learn to fly. I could build a house. If I don't start growing again, challenging myself, I'm going to continue to whither and die. It may not have been my first epiphany, it certainly hasn't been my last, but it was one of my most important and cherished. I think God kicked me in the butt!

I figure the first third of every man's life is spent growing up, getting an education, and reaching some level of maturity without killing himself during those teenage and college years. The second third of a man's life is dedicated to buying a good car, finding a mate, buying a home, planting some trees and fathering a child or two. Every man must also establish himself in his career and learn how to barbeque. Learning to barbeque is one of life's most important skills that carries a man through the rest of his life. The last third of his life is devoted to doing what he always wanted to do, but really couldn't do in the first two thirds. Everyone will tell him, "You can't do that!" But by this stage in life, a man is done listening to what everyone else is telling him to do. We're talking mid-life now, and for some, it is a crisis. Mine had arrived right on schedule.

A quick review of the yellow page listings of flight schools prompted me to visit the local general aviation airport the next day. I found myself "interviewing" flying clubs and wandering around hangers and planes and I was like a kid in a candy store. The sights, the airplanes and the smells of oil and fuel and the noise were all so exciting. Pilots and planes were everywhere! This was Chuck Yeager, Neil Armstrong stuff! I was mixing it up with them!

In all recorded history, in my mind at least, it is pilots who have saved the world...time and time again. It's Jimmy Doolittle; it's Luke Skywalker against the Dark Side, it's P51's taking out German troop trains and it's a B29 dropping the big one on Hiroshima to end W.W.II. Pilots are always called upon to save the world. I wanted to be on the "save the world" team.

"Ralph?"

He was a somewhat slight and geeky kind of man who greeted me in the lobby of Aspen Flying Club. I announced that I wanted to learn how to fly and he led me to his office for a little chat. We sat down, exchanged pleasantries, and he proceeded to explain the curriculum of Ground School and Flight School and how they were best done at the same time.

Then, he took me out through the hanger and together we walked the flight line of airplanes used by the club. What beautiful birds! He spent a lot of time with me. No pressure either. I got his business card, thanked him and left to ponder the day's events.

The next day, I found myself in a conversation with a friend who was a pilot. I recounted the previous day's events to him. He said, "You need to look up this one instructor out there at the airport and see if he'll take you on as a student. He's very busy but he is the very best there is." "What's his name," I asked? "Ralph, I think," he said. "Ralph!" I exclaimed. I thanked him and we parted. Later, I pulled that business card out of my pocket and looked at the name of the man I'd met the previous day. Wendal Ralph! The adventure had begun! I was growing again.

I was getting nauseous! Wendal Ralph and I were in a Cessna 172 making uncoordinated turns over the Eastern Plains of Colorado on Lesson 1. Wendal was demonstrating the 3 axis of flight attitude and how in a coordinated turn, everything was in harmony and that in an uncoordinated turn, it wasn't. I was turning green, my stomach was in the back of my throat and my ability to learn anything had vanished fifteen minutes earlier. I was about ready to explode when Wendal's instincts recognized the looming crisis and he announced, "That's all for today's lesson; we're heading home."

Fighting a very stiff, direct crosswind, Wendal put the plane down on the runway with the left wing low and we touched down on only the left main tire. It appeared to be a controlled crash but we taxied in without a problem. I never knew landing on one wheel in a crosswind was proper technique and Wendal had made this feat look remarkably simple, which I knew it was not.

I apologized profusely for my condition and my embarrassment showed as we walked in from the tarmac back to the club. I had been in small planes before and had never had a problem but I was seriously having second thoughts about learning how to fly. My stomach was not built for this kind of abuse! Wendal calmly remarked that I'd soon get my "sea legs."

My local pharmacist assured me that I had the best product on the market so the next day, 1½ hours before my next flying lesson, I took four tablets to combat my anticipated nausea. We took off; Wendal gave me the controls and watched me sheepishly as I fought to control the aircraft. It took my full concentration to try to fly this thing. I was all over the sky…up, down, right, left. I could not fly level or hold a heading or altitude. Wendal announced with a laugh that he was about to get sick this day, and then started giving me a few pointers. After we landed someone asked Wendal how I'd done. Wendal said, "He's finding the airplane." I went home exhausted, collapsed into bed and slept for four hours. I was still half drugged but I had not gotten nauseous.

The next lesson I completed on three tablets and again slept soundly afterwards. The third lesson I did on two tablets, the fourth lesson on one tablet and the fifth lesson I did without any medication and I did not get nauseous nor need any sleep afterwards. My "sea legs" had arrived and I was learning, growing, challenging myself and having the time of my life!

They say that any landing that you can walk away from is a VERY good landing. They also say that a GREAT landing is one after which you can use the airplane again. Weeks later, I was one thousand feet over Centennial Airport with Wendal Ralph on my final approach trying to learn how to make great landings. "It's pitch and power," Wendal said, "use power to extend your approach and pitch to control your speed." I was getting it. On the next lesson, I made five landings all without any assistance from Wendal. I was sweating bullets and concentrating like I never had concentrated before. It seemed I was just seconds away from disaster and certain death. Wendal was ready…right there to pounce on the controls and save our lives if need be but it wasn't required, and after the lesson, in a post-flight briefing he said, "I never touched the controls, you did them all without me." It was a great day and very satisfying to master this part of learning to fly. And, we could use the airplane again!!

And, so the adventure went; flight lessons twice a week during the day and ground school twice a week at night. They say that learning to fly is the *second* most fun thing a man can do. It's learning so many different skills and learning so many different regulations and it takes physical coordination to do it. It's physics, navigation, weather, chemistry, communications and planning. It's multi-tasking like you have never done before. It's challenging. And, Wendal Ralph was and is the best pilot and instructor there is.

After twenty-one point six hours of flight instruction and a checkout with another instructor, I was ready to solo. Time to cut the strings, wave good-bye to Wendal and "take 'er around the patch" by myself. It's like taking the training wheels off or taking the car out for the first spin after one has learned to drive. Except this time, you can kill yourself. The required three landings and take-offs all went fine. I felt great, taxied in, tied the bird down and walked in to the club. Wendal had watched them all from the tower and greeted me. He winked and started to ask…but I cut him off short and exclaimed, "Yes, we can use the airplane again!" It was still basically all in one piece. My shirt tail was ceremoniously cut off, dated and signed by Wendal as a souvenir. Hey, it's a pilot thing! I took my FAA written test, oral and flight test and earned my Private Pilot license after completion of the Ground School and seventy-seven hours of flight instruction. I was a pilot!! I was free to go out now, without an instructor, and legally kill myself in an airplane. The rest of my instruction was learning how not to do that.

Spin Training

Take a bug. A house fly is best. Throw it into the toilet. Flush the toilet. Watch the fly—as it swirls round and round, down and down, and gets closer and closer to oblivion. That's what spin training is all about. If you were an angel, sitting on a cloud above Wendal and I, that is what you would have seen as we spun our Cessna 152 above the plains of Eastern Colorado. Spin training used to be required of all Commercial Pilots but too many were getting killed in the maneuver so the FAA "relaxed" the regs and no longer requires it. Wendal was giving me spin training because, if we survived, it would make me a better pilot. I'd be capable of righting my aircraft from an "inadvertent unusual flight attitude." Though I had volunteered for this, I had dreaded this day for quite some time.

The game is started at least three thousand feet above the ground. The throttle is retarded and the nose is raised until the airplane slows to a point where there is no longer enough airflow over the wing to provide lift. The plane then stalls and enters a spin. Game rules dictate that the plane must spin three times before one "arrests" the spin and flies the plane out of the spin in a straight and level attitude. And, the game is lost if one continues in an uncontrollable spin into the ground. Wendal warned me, "This is going to be dramatic." Wendal then entered into the first of two spins for demonstration. I immediately decided I did not want to play this game anymore. It was frightening! I wanted to go home!

With great reluctance, I did the next three spins. I felt like a fly moments from oblivion as the ground spun upwards towards me. My hands and feet furiously manipulated the controls first to stop the spin, then to gently raise the nose and restore the plane to normal flight attitude. "Stress" the plane too much in this maneuver and one risks breaking it apart in midair. After three spins, I had sufficiently demonstrated that I had mastered the maneuver and I had had enough! I didn't want to do another spin for the rest of my life.

Emergencies

My training was progressing and after each flight lesson, the thrill and joy of flight stayed with me for days afterward. I was on a continuous high from one lesson to the next. The ground school was interesting and I was having the time of my life. Becoming a pilot is fun, challenging and a lot of hard work. Every lesson was exciting!

Wendal and I were flying over the Eastern Plains when he explained that today's lesson would be to learn how to handle an engine fire while in flight. He calmly explained that an engine fire, while in flight, was the absolute worst of all emergencies a pilot could have. Immediate action was required if a pilot wanted any chance of survival. The first action is to shut off the fuel to the engine, then close the cowl flaps, turn off the master switch and quickly put the airplane into a vertical dive. The dive is necessary to rapidly gain enough airspeed to extinguish the flames. The velocity of the wind essentially blows the flames out. The first and last parts of this maneuver are the most interesting. To quickly put the plane into a vertical dive, one has two choices; push the yoke in and go weightless as the nose goes over and your stomach tries to exit your mouth, or execute a "wing over" turn to enter the dive. Wendal chose the latter and we were headed straight down for the ground. The airspeed needle quickly climbed towards the red "never exceed" range. Once the airspeed climbs above 130 kts. in the dive, the flame is presumed to be extinguished and one can maneuver out of the dive into a normal flight attitude. At that point, one is faced with the second worst of all in-flight emergencies...a dead engine at low altitude over hostile territory. It was a lesson I won't soon forget.

The flight training progressed from spin training to mountain flying to high performance aircraft with retractable gear and constant speed props. I flew higher, faster, further and more complicated airplanes. Eventually, I arrived at the next inevitable step, the Instrument Rating required of all commercial pilots. Though the "commercial ticket" isn't necessary for recreational flyers like me, all the Certified Flight Instructors assured me it makes one a better pilot. And, it allows one to fly in the "soup" (cloud) when one has to.

Instrument Flight

When built, the Houston Astrodome was fully enclosed. It was seven hundred and ten feet in diameter and had a ceiling height of two hundred and eight feet. It seated sixty-two thousand, four hundred and thirty nine football fans. Immense! Imagine if you will, that you are in a small remotely controlled airplane and that you have just taken off from the fifty yard line and are headed for the goal post at the end of the field. Air Traffic Control has instructed you to fly through the uprights, execute a left turn heading 090 degrees, climb to fifty feet, then turn to 180 degrees and climb to one hundred feet. You are then to proceed to seat X, then to seat Y, then to Z, then split the uprights and land right where you took off. No problem! You can do that. But, just as you clear the first upright after your takeoff, somebody turns the lights off. That is what Instrument Flying is all about.

Instrument flight training doesn't start until you have nearly two hundred and fifty total hours under your belt. You need to be proficient in flying, navigating and communicating before you're ready to train for IMC (Instrument Meteorological Conditions). You can't see a thing when you are in the clouds.

Instrument flight training is a minimum of forty hours in the dark, under the hood, groping your way around the sky by instruments alone. You are a blip on a radar screen hundreds of miles away. Your job is to fly to an electronic point in the sky, then another and another and the FAA expects you to be there at a precise moment in time. If you aren't, you can lose your license or your life. You do all this without any reference to the outside. You don't see the ground, the sky or anything but your instruments. Your stomach, brain and inner ear tell you one thing while your instruments tell you another. You learn what spatial disorientation is, how to fight off nausea, and how to set up your instrument scan. You learn how to execute a hold and enter a pattern and how to navigate, communicate and aviate all at the same time, in the dark, while handling nausea and emergencies of every description. You learn how to fly the ILS (Instrument Landing System) by lining up the needles on approach, what "minimums" are and how to execute a "missed approach." You learn how to fly an airplane by yourself, through all kinds of weather from A to B to C. And the old pros, the best of the best, will tell you that Single Pilot IFR (Instrument Flight Rules) is the hardest thing in the world to do. Take away their autopilot, and most simply refuse to do it. It's too stressful and dangerous! It was the hardest thing I had ever done…but, earning my Instrument Rating was another satisfying notch in my flight bag.

Glass Cockpit

Long after I earned my Commercial Pilot's License, technologically advanced aircraft entered the general aviation market and soon found their place on the flight line at Aspen Flying Club. These new birds were quite something when compared to the 1950's technology we had all been flying. They had sleek new wings, composite fuselages, computerized engines, digital avionics with GPS and moving maps on big CRT screens in the cockpit. Some even had ballistic parachutes. Cirrus and Diamond Aircraft were the first of these hot new birds. Turn the key in these airplanes and their cockpits lit up like the space shuttle! They are commonly called "glass cockpits." They were gorgeous and I embraced them from the very beginning. Learning to fly these new birds was exciting and challenging. They were computers with wings! The 21st Century had finally arrived in General Aviation and at Aspen Flying Club.

The Save the World Team

I miss the "save the world team" I was a part of. It was a fraternity of men and women all aspiring to become great pilots…all good friends…all comrades in arms. The airlines hired Wendal away from me. He was too good and they grabbed him. But, there were other instructors and lots of friends. There was Schoonover, Everard, Kelly, Naife, Batdorf, Bubb, Stout, Gabel, Osborne, Ramsdell, Gensler and others. There was Glenn

Endsley, the FAA Examiner who made us all sweat bullets with every new rating we earned. They were all great pilots then and most are even better pilots today. We were all there at Aspen Flying Club at that same moment in time. Today, they're flying airliners, regional and corporate jets all around the world. Some are in fighter jets over the skies of Iraq and God knows where. Some are still flight instructors, some have retired and some are flying desks. Others, like me, have left and pursued other challenges. But somewhere in cyberspace, on several FAA databases, one can still find my name and their names among the likes of Chuck Yeager, Neil Armstrong and others on the "save the world team."

***

The Old Courthouse

Ft. Myers, Florida—2007

I got word yesterday that my hearings today would be conducted in the Old Courthouse instead of the new Constitutional Complex where I had conducted all my other hearings. So, this morning I left Cape Coral and drove across the river into downtown Fort Myers and found the Old County Courthouse...a stately brick building with tall gothic columns in the front, a big banyan tree and a live oak with Spanish moss in the front yard. The building was erected in 1915, the same year my mother was born, and it is on the National Historic Registry.

I climbed the stone steps to the double oak doors and entered into the main hall where the receptionist smiled and greeted me. The reception area had nice marble floors, a soaring ceiling and two sitting areas for visitors with wicker chairs and wicker tables. Along the back wall were five oak and glass cases housing mementos from each of the five districts in Lee County. At the far end of the main floor were the stately offices and conference rooms of the five County Commissioners. It all seemed perfect and fitting for an old courthouse in the South. I walked to the other end of the building and took the steps to the second floor to find my hearing room but got distracted by an auction going on in the County Commissioner's chamber room. They auction off foreclosed homes and hold tax sales every Friday, I was told. It was quite a scene and quite interesting to listen to the cadence of the auctioneer's voice as he tried to coax each bidder higher...a sign of the times in this economically depressed part of Southwest Florida.

I found my hearing room. The walls were of oak and there was a big oval conference table in the room with chairs for perhaps ten people. Today, I would be the acting Special Magistrate for Lee County. It would be my job to conduct hearings for people protesting their property assessments. To qualify for the job, one had to be a State Certified Appraiser in good standing and not hold any elected office. On that basis I qualified. I enjoyed the job and found it interesting. And with it, came a certain air of dignity and respect which I enjoyed. I had made a simple inquiry earlier in the year via e mail and to my surprise, a large envelope arrived six months later with a contract in it, a detailed explanation of the state statutes governing property assessments and what my duties were. I signed the contract and committed myself to one day of hearings each week from October through February. Shortly, the Property Appraisers showed up along with the first of this morning's Petitioners and I started the procedure. I conducted the hearings for the morning and ended the session about 11am. With my next hearing at 1pm, I had plenty of time for lunch at the nearby Quiznos and then an exploration of the innards of the courthouse.

The Courthouse had tons of old photos and documents depicting the history of Lee County. It was all quite interesting. I really admired the old Southern Gentlemen of the late 1800's. Captain F. A. Hendry, in particular, looked so distinguished in his rumpled suit, straw hat and snow-white mustache and beard. I vowed to grow a white beard like his and wear a straw hat when I grew older. It appeared the "Colonel Sanders" look was quite the style back then.

I went back to the Commissioner's hearing chamber and it was empty so I went in. The focal point of the big oak paneled chamber was a six-foot-tall portrait of General Robert E. Lee on the far back wall... right in the center and above the oak pulpits and seats of the County Commissioners. The portrait captured one's eye immediately and it dominated the room. He was magnificent in his Confederate uniform! I found myself awe stuck by the General's portrait and surrounding chambers. I felt a sense of history and reverence there in that room as I stood alone gazing upward and I could not help but wonder just what chain of events had brought a man from the mountains and plains of Colorado to the position of Special Magistrate and this hallowed chamber in the deep South.

"Mr. Rossiter!" Alan's booming voice broke the silence and startled me. I spun around. "Yes, Alan, what do you need?"

"We're ready to start the afternoon hearings," he said.

"OK Alan, I'll be right there."

I walked back to the hearing room and concluded the afternoon hearings. I left the old courthouse but I couldn't stop thinking about the General's portrait as I drove home.

***

The Big Clock Is Ticking

Cape Coral, Florida—2008

The big clock in the sky is still ticking as I stare out the window of my home office, day dreaming; lazily enjoying the view of yet another sunny day in Cape Coral, Florida. I relocated to sea level from the mile-high Rocky Mountain area. I'm here chasing another dream, from another epiphany...and my thoughts are wandering. Past events come into my mind, dance around and then are replaced by more thoughts from the past. My thoughts had wandered back to my flight training days with Wendal Ralph years ago and the waters of Lake Buckatabon. I concluded that it was that first bluegill I'd met as a boy at camp that instilled a love for fishing and eventually brought me here to Cape Coral, the old courthouse and that spot in the Commissioner's Chambers in front of General Lee's portrait. What a journey it has been!

My love of fishing all started on that warm sunny day in Northern Wisconsin where I discovered bluegill, fly rods, boats and the joys of the water. There have been thousands of fish since then in hundreds of lakes, streams and oceans all over North and Central America. Though real estate has been my profession, flying and fishing have been my passions. They have taken me to some very special places.

Epiphanies made it all happen for me. They changed my life. They come to all of us like a bolt out of the blue. They wake us up out of deep slumbers and spur us into action. Why, I can do that! I can go there! I can go down that road! I can build a house! I can learn to fly an airplane. I can fish the sub-arctic. I can go to Alaska for salmon or the jungles of Costa Rica for tarpon. I can move to Florida. I can do a million things and you can too if you will just listen to those voices within you.

I am a US Coast Guard licensed Charter Captain now. Yes, another epiphany. I spend my days in search of tarpon, snook, shark and redfish. I'm a fishing guide for hire, a water taxi and occasional tour guide when I'm not appraising, selling, flying or serving as a Magistrate. I'm in a sub-tropical paradise of sun, sea and sand. I've followed my bliss and fortunately, my wife has been gracious enough to come along and share the adventure.

The big clock in the sky is still ticking as I stare out the window of my home office, day dreaming, enjoying the view. My thoughts are focused again on the future and what events might transpire before I die. The list is shorter this time: the Caribbean, Africa, my first bonefish on a fly rod. I envision that big clock in the sky...ticking away, until that moment, at some unknowable point in time, when it suddenly stops ticking. But now, I'm older and wiser and I listen more intently to those voices within me.

Hey! Now I'm sixty-one years old!! I still have things I want to do! The world is a big place. Life is full of opportunity and adventure. There are sights to see, things to do, places to go, and things to learn. If I'm to accomplish all this, I had better get going.

I hear a quiet voice within me. Listen! I hear another epiphany coming...

FOLLOW YOUR BLISS—

***

Bill Moyers: *Do you ever have the sense of...being helped by hidden hands?*

Joseph Campbell: *All the time. It is miraculous. I even have a superstition that has grown on me as a result of invisible hands coming all the time—namely, that if you do follow your bliss you put yourself on a kind of track that has been there all the while, waiting for you, and the life that you ought to be living is the one you are living. When you can see that, you begin to meet people who are in your field of bliss, and they open doors to you. I say, follow your bliss and don't be afraid, and doors will open where you didn't know they were going to be.*

My general formula for my students is, "Follow your bliss." Find where it is, and don't be afraid to follow it.

Joseph Campbell, *The Power Of Myth, pp. 120, 149*

BIOGRAPHY

FRED ROSSITER

Professionally, Fred Rossiter has spent the last thirty-six years of his life in the real estate industry as a licensed Real Estate Broker and a Certified Residential Appraiser in two states, a custom home builder, investor and homeowner. Fred has served as a President and Director of two homeowner associations, built a community park and saved forty acres of land from development for use as a wildlife preserve.

On a personal note, Fred and Susan, his wife of thirty-eight years, have built a family with two beautiful and accomplished daughters, Shannon and Katy."*We've been fortunate and enjoyed every minute of it,*" says Fred. "*My family has been a great joy to me! It's what life is all about.*"

Fred has a led a rich and exciting life."*It's been a life of adventures, challenges and change. There is always something new to do whether it's pursuing salmon or arctic char in Alaska, building your first house, learning to fly, going to the sub-arctic or Costa Rica, or my latest adventure…. becoming a USCG licensed Charter Captain and Tarpon guide in SW Florida.* "*Life's an adventure and the clock is ticking.*"

"*Epiphanies? My life has been a series of them, one after another. One word that describes me? Restless!*"

Visit: FredRossiter.com, BrokerFredRossiter.com and
CaptainFredRossiter.com

CHAPTER EIGHT

WAR PAINT
Regan Rosburg

Names have been changed...all except mine.

After having a difficult time applying my fake eyelash, I decide to have the make-up artist do it. It's only twenty dollars, and I made good money yesterday, so what the hell. I'm staring into the mirror watching the process of paint being applied to my eyelids. We have decided to go with a powder blue color, which I like because it enhances the blue ring around the hazel disk that is my eye. Also, I have chosen to wear a long, blue evening gown with spaghetti straps to start the night. I watch as I'm transformed with color, piece by piece, into a different person. I admire the artistry that is at work; how with an arsenal of brushes, thirty different makeup compacts, four different styles of hairbrushes, and two hairdryers, each one of us girls is able to put away one personality and step into another one.

"Okay, Raven," says Vicki, our makeup genius. She smiles with approval at her current masterpiece, my face. "You want your tattoo done too, sweetie?" She blows a puff of smoke out of her mouth as she asks me this, and I decide to light my own so that the smell doesn't bother me.

"Sure, I guess." Shit. That's another five bucks. Oh well.

The other girls have tattoos as well, but mine is the biggest pain in the ass because of the size and location of it. It's a phoenix, about the size of a salad plate, sitting square in the middle of my lower back. We are not allowed to show our tattoos here in this club. Tattoos are not *sophisticated*, and this is a "respectable" gentlemen's club. I ponder the irony of this as I watch Carrie. She is standing in front of the sink, her hip cocked to one side, bottle of bleach in hand, cigarette hanging like a limp piece of lettuce out of the corner of her mouth. She wears nothing but a bra, and the strap is hanging tiredly from her shoulder. Her brownish-orange, over-tanned skin is glowing under the row of dressing room lights. In twenty minutes she will be unrecognizable…a goddess, a blonde bombshell. But right now, she is trying to get a lipstick stain out of her thong panties. As she weaves a string of profanities, the inch-long cigarette ash holds on for dear life. Like I said, it's a classy joint.

How did I get here? My love-hate relationship with stripping began in college. It started out as a *rationalized* necessity. I had to pay off a student loan that was burdening my father, who had recently become disabled. I could make fast, good money dancing, right? I was curious, adventurous, brave, naïve, and stupid. Dancing did not lead me out of debt. Rather, it was like one long Halloween party. I danced with gang member's girlfriends, drug addicted drop-outs, and poor single moms who were trying to make ends meet. The pay was lousy, but the stories were good. I saw lots of healed bullet and stab wounds, and saw a small Hispanic girl get pushed into a locker because she stole another girl's jeans. Good times.

The tattoo was a symbol of my independence from dancing, from men, and from addiction in general. I got it before I traveled alone to Indonesia at age twenty-five, determined to become inspired for my artwork. I had spent four years earning my Bachelor's Degree in Fine Arts, and after college I settled into a steady gallery job that not only bored the hell out of me, it also sucked my creative juices dry. My trip abroad, alone, was my way of showing myself I could do anything. I wanted to be a different person when the plane landed back on American soil. The phoenix was *me*, constantly reinventing myself. I was always transforming…dying and being born again out of the ashes. It was a promise to myself that I would never dance again.

That was four years and three clubs ago.

"Shit! It's almost seven!" says Ivy. I turn and look at her. I haven't seen her in a while. She has new breasts. They are *glorious*. "My hair, like, totally looks like ass!"

I return my gaze to the mirror, then spin around and sit with my back to Vicki. She opens a small jar of thick, dark makeup. I've been tanning so we have to use a darker color. I swear I can feel the flames around my phoenix hiss as they are smothered and then put out by the makeup. I look at the tattoo in the mirror. Not a trace of it is visible. It's like it was never there.

I look at my face in the mirror. Not a trace of *me* is visible. It's like I was never there.

***

Go that way, really fast. If something gets in your way, turn. Charles DeMar, *Better Off Dead*

I have been at this "classy" club for almost a year. I can't leave. The money is too good. I think back to the first club, when I would leave with thirty dollars and a horrible sense of self…and usually a good buzz from cocaine and alcohol. At least I don't usually feel dirty when I leave here. It's hard to feel dirty when you work five hours and make four or five hundred dollars. The power is exhilarating. The comments roll off your back. You forget the hand that brushed your breast and the bouncer who was looking the other way and didn't see it. You forget the way you breathed down some stranger's neck to get him to shell out another twenty for a table dance. You forget what leering expressions you see through the V-shape of your legs, like you are looking down the sights of a revolver. You forget the lies you told about yourself, like that you love to do "lesbian things," and what turns you on most is the cologne of the guy whose lap you are sitting in. You forget about the hand that tries to wander up your dress, and how you giggle, "Tee-hee! Don't do that, Sam…," and place it back in his lap. You forget about the urge to smack some old man who thinks he's better than you are, simply cuz he holds the cash and *you haven't taken it yet.*

You forget all the derogatory things you say and do for those five hours…If—and it's a big If—you make good money. If you don't, you say something like the following:

"Fuckin' prick!" yells Velvet as she enters the dressing room. She is one of the most stunning women I have ever seen. A tall brunette with a thick, jet-black mane of hair to match her big, brown, deer-like eyes. Her makeup is always dark and smoky; her lips look like they are full of berry juice and about ready to pop. Her skin, the color of a perfectly toasted marshmallow, peeks out of her long, maroon-colored satin gown and elbow-length satin gloves. She's so willowy and lithe that we are all startled when she suddenly launches her purse into her locker. Make-up, cigarettes, and a wad of cash spill all over the floor.

"Ya, right, so this cheap bastard from Fort Collins screwed me outta my money tonight! The jerk keeps me sitting there for forty-five freakin' minutes with a stack of twenties under his beer glass, right? So, I get up to pee, come back, and he's doing a table dance with Jamilla! Then he fuckin' bolts outta here afterwards! And my regular didn't show tonight...and, like ONE table dance the whole night. I fuckin *hate* this place! The guys are such shit-heads! I'm gonna quit dancing! This is bullshit!!!" This last statement she punctuates with her six-inch heel against the lockers. Tirade...over.

Quit dancing?

It's like trying to quit smoking. All your best intentions are there. So you set the date, and you get support from some of your close friends, and you smile because it's a healthy decision. Good for you! Yay! But...wait... then you think about a real job. You think about the eight-hour shift with a half-hour lunch break. You think about working for some lame boss. You think about writing a resume, and about all the interviews for "lame" jobs like waiting tables, courier services, house-cleaning, or retail. Because you have made so much money at one point, you recoil. *You think about earning* (gulp) *minimum wage.*

Then you think about dancing. You think about how you can set your own hours. You think about the excitement. You think about how great you look (by the way, strippers are *always* looking in the mirror when on stage...we are intoxicated by our own beauty, probably more than you are). You think about the power of dancing. You think about the sexual energy that you release on stage, and how it makes you feel. You think about your girlfriends at work, the ones with whom you can commiserate about things that only a dancer would understand. You think about the costumes, the music, the flirting. You think about the night you made a thousand dollars in two hours, and how that somehow might happen again.

And then just like that, you "light up." You start dancing again at a different club, or a different city, with a different name. Whatever. In the end, it doesn't matter. It's all the same shit. You are addicted. Smoke away.

***

It's not what you call me, but what I answer to. African Proverb

The music is thumping outside, the men are starting to arrive. I have high hopes that one of my regulars, Marco, will come in tonight and perhaps take me Off the List. "Off the List" means off the dancing rotation, where you are a man's date for as long as he wants to sit with you. It's a hundred dollars an hour, and Marco usually gives me a couple extra hundred on top of that. I like talking to him because he's not trying to get in my pants, and we can talk about taboo-dancer-subjects, like "Reality." Reality conversations are not encouraged in strip clubs because they are downers. Strip clubs are small versions of Las Vegas...no windows, no clocks, no bitching wives, everyone is imbibing in sexual play and fantasy, the booze and the money are flowing. Here, no matter what the man looks or acts like, if he has enough money, he can sit with the most beautiful woman in the room. Screw reality.

However, for Marco and me, it's different. He goes to Las Vegas all the time for work, and is bored with the clubs and the women. He likes my mind, and pays well for it. So, as asses and glasses flailed around us, Marco and I would chat the night away about politics, spirituality, the differences between America and his native country of Italy, sports, car mechanics, science, and my favorite subject of all...ART.

Let me first just say, I am not a typical dancer. Most of the time I am at work, I feel like I am doing research. I am fascinated by the fact that I am in this world. I'm inebriated by it; I absolutely *cannot* stop myself from coming to work here. Every day is different. One of the things I've discovered is that there are two types of dancers: those who had good relationships with their fathers, and those who did not. If you ask me, the daddy's girls make the most money because they have been infused with the power of having daddy devotion all their lives. In essence, they know how to work it. The other women with the negative relationships with their fathers—neglect, abuse, or loss—find themselves resentful, always trying to please, and back-talking the men as soon as they enter the dressing room. I scribble observations like this in a journal in between sets. I'm the weird one, the dancer that fits into the nerdy clique, I guess. But I don't care. I'd rather be a nerd at this point than have fake boobs.

Back to Marco. According to Jamie—who, by the way, is pleased to announce that she has *almost* humped the entire pro football team this year!! Yay!—Marco is here. He's sitting by stage two, waiting for me. Hell yah, and thank God, I'm gonna actually have a good conversation with someone.

I stand and go to my locker. On each locker is a star made of construction paper, and our names are written in puffy glitter paint. Mine says "Raven." This is the third name I've danced by, but I like it best so far. Ravens are smart birds, sleek and dark, and have tremendous amounts of lore written about them. My name is secretly magic to me...it connects me to my spiritual side in the midst of chaos and debauchery. I open the locker and take inventory of the contents. The top shelf contains makeup, brushes, pictures, panties with sequins, panties without sequins, bobby pins, hair ties, a Santa costume, a low-carb power bar, energy pills, Red Bull, a bottle of gardenia oil perfume, and a towel. I have six dresses, all evening gowns, of different colors and textures. The bottom of the locker contains my street clothes in a duffle bag, and two pairs of platform heels. I strap on the white pair and decide that my toenail polish will need to be done again tomorrow when I wake up at noon. I pull on the blue spaghetti strap dress, dab a drop of oil behind my ears and between my breasts, grab my purse, and check myself one more time in the mirror. Then, in a six-inch heel strut that I've perfected over the years, I breeze past the tornado of hair, nipples, ruby lips and attitudes that make up my co-workers. I walk into the hall, then into the vast room.

The room is lit with a purplish glow. The four stages are surrounded by tables and chairs, all of which are full of men. It's Friday night, which means bachelor parties, regulars, and women who have been brought in by their husbands to "spice up" their marriage. The look that I get from these women is one of both admiration and distrust, and I love dancing for them. I try to show them that it's okay, what I'm doing, and that a woman's sexuality is a powerful thing. Despite the lingering jealousy they may have when they sit down in front of me, I hope that by the time I'm done dancing for them, they see something else. I hope that they see the artistry in the movements, how I hold invisible ribbons of music and let my sexual energy spin around them and into their soul. The quickest way into a soul is through the eyes. If a woman is willing to meet and hold my gaze when I'm four inches from her face, I know I have uncoiled some little doubt she had about the power of her *own* sexuality. I secretly hope she carries it with her, and dances naked alone...for *herself.* I picture her celebrating the private kaleidoscope of colorful energy that will unfurl from within her. As an added bonus, I also can pretty much guarantee that she and her husband will fuck like bunnies all night long.

Ah, the sexiest New York accent is about to enter my ears. "Hey Raven, how ya doin' this evening?" says Jimmy, one of the managers. He is my favorite because he reminds me of Frankie Avalon. Like the rest of the managers, he wears a tailored black suit. He's six feet tall with a helmet of hair shaped into a slicked-back square. Jimmy looks like the kind of man that would take your hand and spin you effortlessly around the dance floor to a Frank Sinatra tune.

"I'm fine, Jimmy." I give him a hug. He smells like sexy cologne. "Looks like a busy night, eh?"

"Yah, sure does. You look gorgeous, Raven, as *always*. So, ah, hey, Marco's here. You were gonna be up in the stake-house in two sets, but if he takes you off the list, let me know."

I wave to Marco, and he signals to Jimmy to take me off the list. Thank you, God. I make my way over to my client, my friend, the only person who listens to me here and thinks I'm smart...Marco. He's in his mid-fifties, has thinning hair and, despite his diet of non-alcoholic beer, a big ol' belly. He has quiet, friendly eyes that look out from behind thick round glasses. His hands are calloused and worn from all of the work he does driving and moving crates. This man works harder than anyone I have ever met in my entire life. Born in Italy, Marco served in the military, then came to the United States for adventure, women, and a shot at a better life. Now, he has three different jobs, and lots of stress. I worry he might have a heart attack, especially since he picks *all* the vegetables off anything that arrives in front of him to eat.

I sit down, light up a cigarette, order a glass of white wine, and we start to talk.

When you work at a strip club, after the initial cheesy, stupid sexual innuendos and giggling, the man will inevitably ask you this question: *"What is a woman like you doing in a place like this?"* It's almost like they feel sorry for you, and yet it fascinates them. They always want to know *how* you ended up in a dress, willing to show your naked body for money. Are you supporting a cocaine habit? Does it (gag) turn you on? Did you get kicked out of your parents'/friends'/sorority's house? Do you have kids to support? Are you paying off school loans? Are you just passing through and work at other clubs, like those naughty clubs in Vegas or Alaska? I suspect they are collecting stories, much like I am, trying to make sense of fantasy.

To be honest, I think it's more interesting to ponder how *they* ended up in a strip club shelling out all their hard-earned cash to a strange woman. But whatever.

I will generally size up the guy and then tailor the answer to the vibe I've gotten from him. "I love adventure, and this is so exciting!" or "Who *wouldn't* want to be surrounded by all these gorgeous bodies, sweetie? Tee-hee!" or "It's fun and keeps me fit," or "I've danced all my life," or simply, "I've got bills to pay, dumb-ass."

But when Marco asked me, I actually told him the truth. I told him because I actually trusted him. He won my trust by being the opposite of every man I'd met so far in clubs. He did it by *not* trying to touch me, by *not* asking for table dances, by *not* saying stupid, vulgar things, and then paying me anyway. He was consistent. To me, he was always kind, to the point, and wise. As sick as it sounds, he was like a father amidst all of the frat boys, cheating husbands, and curious/bored/perverted/culturally conditioned men.

Marco sets down his beer, leans back in his chair, adjusts his glasses, and finally, bluntly asks me.

"Raven, what the hell are you doing here, anyway?"

Behind me, a group of men yell out the classic "Wooo-hoooooooooooooooo!" I turn to look, but I don't really want to see it. The bachelor party's guest of honor, drunk beyond performance, has been placed in the shower. He is dressed in only a pair of board shorts. It looks like the last time he saw a gym was when I was in kindergarten. His face is red from sunburn, and he has goggle marks to match the perfectly defined red sunburn line of his collar. Despite the look of giddiness on his face, I feel sorry for the poor, drunk bastard. He probably won't remember much, and will have only lipstick kisses on his cheeks and forehead as a reminder the next morning. Two voluptuous blondes with matching bodies are rubbing shaving cream on both his shaved head and their overstuffed breasts. They paint the glass of the shower with their grapefruit tits, smearing the shaving cream like two synchronized, dragging tongues. "Woo-hooooooo!"

I turn back to Marco, exhale my cigarette, look him straight in the eye, and say it.

"So I can paint."

***

Life is pain, Highness. Anyone who says differently is selling something. The Dread Pirate Roberts, *The Princess Bride*

I have always been an artist. My whole life has been dotted with awards, compliments and positive feedback on my artistic ability. In college, when I finally walked into the rooms of the fine arts building, I knew what I wanted. I was taking everything *except* art classes because I had the same small-minded mentality shared by the masses: that to pursue an art career was a dead end. "You can't make money." "Cut throat." "Good luck." And still, when I smelled the tempera paints, glue, wax, and ceramic of that building, I walked straight to the fine arts office and changed my major. I called my mom shortly afterwards. Thankfully, she bit her tongue because *her* mother had talked her out of an art career long ago.

I think it was a combination of stupidity and blind faith that made me change my major. That, and a lot of pot.

In college I excelled in painting. I was constantly collecting material from my life's pain as fuel for the work. No one's life is easy, and mine was no exception. Family drama, alcoholism (in both my family lineage and the men I so conveniently attracted into my life), murder, drug addiction, and eating disorders...a perfect base-line for therapy and prescription meds. However, something wonderful happened to me when I picked up that brush. I could turn any pain that I had suffered into something that read like a visual diary. Not a new concept for artists. But as a *new*, naïve artist, it meant everything to me. It was the great "breaking open" of my journey towards healing. I spent time pouring cryptic messages into beautiful imagery and poetry. I became a warrior for myself, determined to figure out my pain through "the work." People thought it was wonderful, and I kept going. It was all I could do.

***

Remember that no one can make you feel inferior without your consent. Eleanor Roosevelt

I've just told Marco the truth, but I hardly believe it sometimes. I feel the phoenix shift uncomfortably on my back, searching for a way out from under the makeup. It pushes up against my skin, like a monkey pushes against the glass cage in a science laboratory...confused and scared.

I light up another cigarette, another smokescreen to hide my unease with what I've just said. Who am I now? I'm a tofu-eating, organic-shampoo-using, yoga-doing, meditating, healthy-eating, cigarette-smoking, drug-doing, alcohol-consuming stripper who paints about the spiritual side she so desperately wants to cultivate. Ha! So *there*! Stripping as a means of painting? Stripping as a means of becoming more spiritual? Stripping in order to support the passionate, real, organic, cosmic side of myself? Hmmmm…it makes PERFECT sense, I decide. I must just need the dark to explore the light. Very dark. A patch over both eyes, standing in the middle of the desert during the new moon…under a blanket. That dark.

Think about it. We all find reasons to rationalize our behavior. Relationships that have turned to shit. Trips we should have taken. Trips we shouldn't have taken. Drugs we shouldn't have done. Drugs we *should* have done. Dreams that we once had, but are now, for some reason, "past their time." Reasons to explain who we are, *while we are who we are.* We all know, on some level, who we want to be and what we want out of life. It's our fear that gets in the way. And honestly, as difficult as it was to dance sometimes, the amount of revelation that painting provided was altogether much more terrifying. Painting showed me the ironic, unstable situation I had put myself into…and yet the more I painted about my desire to break free of my fears and insecurities, the more I clung to dancing. I would grab that pole with all the gusto of a pit bull with her chew toy, and I would grind myself into oblivion.

I have come back stage for a minute, leaving Marco in the club. I sit on the bench, watching the craziness, the re-application of makeup, and the lesbian action. Two dancers are kissing because they have had too much to drink. They are the new eighteen-year-olds that we are all upset have been permitted to work here. Shock value is their M.O…and they are pissing us all off. A few days from now, a dramatic fight (after the club has closed for the night) will cause one of them to shove the other into a locker, and they will both be subsequently fired. This is a good thing…if they didn't get fired, one of the older, hardened dancers would eventually eat them alive.

Strippers are tough. No doubt. We have learned that being a bitch at the right time, with the right guy, can make you a ton of cash. It can get you out of that fight with the six-foot tall, hoofed, buck-toothed, frightening, beast of a dancer who suddenly hates you and wants to kick your ass. Being a bitch at some point can actually save your life. I finally learned how to be a bitch...but it took time. When I first began dancing, I was a doormat. But that's how most dancers start out. The men shit on you, and your fellow dancers take advantage of your naivety, spreading rumors and gossip, creating cliques. It takes a few times of being fucked-over and degraded before you really reach down and say "enough is enough." But I've seen it happen. Once it does, you change, and you change forever. I'm about to see my friend change, and it's fucking hilarious.

Lexus has been working here the same amount of time as me. She is an African American, gorgeous, petite woman. Her muscles rope her entire body. She has beautiful dread locks pulled up into a cascading pile on top of her head, and the gold jewelry she wears is the perfect contrast for her dark black skin. We hang out a lot backstage. I've always liked her. Ancestry of a dominant, powerful woman is behind her eyes, and yet she, like the rest of us, puts that wild mare on the shelf in order to be a sweet, malleable "date." She and I are two nerdy misfits; two strippers who see past the glitz and ephemeral money of dancing...most of the time. Tonight, on what ends up being her last night, proves itself to be a perfect way for her to exit. She is my new role model.

Lex, as I call her, walks in from the club with a wide-eyed, elated look on her face. She and I have spent hours discussing the finer points of club politics, who makes money and why, what the men are all about, the power of dancing/sexuality, the suppression of women, and the dynamic that makes this life what it is. She's as real as you get. I've gotten bits and pieces of her story, and know she is trying to put her life together after bouts of drug addiction. She puts up with a lot of shit she knows she shouldn't have to, and I can tell that a woman like that is not one that would *normally* be trifled with.

"Girl!!! I have fuckin' *done* it!" she whispers to me as she sits down. I scoot on the bench to make room for an ass that is as wide as *one* of my butt-cheeks. Apparently, one of the regulars has given her trouble. There are some men who come in and are "rotating regulars," meaning they move from one dancer to the next over time. I've had my time with this particular loser, Bruce, as well. I remember telling him, "he couldn't pay me enough to sit with his drunk, woman-hating ass again," and that I "felt sorry for both him and his pathetic, miserable existence."

Lex has been struggling financially for some time at the club, and this guy was at the wrong place at the wrong time. Apparently, he had done the same thing to her that he had done to both me and countless other dancers: taken them off the list for a few hours, and then let them be his captive audience as he got increasingly drunk. Once he hit a certain point, he flat-out degraded you as a woman. It was his personal power trip. You couldn't really leave, because you'd been paid to sit. Nice, huh?

According to Lex, Bruce had been sitting there for a few hours making not only the usual woman-hating comments, but also...*racial* comments. Bad idea. He ordered another round of his poison, and she calmly ordered hot tea. Lex quit drinking years ago, so she always ordered spritzers, mocktails, coffee, or hot tea. Perhaps he did not know how much she had endured, how close she was to the end of her patience, how he represented every single misogynistic bastard that she had so sweetly smiled at. Bruce slurred along in his drunken speech, and Lex leaned in, batting her big, dark eyes. It was only after the tea actually began burning his skin that he realized she had poured the entire contents of her tea pot into his crotch.

In the dressing room, she smiles a wicked smile, and I cannot stop laughing. In the back of my mind, I know that this is the end of our epic conversations...the end of nights spent commiserating after work at the all-night diner down the street. I know I'll miss her, but I am SO proud of my friend. She packs her locker in haste, returning to her street clothes and whatever life she had left before walking through the club doors. Her determination to hold onto the shreds of feminine righteousness is, without a doubt, empowering to the rest of us. I watch in awe as she sweeps herself, dignity intact, out of the dressing room...hopefully forever.

***

I want you to hit me as hard as you can. Tyler Durden, *Fight Club*

Things have a way of sinking in slowly. A small drop of dye added to a swimming pool every day will eventually, suddenly, turn the entire pool a different color.

I sit there, alone, without Lexus. I feel the uncomfortable emptiness and unease in my stomach. She got out. She got out? She's not out. She's out. *Shit.* My attention wanders to a chiffon gown in cerulean blue that one of my fellow mistresses is donning. In my mind, I place that color of blue along side the brown background of the splotchy brown carpet, which, when squinted at, is a lovely modeled pattern of rich chocolates, beiges, and complex night-shade plums. I see them shifting around each other, sea foam on shells and beach...swirling colors that would come off of my brush. I wish I had some pencils to jot down the idea...can I remember when I get home tonight? My aching intensifies. I hate it when this happens at work. Aching for the time to create is so much more painful when you know that small window of inspiration might get lost in the smoke and hairspray of your life.

I have mentioned to my fellow dancers that I'm an artist. In fact, there was one time when I was encouraged enough to bring in images from my portfolio. I guarded these images like they were letters from a diary, as indeed, *they were*. I didn't know what a dancer would say about this side of me. (Recently, I had mentioned how I was grateful that I menstruated, because it reminded me that I was a woman with this amazing connection to the lunar cycle. The dancer I told this to, collecting all the doubtful eyes in the room with her, said sarcastically, "Well, honey, what color is *yours,* cuz it must be more special than mine.") Things like cycles, nature, humanity, philosophy and spirituality captivate me so much in my daily life; I have to paint about them. I have to let color and imagination flow from my brush out of respect for the universal beauty that surrounds us all. This feeling *overwhelms* me, keeps me up at night, wakes me up early, and makes me get home from dancing at 3am only to wake up at 9am so I can get in a few hours of painting. I carve my promissory sentences into each painting...promises that someday I will be an artist and not a dancer...that I will be healthy...that I believe in a higher power...that I will travel and be happy and be in love and be empowered. Surprisingly, when the other dancers saw this work, they were actually quite lovely about it. "You did this?" they would say. "What are you doing here?"

Soon, the dancers started to connect me, Raven, with my "day job" of being an artist. I had dancers who would introduce me to men in the VIP room who were serious art collectors (self-proclaimed...who knows). Of all the men who said they wanted to buy my work, four actually did, Marco included. Most other men were full of the manufactured, alcohol-induced, fantasy-land promises that never really came to fruition. But that's okay. It's all part of the game.

Also, of course, there's Sandy, the petite blonde Belle of the South with whom I dance. She is *so* impressed that she says, martini in hand, "Giiiiiirl, I'm gonna get you on Oprah!!!" She goes on and on to a collection of men who are lounging on overstuffed chairs and couches. They are captivated by her Southern drawl and high, shelf-like breasts. Her face is cute, her eyes are doe-like, and her candy-sweet demeanor gets her fists full of cash. (Tee-hee! Blink-Blink!) Back-stage, she cusses like a sailor. "Sweetie-pie, I have connections to that woman, Ms. Wimfrey, an' her show! The world needs to see yer art! I'm gonna get yer work on that show, I promise! I'll phone you, sweet darlin'!"

I was, at first, elated...later realizing she was full of shit. But we believe what we want to believe. **We can consciously take what people say as either a vitamin or hemlock.** It's our choice how we assimilate other's words and actions into our lives. I used her excitement to push myself to be more openly talkative about my hidden passion, my first love...my art.

The thing is...all of these experiences have been gathering up inside of me, this encouraging knowledge of who and what I could be...if I would just let go a little and have the faith that I desperately paint about. I have seen it work in my life; at times, I will ask for something, and it is given. This truth—this hard, nugget of truth—is making this place intolerable at times. I feel a rift forming in my heart. It is becoming undeniable and louder and louder...

But a drink will fix that. I stand up to walk back onto the floor. Marco will be leaving soon, and I will be back on the dancing rotation. The one outlet, the one thing that gets me as high as painting does is available to me here. Dancing.

***

The body says what words cannot. Martha Graham, Choreographer

The best feeling in the world is having an audience who adores you, and you adore them right back. If the reason you adore them is all about the cash in their wallets, however, it does put a damper on things. I step onto the main stage. Thoughts from my inner twin, my artistic heroine, are in my head still. The wine didn't kick it. Time to let her go. I need to let her go quickly, or else I can't do this. I need to become Raven. Suddenly I have one of those artistic visions of mine: as I step forward, I am unstitching a small, square patch of skin on my stomach. The sutures come out and the solar plexus gateway to my soul opens. This is where I keep my spirituality, my higher self. In my mind, as I open it, three ravens fly out. I stand there naked except for shoes and a thong. Now I'm empty. Now I can dance.

Next, the perfect things combine to make magic: 1) A collection of men who are intent on spending money and are not too drunk, 2) confidence in my dancing skills, 3) a feeling of sexiness, and 4) the perfect songs. I prefer the moody, slow, sultry songs…the ones that build up from the beginning, like sex itself. I move along the glass at first, gathering the invisible winds needed for motion. I can feel them, I always feel them…they are ribbons of sexual energy, mine for the taking. Foreplay has begun. I put my thumbs under the spaghetti straps, slowly pulling one down, then the other. I spin around on six-inch towers, switching my movements between slow and catlike to a quick, breathless touch to the first man. It's all in the eyes…*all* in the eyes. I get closer to him, look into his eyes and feel he is a good man. We exchange something, an understanding, an appreciation…it feels good to me. I slither down onto my belly and roll onto my back so I can look up-side down at the next man. I draw my arms up under my breasts, cupping them, giving him the sultry glance. I feel energy ripple out of me like a pebble dropped into a pool. I imagine it cascading and splashing up onto each one of them, wetting their shirts, staining their clothes, making them mine. I have made an impression on you…I am all you are thinking about, aren't I? I'm everything you are looking for.

I work my way around the stage, guided by the slow thumping of the music. I can honestly say that each one of them is looking at me with such intent, such focus, that I'm beginning to change. Nothing else around us exists except that song, my rippling, flowing body, and their gazes. I am mesmerizing. The woman at the table with her husband stares, mouth open, in deep…what is it…what is this feeling I am collecting? Suddenly I realize it…it is the admiration of art. They are the audience; I am the self-creating art piece in front of them. Art…there she is again, my twin, whispering in my ear as I dance. I thought I let you go five minutes ago? The music stops and for a second, I look around and gather the last few glances from each person at my stage. The stage has a pile of cash, as does my g-string. But what takes my breath away is the fact that they all pause…and a sincere, humble, grateful "thank you" comes from each one of them.

I am *high*. I *love* this. I *love* this attention. I *need* this money. I need this feeling to last and last and last because it is easy validation of my worth. It proves that I am okay. On the surface, I am just fine. There are no little written-out promises on my skin, no visual images of who I am inside. The only way they might have a clue is the phoenix, and she's muzzled right now. My money is my reward. My movements are the art. My body is the canvas. I can show this to everyone here and they approve.

I cannot show my paintings to everyone…I would feel too naked. Too exposed.

***

The truth will set you free. But first, it will piss you off. Gloria Steinem

It's now 2am…the club is closed. Standing in line to cash out my chips from Marco, and to tip out. I made five hundred and sixty-two dollars tonight. After all the settling up with the club, I should walk out of here with a little over five hundred. That is better than average. Not bad…not bad at all. All the other girls are standing around. Things quiet down and become less interesting after hours. We've removed the fantasy. Evening gowns have been swapped for street clothes, makeup has been removed, eyelashes pulled off, hair brushed out. We group ourselves into little cliques at this time of night. I am, of course, alone. Lex is the only one I would've felt like talking to. In such a transient job, you gotta be careful who you become friends with, because they could leave at any moment.

I am lost in thought, not sure how it happens, but suddenly I tune into the girls who are closing out with Jimmy, the sexy manager. One of the girls, Shilo, and I used to go to high school together. Her new boobs are pretty fantastic. She and I acknowledge each other, but we are not really "friends." The other girl, Amber, was with her the whole night while they were off the list with a couple of young, rich, and remarkably good-looking guys. I had noticed them earlier in the evening. The champagne was flowing, as were the drinks, trays of food, and the table dances. Both of the girls were off the list for at least four hours, which means four hundred dollars *per girl*. One thing is certain: those boys dropped *a lot* of cash on them, for sure. I could be jealous, but I'm on cloud nine about how much money I raked in tonight.

Except…I overhear…apparently those handsome boys paid the bar tab, but forgot to pay for the hours the girls were off the list. Needless to say, the girls are PISSED. Jimmy is pissed too. We have all been screwed over at some time or another, but nothing like this. We all feel for the girls as we sit around smoking cigarettes, waiting with wads of cash. I've finally cashed out my money and grab my bag, when suddenly a girl runs out of the locker room with her cell phone. "They're at the diner! Those guys are at the diner!!!"

I'm walking out the door, when Shilo rushes up beside me. "Raven, can you take us to the diner? We wanna talk to those guys and get our money!"

I don't even think twice. Fuck those rich guys, of course I'll give them a ride.

We pile into my small pickup truck and I drive a few blocks to the all-night diner that Lex and I used to go to. I feel a twinge of sadness. The place is full, but I know she is not there. I wonder where she is, and know that I'll probably never see her again. I turn off the engine and the girls and I get out of the car. I don't want to get involved in this, but I'll at least wait and see if they need a ride back anywhere. She's kind of like a little sister to me at this moment. We protect each other. I'm proud of them, standing up for themselves. I feel a sense of female empowerment as we open the door to the diner.

There they are, stuffing their faces with burgers and fries. They look up as one of the girls yells "hey!" and makes her way down the aisle. Oh shit, I think to myself. Two slightly drunk, angry strippers who are owed money? I feel a "scene" happening. The two walk over, standing with locked legs and hands on hips, looming over the table. Voices are raised. People stop eating and turn to stare at the two raving beauties in street clothes and glitter that are holding up one finger, doing the "spiral-head, oh-no-you-didn't" thing to these two young men.

"…look, it was a misunderstanding! Jesus!…"

"…yah, whatever…I don't care…who the fuck do you think you are…"

"…didn't mean to cause any problems for you ladies, but FUCK…"

"…dude, let's just go back and pay our tab…."

"…yah, you *do* that, understand, you cheap asshole?"

It's all happening pretty fast, and I'm just standing here. Some people turn and look at me, but I just kind of shrug with my expression. The girls walk back over to me and seem a little more calm, but only a little. Shilo explains that it was a misunderstanding and they said they didn't mean to leave without paying that part of the bill, and are going back to settle up. The guys seemed still angry, but I guess it could've been worse. The girls walk outside to wait and smoke. As the guys approach, one of them gives me a dirty look and says something under his breath about my friends. I know somewhere deep inside that those assholes left on purpose without paying, and are pissed that they got caught. I can't take it anymore.

"Look," I say with a calmness that surprises me, "it's all good. The manager just wants you guys to get back there to pay the tab. Next time you leave, make sure you pay your fuckin' bill."

"What?" says the first. He has an ivy league thing going, a preppiness...an "I'm better than you," attitude that hangs around his body like a thick cloud of smog. He walks up to me, looks down on me, and says, "What?"

"You heard me," I say.

"Who are you? You're just a fuckin' slut. I make two hundred and fifty thousand dollars a year. What do you do? You're just a fuckin' stripper."

Rage *boils* inside me. A hot sensation of tears, anger, and frustration is stuck in my throat. I look him square in the eyes and say it: "I GET PAID TO SIT WITH FUCKS LIKE YOU!!"

For a split instant, before I spin around on one heel to march back to the truck, I catch a look of shock on the bastard's face. We share a realization of the power game, and who has the upper hand...neither of us. I feel sick to my stomach. My hands are shaking as I put the key in the door of my truck and climb inside, slamming the door behind me. I roll down the window to let my newly lighted cigarette smoke escape. I am desperately trying to stifle my tears, the screams, the sobs that are in my throat. Through the open window, I hear the two girls talking to the guys. "Don't worry about her...she's not with us...we're sorry for making a big deal out of it, baby...just come back to the club next week and we'll take care of you again...tee hee..." These bitches I had respected five minutes ago, the ones I had just fought with, and FOR, are chatting up the guys to come back next week.

It has finally happened.

I stand on the top of my epiphany as though I'm balanced on the sharp point of a needle. It HURTS. A new feeling sweeps over me, seemingly in an instant, but indeed it has been happening for some time. One drop of dye too many has suddenly turned my pool a different color. Now I'm drowning in it, and I can no longer stand it.

What am I afraid of? Who am I afraid of becoming? This bastard has just reduced everything I am, all that I have been through, all that I hold dear to myself, to the words "stripper" and "slut." I keep hearing those words ringing over and over in my ears. He doesn't know the passion that I keep alive everyday, the creative storms in my spiritual weather, the drive and ambition that keep me picking up that brush. He doesn't know about my phoenix, my smothered firebird that keeps choking on the ashes every time I cover my mouth when I should yell…every time I smile instead of slap some jerk…every time I downplay my artistic potential. I am so mad at this man, but it is clear that I am angrier at myself for not listening to my truth. I've become a masterful player in the game…so masterful that I have lost sight of the rules. My rules when I began were to get in, and then get out. Yet, because I have been lying to myself, I have begun to believe the lies that others have told me about what I'm capable of. If you stop listening to your own voice long enough, you stop hearing it altogether. Where the hell did I *go?*

Suddenly it is clear how I truly have fractured myself into two people. I have two lives, two energies, two destinies…which one am I going to feed from now on? I have been splitting my energy between light and dark, between painting and dancing. I cannot live in two worlds anymore. My intention has always been to create beauty, and yet *the way* I have been fostering this process has been to exploit myself, to reduce myself and my talents to nothing more than a pretty face, charm, and physique. My intention is not in line with my actions. I have become separate from my true path: my painting, my art. What I realize in that instant is how precariously close I am to losing myself forever to the darker side of myself. Painting is creation. It is light-generating, exploratory, and life-giving. Dancing, drinking, drugging, smoking, dating the wrong men, and swallowing my opinions—no matter how I try to sugar-coat it—has been pulling me down into darkness.

Dancing has taken so much courage all of these years, but has ended up leaving me empty and fearful of following the creative path. The shocking reality is that painting, not dancing, is going to require *much* more courage than I have ever used so far. I can no longer lie to myself about how afraid I am to *let go and do what I am afraid to do*. I want to be free. I want to be the one who gets out. I want to be like Lex. I want, suddenly, so much more than that club can offer me. I want *authenticity*.

I wipe the tears from my eyes, then I look into the rear view mirror at the two jackals and their sheep. I blow a puff of smoke out of my nostrils, and look at myself in the mirror. My twin looks back at me, her eyes smoky and glossy from tears. I feel the phoenix burning off years of resentment, years of anxiety, years of avoidance. My skin burns with determination. All of the makeup in the world cannot paint over the face that stares back at me. She is radiant.

I put the truck into first gear and peal out into my new, uncertain life, flames licking at the road behind me.

God help you if you are a phoenix, and you dare to rise up from the ash.
A thousand eyes will smolder with jealousy while you are flying past.
Ani Difranco, *32 Flavors*

BIOGRAPHY

REGAN ROSBURG

I grew up in Monument, Colorado, affectionately known as "Mo-Town" to all who lived there. In 1995, I attended the University of Colorado in Boulder. I continued to pursue my artistic longings in college, earning a BFA in painting and photography. After college, I traveled to Thailand and Indonesia alone to "find myself." For five months, my eyes opened to different cultural beliefs and traditions. I began to feel self-reliant, and was inspired to continue exploring different themes with my art. One of the themes that surfaced after being in Bali was the connection of humanity to its natural surroundings. This began to fuel political and environmental themes, yet I looked at it through a softened, scientific and philosophical lens.

My work has been featured alongside Rebecca DiDomenico, Anna Maria Hernando, Tracey Krumm, John Matlack, Terry Maker, and Jason Thielke. I have shown at the Boulder Museum of Contemporary art, as well as galleries in Florida, Santa Fe, NM, and Indonesia. I am currently represented by Art & Soul Gallery in Boulder, Colorado. I also show in my new haunt, Denver, Colorado, where I teach private and group painting lessons. Oh, and I'm a bartender (all the power and sexiness of a dancer, but without the removal of a dress...). Every other year, I still travel alone for months on end to Indonesia, and keep my connection to the Earth by going for long hikes, runs out in nature, and a daily yoga practice.

My paintings are created from resin and mixed media, incorporating found objects with photorealistic painting. The process is intensely laborious and detailed, and has taken nearly a decade to perfect. I work closely with an entomologist, using sustainably farmed insects that are prepared and then imbedded in the paintings. I do this in order to bring a more realistic representation of species that are affected by global climatic temperature shifts. I create small environments that reveal themselves slowly, posing the viewer to question what he or she brings to this world, and how he/she plays both a specific and general role as part of the global ecosystem. To quote my artist statement, "Our ecosystem is a grand architecture of cycles and coordination, of adaptation and natural selection, of migration, persistence and chance."

No, I'm not a hippie, and I don't smoke "the pot" (…um, *anymore*… but I do want a '73 Scout that runs on biodiesel). As the environmental and human consciousness issues that fuel my work continue to move into a global spotlight, I continue the work I have always done in order to be a part of that dialog. Art is a gateway into that which we do not understand, unlocked without the use of words…only the eyes and the emotions are necessary to enter that world. As time ticks by on our spinning planet, I am happy to help the discussion continue in a direction which brings awareness, strength and hope.

Visit: www.reganrosburg.com, or go to www.artandsoulboulder.com to see show images and schedules.

CHAPTER NINE

MY RIGHT BRAIN
Joe Milner, Lt. Colonel, USAF

All truths are easy to understand once they are discovered; the point is to discover them. Galileo

There are many places we tend to think of when we imagine being in a special place which has an innate ability to bring out our creative side and inspire us; a Hawaiian beach at sunset, high in the Rocky Mountains in an aspen grove in the fall as the trees burst with color, or maybe just a simple view from high atop a skyscraper at dawn. One area not commonly recognized as a creative or enlightening area in which to be inspired is a desert war zone. As a matter of fact, just the opposite is expected. This just proves the backdrop which leads to an epiphany moment can come in any form, any location, and any time. It does not have to come at a special time and place in which you have set things up for it or strived to create the perfect moment. It can and will happen when you least expect it, but are most open to it.

To understand how my epiphany moment came about, let me tell you a little bit about how I got to Iraq today. As a child growing up in Atlanta, Georgia, I was your average classmate. I was neither at the top of the academic charts, nor frightening my parents that the middle of their three children was in any danger of failing school. I was just average. Some classes were easy such as writing and history, but I struggled in others, especially science and chemistry. I loved math; the concepts came so easily I could listen on Monday, daydream the middle of the week away and ace the Friday quizzes. I was your typical high school athlete playing football and basketball well enough to letter on the team, yet never the star.

The approach of my high school graduation brought me to a crossroads as to what to do after graduation. I had reached a point in my life where I did not want to go on to college, so I looked into what other options there were out there in the world. I always excelled in a team environment and while my parents encouraged me to consider college, I knew that I was not ready to take on four more years of school. So I visited the local military recruiting offices. I was interested in becoming a police officer and the recruiters made my choice easy. The Navy wanted me to serve a full four-year enlistment, doing something other than law enforcement before they would train me to be a police officer, and that crossed the first service off the list. I was living by an Army post at the time and knew neither the Army nor the Marines was the place for me. On to the Air Force recruiter I went. As a result I am now a career Air Force officer with over twenty-six years working in military law enforcement. I started out by enlisting in the Air Force Security Police and after a few years decided it was time to begin to get my degree, and I headed off to the base education office. I applied for and received an appointment to attend the US Air Force Academy to earn my bachelor's degree and my commission as an Air Force Officer.

While I was at the Academy, I took the first of many batteries of tests cadets and officers take at various stages of their career designed specifically to help me understand and define my personality traits as well as my style of leadership. As a profession, the military continually studies leadership and history in an effort to develop and enhance our leadership skills, so these tests are a natural outshoot of this development. These tests range from the Myers/Briggs personality tests to color association tests, all of which are supposed to help you understand more about who you are and what are your natural personality traits.

One small problem is that they are frequently used to point out how similar we all are or, in my case, how uncommon you are in the "common" personality profiles of officers. I was never categorized in the average group for Air Force officers; as the standard assessment showed officers tend to be very logical, analytical thinkers with great critical thinking abilities. I always came out as a more subjective versus objective thinker and I am a "people person." I love people. I always rated very high in my interest in others and my ability to use my sensing and judging characteristics to gather specific, detailed information about others. I then turn this information into supportive judgments because I want to like people and have a special skill at bringing out the best in others. I also rated very high in my ability to read others and understand their point of view. Many of my peers have noted that people like to be around me because I have a special gift of invariably making people feel good about themselves, which in turn makes units I am assigned to or commanding perform well.

While my personality has always helped me lead Airmen, the other aspects of my professional work required what appeared to me to be extra effort on my part to achieve the same levels of proficiency and competency as my peers. While I studied hard to barely pass exams at the Academy in the nine core engineering courses, many others breezed through the work without a hitch. As I struggled to just get my mind around how these formulas all worked together to explain how an aircraft engine took in air and produced thrust to make an airplane fly, my contemporaries were easily morphing several formulas together at once to show why an F-4 Phantom should have theoretically never flown in the first place. While my classmates were off studying by themselves, I found myself frequently back at the professor's office asking for extra help to just understand the basics. I even failed, and had to retake three of the nine core courses and was at the very brink of automatic disenrollment before I managed to understand just enough of the concepts to pass the remaining six courses, but just barely. I never really worried about why others could so easily understand and gain these skills and I could not, but I did always wonder what the real difference between us was. Little did I know that it would take over twenty years before I would finally discover the difference and understand it.

After the Academy, I returned to my previous career field of the Security Police, now as an officer. I found that though I no longer was in an academic world, there were still subtle differences between myself and my fellow officers. A prime example is how my peers could rattle off directions with precise distances and measurements to get a lost motorist from the runway to the commissary without blinking an eye. I would think about it for a second and give them the same general type of directions, but mine were definitely different. I would point in the direction they needed to start, mention a landmark versus a distance they wanted to travel to, then make an arm motion of the direction they wanted to turn (sometimes saying the wrong direction, but displaying the correct direction with my hands) until I had drawn for them a visual map of where they were to go. I also found out I had an excellent memory for faces, but was equally terrible with names. I would meet a person and I really had to work hard to remember their name. Luckily for me, we wear name tags in the military so I at least have a built in memory jogger to help me try to remember names; but no matter what method or intensity I put into trying to remember names better, they never have stuck with me. I chalked up most of it to the fact that my peers obviously were smarter than me or just plain more talented, but there always seemed to be something else I could not quite put my finger on.

As the years rolled past, I learned to compensate for most of the areas I had difficulties in by using little gadgets or routines to help me keep track of things. I found that if I do not write things down, I will forget them within seconds of a conversation. This usually meant that I would not think of these things again until I either ran into the person later or until I was asked for a product or status of a project only to stare blankly at the person and apologize for not accomplishing the task. This did not go over well with my superiors, so I started with a day planner and was then an early graduate to the world of PDA's and other information storing gadgets. I learned everything about them, spent hours in-putting everything from appointments to phone numbers to task lists in them and used these gadgets not because they were fun or cool, but for survival! The benefit was that I quickly found myself known around the office and in the community as a quasi tech-geek and information storehouse for how to make numerous programs or gadgets work at their most optimum level.

I also used routines to help me keep track of items like car keys. I always set a place for them when I get to a new location or environment and always put them in the same place if I wanted to be able to find them again in a timely manner. To this day if I set an item down at a place other than its designated location, I am more than likely going to forget where it is and spend more time finding it again than I usually have. The same thing goes for my storage of papers or files. I do not "file them" in the traditional sense; I "stack them" on my desk in piles or in deep drawers of my desk. As the pile grows, eventually I go through it and get rid of some items, but if I take them out of the pile and put them in folders, I normally forget what system I used that day to categorize them and they are "lost" until I search long enough to find them again.

In a world of professional officers, I have a mental system that defies my peers and their much more structured organizational skills and they often chide me for my apparent lack of organization. Many of them have been frustrated over the years when I was not present, but they needed to find an item or file I had in my possession and they had to go through my stacks to find it. I have received numerous phone calls asking me where an item was and if I used my system, I have always been able to tell them which stack it is in and where in the stack to look for the item. I was always sure to find what they were looking for, much to their dismay, but not without my share of ribbing for how things were "organized."

All of this brought me to where I am today and the events that led up to my epiphany moment. I was notified in March of 2007 that I was to be deployed to Iraq in September of 2007 for a year, to work in the Multi-National Security Transition Command-Iraq as part of the Ministry of Interior Transition Team training the Iraqi Police. I was selected to lead the force protection element responsible for the safety and security of the ninety-three Coalition personnel working out of the Ministry of Interior headquarters and mentoring my counterpart, an Iraqi Brigadier General, on security and anti-terrorism operations for the headquarters. I expected my year to be busy, sometimes frightening, but I never thought I would be hosting personal revelations of the type I have experienced.

The backdrop of a war zone brings with it a wide variety of times and circumstances, ranging from the hectic chaos of a frontline headquarters to on-the-edge of your seat experiences when you are out on a mission protecting your comrades-in-arms as they are conducting operations in unsecured or hostile areas. But then come small moments of resting and recovering which can lead to introspection and learning. During my first six months in-country I found that I did have a little time, usually late in the evenings, to rest and relax but found myself with few activities to take up this time. Halfway through my year I returned home for fifteen days of leave and while I was home, I mailed a beginning drawing lessons kit to myself to take up a multi-year dream of learning to draw again like I used to when I was younger. I never forgot the fun and enjoyment of drawing, but it slowly had taken a back burner to athletics, homework assignments and the myriad of other activities high school students get into. It wasn't until I had been in the military for a few years that the itch to draw again was back, but by that time I was married and then became a father to our three wonderful kids. The battle of "not enough time to do everything I wanted" meant making a choice of how to use my time and deciding to spend time with the family always came first. Drawing went on a back burner for many years, but I never lost the desire to draw and to this day get a thrill just walking through a hobby or art supply store looking at the art supplies.

Now in Iraq, I had a little time on most evenings, not much, but enough and I wanted to use that time to begin drawing again. I originally began a program which led me through many of the basic exercises on learning to see and draw, but it never held the same excitement or enjoyment that I had remembered and expected. It was during this time that I mentioned my endeavor to one of my office coworkers back in Colorado and she mentioned an outstanding book on drawing titled *"Drawing on the Right Side of the Brain"* by Betty Edwards. She told me she used this book as a basis for teaching drawing classes at the Academy.

After hearing her excitement and high praise for the book, I immediately ordered it online and two weeks later was reading about a subject that went far beyond just learning to draw. As I read and worked through the first part of *Drawing on the Right Side of the Brain*, I was fascinated by the book's approach to learning how to draw. The book explained some of the research on how our brain is wired together to form the verbal and analytic left side of the brain and the nonverbal and global right side of the brain. The more I read and started doing the exercises, the more I saw of myself and the major difference between myself and others. *I finally hit a stunning moment when my epiphany broke through and I realized the difference. I am a primarily right sided person!* Eureka! It was an "I could have had a V8" moment when I realized what had been right in front of me for so many years, but unseen and unknown. No wonder the linear thinking and concrete ideas of my contemporaries never made sense to me, since I learn by seeing and doing; drawing mental images to relate to ideas and always working off my emotional or "gut" feeling for what is the right thing to do. I was so ecstatic I had to jump up from my desk and walk around my little room as my excitement was almost overwhelming. Thoughts rushed into my mind as I began to connect the implications of a right-sided brain to the reasons so many of my actions were "different" from my peers. At a very personal level, I also felt very special just knowing that I had a unique primary means of processing my world picture that was not "average." Now I understand the difference and it was drawing as a means of relaxing and winding down at the end of some stressful days that brought it out.

Over the next several days that feeling of being special and unique stayed with me. I continued to look back into my past and realized I should have caught on when I was at the Academy as to the difference between myself and the majority of other cadets and officers. As I struggled with the engineering curriculum, it took an unorthodox fighter pilot who was my instructor for, of all subjects, thermodynamics of engines, who was able to paint a bigger picture on how the formulas all fit together in a larger scheme better than any of the engineering formulas had made clear to me. Once I saw the whole picture, I could understand the parts and how they fit together. I can now see that my verbal and very descriptive directions for motorists with lots of hand motions was a reflection of my tendency to draw a visual picture for the person I was talking to, not an inability to know how to get there. It is just a different way to express myself and my thoughts.

The same is true of my organizational skills. I use a more complex and non-linear method to keep track of where things are or should be. I look for the relationship of things to one another and order them that way versus an analytical method. That also explains why an analytical mind could not make sense of my methods as they were completely as foreign to them as their methods are to me. My brain runs simultaneous thoughts and ideas and not successive patterns, so the lists I have to maintain are not because I am scatterbrained, but because I am running analogical thoughts in a track where others are expecting a digital response. My ability to remember faces over names is from my propensity towards non-verbal learning versus the verbal or symbols (written language) ability to "see" the name in order to remember it. I see the face, but not the name!

What a breakthrough discovery this has been, but it took until now to finally understand. Where does this lead me from here is the next question? Since I have only discovered this side to me a few weeks ago, I am not totally sure yet, but as I have continued my drawing lessons, I am learning to enhance my ability to use and open the right side of my brain. I have found that I love to listen to music as I draw. This enables me to eliminate distractions and allows me to focus on the lines and edges which lead to a picture or drawing. I am more diligent in my lists as a means of keeping myself straight in a linear world. I enjoy the freedom of not only being different in a personality sense, but in my method of processing information. I realize why I have to focus to stay on task because I have learned that daydreaming is a common right brain activity. But most importantly, there is freedom in understanding. There is freedom in knowing that you're made uniquely different, and it is not only okay, but pretty cool!

BIOGRAPHY

JOSEPH "JOE" MILNER, LT. COLONEL, USAF

Lieutenant Colonel Joseph "Joe" Milner is the deputy commander of the 10th Mission Support Group, Headquarters 10th Air Base Wing, United States Air Force Academy, Colorado. He leads 1,900 military and civilians assigned to seven squadrons responsible for civil engineering; morale, welfare and recreation programs; military and civilian personnel, communications and computers; security forces; transportation, supply and contracting for more than 14,000 military and civilian personnel. He is currently deployed to Iraq as the Ministry of Interior Force Protection lead mentoring Iraqi general officers on force protection/antiterrorism while directing force protection for 93 Coalition personnel in Baghdad's "Red Zone."

He was born in 1964 in Atlanta, Georgia. He graduated from high school in Columbia, South Carolina, in 1982 and immediately enlisted in the United States Air Force as a Security Specialist. He was selected to attend the Air Force Academy Prep School in 1984 and subsequently entered the Air Force Academy in 1985. He was selected by the Air Force Institute of Technology to attend the University of South Carolina and he earned a Master's Degree in Criminal Justice. Lieutenant Colonel Milner is married to the former Kimberly Zaiger of Colorado Springs, Colorado. They have a son Andrew and two daughters, Jessica and Sarah.

EDUCATION:
1989 Bachelors of Science degree, U.S. Air Force Academy
1995 Masters of Criminal Justice, University of South Carolina
1996 Squadron Officer School
2003 Air Command and Staff College
2003 Masters of Military Operational Art, Air University

AWARDS & DECORATIONS:
Bronze Star

Airman's Medal
Meritorious Service Medal with four oak leaf clusters
Air Force Commendation Medal with two oak leaf clusters
AF Outstanding Unit Award with one oak leaf cluster
AF Organizational Excellence Award
Air Force Good Conduct Medal
National Defense Service Medal with Bronze Star
Armed Forces Expeditionary Medal with Gold Border and
one oak leaf cluster
Iraqi Campaign Medal
Korean Defense Service Medal
Air Force Overseas Ribbon (short) with one oak leaf cluster
Air Force Overseas Ribbon (long)
AF Longevity Service Ribbon with four oak leaf clusters
Basic Training Honor Graduate
Small Arms Expert Marksmanship Ribbon with Bronze Star
AF Training Ribbon

CHAPTER TEN

ANGELS ALONG THE WAY
Jane Jones

*A*rt *is a kind of innate drive that seizes a human being and makes him its instrument. The artist is not a person who is endowed with free will who will seek his own ends, but one who allows art to realize its purposes through him...To perform this difficult office it is sometimes necessary for him to sacrifice happiness and everything that makes life worth living for the ordinary human being.* Carl Gustav Jung

Childhood Desire vs. Compromise

I was a child of the 1950's and grew up thinking that the world was a pretty okay place. My favorite pastimes were reading, playing with my dolls and coloring in my color books and on whatever paper surface I could dream up. I wrote stories and illustrated them. For school projects I drew and colored and cut and pasted. If it involved art or craft I was involved. My favorite summer memories are of attending an art and craft program at the neighborhood park. For a few cents I could paint, braid lanyards, create mosaic trivets and a myriad of other things that my mother displayed in our home. We (my sister and I) whiled away hours at the park. No one gave it a thought that dangerous people might be lurking there, watching children—those people were just in fairy tales. Of course Mom checked on us, but we were outdoors, playing with friends and I was making projects. We would go home for lunch, tell Mom about what we had been doing, and then return to the park for more fun. It was heaven!

My parents (mostly Mom) encouraged my creativity and other family members probably found it entertaining. I had lists of ideas with descriptive little drawings of what I hoped the outcome would be. My imagination ran non-stop. I was creative, but I didn't draw very well. I thought that either you were born with the ability to draw, or you weren't. And artists, only real artists, could draw. I couldn't draw, so being an artist wasn't an option for me.

My parents weren't "creative" types. Mom was a homemaker and did all of the secretarial work for my dad, who had his own business as a machinist. I didn't understand that he was actually very creative. We didn't talk about it; it was how he made a living for his family. He invented and developed machinery and products and created several businesses in the course of his life. The word "creative" was not used to describe him; it was a part of his past but his gifts were minimized. Being a hard worker was the more important characteristic for someone of his generation, and he did work a lot. We didn't see him very much, but his creativity was supporting us.

He had dreamed of being a doctor, but finances were tight for his family and it was out of the question. He and my mom grew up during the Great Depression and learned to "make do" with everything, including their dreams. But my father also had dreams for me; he wanted me to be a doctor. I was smart, good at schoolwork and I wanted to please him. Now that's a recipe for a loyal daughter, to follow her father's dreams. But then when I was fifteen, he died, and my way of keeping him close was to try to live his dream for me. His death began my understanding of the permanence of death and the fragility of life.

Unfortunately, he was an alcoholic, and before he died life had been quite turbulent. After he died it was just assumed that the difficulties that he had brought into our lives would end. There was no funeral; no event really to mark his death, or life. His achievements, his dreams, and his flaws were all conveniently swept under the carpet, unmentioned. There was never a word about his creativity. Any character traits that I displayed that were like his were quickly criticized.

My father's sister, my aunt, was creative. She was a pianist, who was raising a family. My mother and aunt didn't get along, and when my aunt would try to champion my creativity and apparent lack of order in my room and on my desk, my mother quickly criticized her, and tossed aside my creativity with it. My mother loved order and a very clean house. Creativity frequently looks like chaos and that was anathema in my mother's world. So I became creative in ways that would be acceptable to my mother and channeled it into home economics classes and sewing. I was so lucky that my junior high and high schools had great programs.

I was too intimidated to take art classes because I wasn't an artist. But I was creative and expressed it through making most of my clothes, and then learning how to design my own patterns. When I was working with fabric I was genuinely happy.

But, I still wanted to please my father, so I took all the biology and science classes my high school offered. Since I went to a high school in a fairly wealthy neighborhood, lots of interesting science classes were available.

During those difficult teen years there was a person who came into my life who was the first person who really nurtured my creativity. She was my best friend's mother, Jacque. She was the mother that I really longed for. She was creative in so many ways and shared that with me. She encouraged my ideas, and validated the person inside of me. She was the mother of my heart, and supported me until her death in 1994. I truly believe that God put her in my life to keep my heart's longings alive.

Lessons in the Fragility and Power of Nature

Next would be college. I tried art classes, but I was very shy and it seemed that everyone knew so much more than I did. A bad encounter with an art instructor was enough to discourage me; at least that is what I thought for many years. The teacher was gruff, and certainly not nurturing, and accused me of cheating on a test, which was something I had never done. I turned away from the artist's path. I now think, with the perspective of many years that I was so fragile that he scared me, and perhaps at the deepest core of me I knew that I did not yet have the strength to deal with the power and intensity of my creativity and at the same time go so much against my family's wishes. I quickly left art classes and my artistic self behind in favor of my other love; biology. For five long and difficult years I toiled away on a degree in biology. I could do the work, and I loved learning. Most importantly however, I gained an incredible appreciation for the strength, wisdom and fragility of living systems. But I was living my father's dream, not mine.

Finding the Road

While I was in college I worked in a shop that sold lovely antiques, and hand-made painted wood items such as small bookshelves, planters, plaques, key holders, and pie boxes. The paintings of fruits and flowers that decorated them were really charming and I was fascinated with them. I admired the free, light and airy way they were painted; as if the creativity of their maker just flowed onto them from the brush. I purchased a few of them so I could enjoy them, and so I could study how they were painted. Those lovely hand-made objects were some of my favorite things.

After I graduated, I never wanted to see another beaker or Petri dish, EVER! When I found out that my father's parents had left me a few thousand dollars, I decided to open a needlework store. It would be a business, like my father had established, and it would revolve around threads and fabrics and creativity! I was on the road to happiness again. I met new people, taught classes, designed projects to teach, accepted commissions and I could be as creative as I wanted to be! I was good at that. After a few years, however I got very tired of having to keep regular business hours. I had a great shop to play in, but sometimes it felt like a cage.

During those years I began to paint; not "fine art" but decorative art. The charming painting on the antique store items led me to think that maybe I could do something like that, so one day, in what was a very bold move for me, I walked into a craft shop and signed up for a decorative painting class. I'm pretty sure that God took me by the hand and led me into that shop to sign up for classes, because there is no way that I consciously thought I could paint. I am eternally grateful that I followed the nudgings of my inner voice. I was lucky to meet one of the loveliest teachers I have ever known. She encouraged me in everything I wanted to paint. From the first piece of fruit that I painted, I was on a roll. I painted on anything and everything. If it wasn't moving, I was considering a design for it! But since I still couldn't draw like an artist, I was using patterns that other people had drawn. I would enlarge them or manipulate them in some way, but I was not really doing the drawing myself. It was creative, however, and I loved painting, so I was happy with it.

I was increasingly unhappy with my retail business, so I looked over the parts of the business that I liked and where I made money and decided that a retail business was not what I wanted. I transitioned to teaching and designing and selling to other shops around the country. I really enjoyed what I was doing, and I loved the freedom of being away from the shop. But I found that I had to design within certain traditional parameters in order to sell, and that became very confining.

Allocation of the Gifts of the Earth

I started to design for another needlework company as well as for my own. I, and other artists, created designs for new products, and then the actual product development was done in Haiti. I thought I was going to have the experience of going to a tropical island, and I was very excited about how exotic and fun it would be. I had no idea that I was headed to a poverty stricken Third World country and that it would change me forever.

The people that I met and worked with were sweet and kind, and very good at making the products from my designs. They did not complain about their lot in life; they laughed with me, told stories and in the afternoons, they sang Christian hymns! I asked why they sang and I was told that it was to keep them awake and alert because they had probably not eaten since some pitiful breakfast. That would probably be their only meal of the day. I was shocked. Here were people who were lovely…and starving.

The people from the company that hired me took me around the island and pointed out where the rich lived, and where cattle grazed. As we rose in elevation, the beauty of the tropical island was exquisite and lush and rich with bounty. Enough bounty that some of the vegetation had been replaced with grasslands to feed cattle! Cattle whose meat was shipped to the United States! Not far away, people were starving, but cattle were getting fat. That really didn't make sense to me. The answers to my questions about why that was happening always came back to money. And my thoughts always came back to the wonderful people that I met and got to know there.

Finding Love and My Missions in Life

Shortly after my trips to Haiti, I met the man who would become my lifelong partner. John and I have been married for a long time, but I rarely call him my husband. That seems so limiting, and well, traditional. And we have not had a traditional life. Recognizing him as the love of my life was truly an epiphany!

When John and I married, I began a part of my life that included great discoveries. He introduced me to some friends who were vegetarians, as I had been for several years. But nutritionally, I wasn't very good at it. One of the friends he introduced me to was Marsha, and she was the queen of vegetarian nutrition and taught me so much and pointed me toward a marvelous book, Frances Moore Lappe's *Diet for a Small Planet*. I not only learned a lot about how to be a more responsible vegetarian, I learned some very good reasons about why to be a vegetarian. (This was in 1986, so it was long before the "Go Green" movement that is currently popular.) Lappe presented information about world food politics and how food is grown for those who can afford it, not necessarily for the people who live on or near the land where the food is produced. It answered all of my questions about why cattle were getting fat on Haiti and people were starving.

In college, I had learned about organisms and ecological systems, but had never considered that Earth is one planet with abundant, but limited resources. Nor had I considered that the allocation of those resources is based on economics and greed, not need. I was not politically active, but I knew that with each bite that went into my mouth I could support the values that I hold dear, and do my best to not contribute to the problems caused by a meat-based diet. That small, rebellious act of protest has been my quiet statement, every day of my life for about thirty years.

John was so supportive of my creativity and helped make it possible for me to go to interior design school and I loved it. I had wanted to do that even when I first went to college. It seemed like a wonderful direction for my creativity, and one where a person who could not draw could still create. I was wrong however about the drawing part of that thought. There were several classes where I had to draw, but it was disguised as drafting. While I was measuring and making sure my lines were all straight and perpendicular, I accidentally discovered that I could draw! I remember looking at a room elevation that I had drawn and realized that I had made some very lovely drawings. While I had always been creative, I never thought I could draw. That was part of why I didn't take art classes in high school. I believed that if I couldn't draw, then I couldn't ever be an artist. And, since there weren't any artists in my family, there wasn't anyone around to tell me any differently. For me, this new realization was like discovering gold. This was an epiphany! I might actually be able to draw! That began a slow process of setting the artist in me free!

Interior design school was very expensive and so I took what I thought would be a couple of semesters off. One evening during that time I went into a bookstore to look for something interesting to read. I didn't know what I was looking for; I was just looking. I overheard one woman going on and on about a book to her friend. She said absolutely glowing things about the book in her hand, and so when they drifted off, I took a look at it. It was *Portrait of an Artist: A Biography of Georgia O'Keeffe* by Laurie Lisle. It seemed like it might be interesting and it had just gotten a wonderful review, so I purchased it.

Desire and Dreams Meet Passion

As I was reading about O'Keeffe's life, I was discovering myself. Her thoughts were my thoughts. I completely identified with so much of what was written into that book. My heart was soaring! John and I were in the car going somewhere and I was reading my precious new book. I remember so clearly saying, "John, this book is me! It's what's inside of me!" I knew without a doubt that whether I could draw or not, I HAD to go to art school. I could do it, or spend the rest of my life wishing that I had. The women in that bookstore turned out to be angels that I never even met.

Being the wonderful and incredibly supportive man that he is, John worked with me to change our finances so that I could go to art school. I found the best one in my area and they accepted me! My secret dreams were coming true.

There were a couple of bumps in the road however. I was close to getting what I wanted so much, and then my husband's job transferred us to a town in northeastern Wyoming! I was devastated...for many reasons! But I was on my track to learning to be an artist, and nothing was going to stop me. I have always been good at teaching myself, so I bought books and art supplies to take with me. Since I knew no one, and John would be out in the field for several days at a stretch, I decided to create Jane's Personal Art School. Then, just as I was getting going with my studies, John's job disappeared and we were headed back to the city! I was thrilled; he was devastated. We moved into a duplex the size of a shoebox and both went back to school.

It took me a while to feel comfortable at the art school. I was so afraid that I would fail. For the first time in my life I was faced with my worst fear, "What if I cannot do that which I long so much to do?" If I couldn't become an artist, I thought I would just be a hollow shell of a person. Some days I was so scared that I could hardly get myself to class. I would head out on my usual driving route, and then I would miss a turn, correct my route, and then miss another turn. And it's not like I didn't know my way around, I had lived in this city my whole life! My fears were literally driving me away from my dream. Fortunately I was VERY determined, and I got to school anyway, late, but there.

In my first figure drawing class I worked for three hours to make a drawing of the nude person at the front of the room. I agonized with every stroke of the charcoal, and it truly was my very best effort. I am not kidding; the drawing that I worked so hard at looked a lot like the outline of a homicide victim at a crime scene! Fortunately the school needed money, so they didn't evict me! I kept showing up in class and trying and trying and trying.

Since just figure drawing wasn't enough torture, I also had to take a traditional drawing class every semester! The teacher for the first semester was a wonderful woman who was tough, but patient. I was finishing a drawing of a still life and she came around and looked at it and said something positive and I responded with, "But I really can't draw." Her very quick response was, "Whoever told you that, was lying." With that one comment, she stuck wings on my shoulders and sent me flying! I could draw! That was a moment I will never forget and will always be grateful for.

***

It seems that at just the right moment, God has always put just the right person there for me. I kept showing up, and the person was there for me. An epiphany was given so easily and directly from this great teacher!

While I was in art school I felt like I had finally found "my people." I felt like I fit in in a way that I had never felt before. I worked hard, learned a lot, grew, and honed my skills. It was an incredible time in my life. When I graduated I was ready to leap into life as a professional artist and since I was in my mid-30's I felt like I really needed to get going.

The artists' path, I found out, is wonderful, but hard. Harder than I ever imagined it could be. Oh, people told me it would be hard, but I had been working hard for years in my own business. I was used to hard work...I thought! But I can tell you this, when I am possessed by incredible creativity and passion, there is nothing else on this earth that I want to do. The rewards are great, but require patience and determination.

Commitment and Determination

During the first year out of art school, I submitted my portfolio to several galleries and found out that rejection is a huge part of an artist's life. By the end of the year I was pretty discouraged. But there was a person who just kept after me to submit my work to a very nice gallery in Denver, where I lived. I just wasn't up for more rejection, but this person kept after me. So in December, I finally said, "Okay, fine, I will send in my portfolio, get the rejection, and begin again in the New Year."

Just a couple of days after sending the portfolio, I got a call from the gallery owner asking me to bring a few paintings in! She wanted to show them to some interior designers who worked on hotels. As a result of that connection I began doing commissioned paintings for Marriot and Sheridan hotels for three or four years. I quit my day job and never looked back. The person who pushed me into submitting the portfolio to this gallery was an angel in my life. She came for a brief time, and then departed.

The gallery owner showed and sold my non-commission work and I was on my way as an artist. I had a pretty good understanding of how to make a painting, but I needed to decide what I wanted to say with my work. Fortunately, life had prepared me for that. The thoughts and ideas that continue to be important for me to communicate in my artwork are:

1. The beauty of nature. Not just the prettiness of nature, but the infinite possibilities, colors and details.

2. The life-force of living things. They are tenacious and determined to live

3. The fragility of that force. It can be gone in a moment. Death is always a possibility. But in that is a great appreciation for the moments of life.

4. Nature is the foundation of all physical life, and a fountain for emotional and spiritual life.

5. Nature is bountiful in so many ways, but people can corrupt it.

I have been a professional artist now for twenty years, and the things I have learned along the way are:

1. Follow your dreams, no matter what!

2. Find at least one other person who will encourage and support you and your dreams no matter what happens. Tell the others to keep quiet.

3. Angels will show up to help and guide you. They look like everyday people and speak in everyday voices, so PAY ATTENTION!

4. Epiphanies happen in ordinary places, on ordinary days. Keep your eyes and heart open.

5. Be prepared for your dreams to come true. Get the training, learn what you need to know, meet the right people. When opportunity knocks, have your bags packed for the adventure!

6. Be patient while you prepare.

7. Life will give you every opportunity to resist your dreams and success. Be determined and committed to your path and your dreams.

8. NEVER, EVER QUIT!!!

Life's Work vs. Life

There is no greater exhilaration than being fully and completely engaged with creativity and my passion for painting. I become a tool for inspiration. There is no ego involved; I am just the tool for the expression of The Idea. I feel like I am doing the work that I was sent here to do and there is a sense of Divine timelessness and purpose. The rest of the time I work out of commitment and determination to do what I believe I was put here to do. And sometimes it is simply work. At those moments, I rely on my passion for what I am trying to communicate in my work to pull me through the long hours.

Then there is life, with its errands, phone calls, weeding the gardens, grocery shopping, and the other mundane things that are necessary to live. They must be done. But they can be squeezed into small spaces of time so that they don't interrupt The Real Work.

But people, they are in another category; a messy category. There are those who truly understand my commitment to my work and accept and love me anyway. And those who do not; and they have pretty well sorted themselves out of my life. There were some tough choices involved. I have some regrets about them, but ultimately I chose the life and work that I believe I was put here to do. My mother would call my choices selfish, but I don't think they are. I prefer to think of them as self-ful choices. Ones that were made by knowing who I am and what I am here to do.

The people in my life who love and accept the limited time I have for them are very precious to me. They understand that our relationships and connections are either through phone or email. Most of them are very engaged in their own creative journeys. I didn't intend to have mostly artist friends, but they are the ones who understand and support who and what I am, as I do them. We are birds of a feather. The friends and family that are not following creative endeavors have simply come to accept how things need to be along with my limitations and are all the more special to me because of their generosity in allowing me to be who I am...without guilt or regret.

By its very nature, a creative life is an alone life. In the alone time there is great possibility for creativity and inspiration to visit, so it isn't lonely time. It allows for the tiny quiet voice to whisper the seed of an idea, or for a fully formed image to simply appear in imagination. It's time for sensitivity without the intrusions of the world, and it's time for getting down to the business of making the images appear in paint. It is time that is ripe with possibility. It is a time when perhaps epiphany will brush by.

BIOGRAPHY

JANE JONES

Born in Denver, Colorado, and continuing to live near there, Jane Jones is known for her simple, uncluttered, richly colored floral and fruit still life paintings. They are presented with jewel-like colors against solid backgrounds gradated with light that highlights the intensity and special qualities of her subjects.

In 1976 she earned a Bachelors Degree in Biology but returned to school to study art and to obtain a Masters Degree in Art History. An avid gardener, she is fascinated by the beauty of transformation in the cycles of life and death. Her art reflects her academic studies as well as her passion for the power and fragility of life.

She taught art history for many years at Red Rocks Community College near Denver, and continues to teach painting and color theory at the Art Student's League of Denver and in workshop venues around the country. Her book *Classic Still Life Painting* presents the Old Masters' painting technique of underpainting and glazing with oils and she has produced several instructional DVDs.

Her work has received several awards at the Salmagundi Club and National Arts Club, both in New York City and she is listed in several Who's Who publications. Feature articles have been written about her and her work in *American Art Collector, Southwest Art* magazine, *International Artist* and *The Artist's* magazine, where she is a regular contributor.

Jones' paintings are in the permanent collection of the St. Louis University Art Museum and have been exhibited at the Gilcrease Museum, the National Museum of Wildlife Art, the West Valley Art Museum and the Colorado History Museum. Her work is shown in galleries in Scottsdale, Arizona, Santa Fe, New Mexico, Houston, Texas and Palm Desert, California.

Aside from her professional life, the activities that give her the most joy are sharing time with her husband John, and their furry family of cats and dogs. The best times are spent on long walks and working in the garden while playing with the animals.

Her paintings can be viewed on her website where you will also find information about her book *Classic Still Life Painting*, and instructional DVDs.

Visit: www.janejonesartist.com

CHAPTER ELEVEN

SCHEHERAZADE
Judi Lightfield

Poker players look for a "tell," something that gives a player's hand away. It's a gesture, a tic, a habit that signals a good hand or a bluff.

Some people have a "tell" in normal conversation.

When I listen to them speak, they'll tell me what's important; what they value.

Some people have a numeric "tell." They'll tell about their bank account, net worth, how much they weigh (or don't weigh), how many phone messages or emails they have received. What they paid (or hadn't paid) for something.

Some are more circumspect with their "tells." They casually drop the name of a celebrity, a hot-spot vacation, a famous event attended. An artist friend keeps a tally of the number of trucks it takes to move his shows around; three forty-foot trucks to Kansas City. Seven trucks to Colorado Springs. He gets so excited when he hears of another sculptor's truck loads. I had never thought about art in terms of truckloads.

I know my "tell." It's stories. A miserable trip to the Division of Motor Vehicles can be turned into a hilarious comedy of errors. A simple mistake can be a life lesson. A tragedy can be repaired through the creation of its story.

My life has more stories than could fill this book. All kinds, all colors; lighthearted adventures, love stories and tragedy. But I return to my first story. The story of telling a story.

All sorrows can be borne if you put them into a story or tell a story about them. Isak Dinesen

***

This is New Jersey. I grew up during the Cold War. The Cuban Missile crisis, race riots and Kennedy's assassination were the background noise of my childhood. We had air-raid drills in school. In case of nuclear attack we were suppose to curl up under our desks. I had seen the photograph of a nuclear strike, the enormous mushroom cloud. In my own mind the desk wasn't doing it. The flimsy wood and metal weren't saving me from ultimate destruction. I was the one badgering the teachers. They weren't telling me the truth.

Second grade was supposed to be for reading, writing and the new math. I missed a lot of school that year; I was sick with tuberculosis. Consumption was the fashionable name. Famous people had it and stayed at sanatoriums. Thomas Mann wrote about it in *Magic Mountain*. Puccini's heroine, Mimi, has it in the opera *La Boheme*. Edvard Munch painted his sister with it in *The Sick Child*.

It was less glamorous when I had it. It had been nearly wiped out and was rare. For me, being sick and bedridden meant brand new coloring books and boxes of crayons. A new box of sixty-four had an oddly pleasant smell and looked so neat, every crayon standing up straight and even in their stadium seating. A new coloring book held so much potential; every page was a discovery of shape and color. Eventually I started to color outside the lines and with more than crayons, but these are my first memories of drawing.

The disease itself left lesions on my lungs. Unlike the scars on my knees from learning to ride a bike or the scars on my hands from being careless with sharp objects, these scars were invisible to others.

Sometimes a disease doesn't seem as bad as its cure. I got over the illness, but every two years I had to be tested for a re-occurrence. The first test was just four little pricks, which would swell up. The next was a large needle in my arm, which again would swell up. The last part of the routine was the worst. A large school bus would come and pick up me and the other three children that had had TB. We would be on this bus for a long time before we came to the New Jersey State Mental Hospital. We were ushered to the basement, and had to put on hospital gowns and wait for a chest X-ray. It was the waiting in a hospital gown that got to me. I always wondered if I would get my clothes back and if I'd be allowed back on the bus to school. How did any of these people know if I was a visitor or resident? How could they tell us apart? This went on every two years from the age of eight to eighteen. Every two years I would sit on a bench in the basement of the New Jersey State Mental Hospital wondering to myself, "How do they know?"

I finished high school, barely. The last week when all the other seniors were cutting classes I had to be there. I hadn't actually been in class enough to meet the state attendance requirements. But I made it and I was ready to be free.

***

This is Boston, Massachusetts, 1973. This is me on my own for the first time in my life; my first big city. My first apartment, roommates and all. It was economical, laid out in a straight line, bedrooms on either side of a hallway, kitchen in the back with a fire escape exit. I had two roommates, Terri and Shirley. Terri worked in a clothing boutique. Shirley was a law student. One night they got into an argument about race. Shirley actually called Terri a racist. The next day Terri was home alone. The building had an entrance with a security system and mailboxes with our names. Someone buzzed and asked for Shirley. Terri, wanting to prove polite, let him in. He knew Shirley. He was black man. Terri wanting to prove she was not a racist, let him wander around the apartment while she stayed in her room talking on the phone.

When I got home there was another argument going on. It seemed that while Terri was on the phone the man had found the rear exit and left with all my good stuff. I walked in and my room, closest to the back, had been ransacked. Television, stereo, jewelry—everything had gone out the backdoor with the black man.

The police came and started a report. The three of us sat at our kitchen table with four of Boston's finest standing behind us. Terri was looking at mug shots. The tension in the air was so thick I could barely breathe, and I couldn't understand why. Terri, Shirley, me—mug shots—four cops. Why all the tension? I noticed the wicker bread basket on the table and in it a nickel bag of marijuana. As casually as I could, I took a napkin and placed it over the pot. The tension broke. No arrests were made that day. One of the cops asked Terri for a date.

My first set of transportation problems. Auto insurance was impossible. I had already totaled two cars and had racked up a few tickets. I worked downtown and the T-train, the regional mass transit, was OK. The line went underground and every time it did the lights would flicker off. Invariably when the lights went off my tushy was pinched. When the lights came on I stood in the middle of the train glaring at everyone. I could never figure out the culprit. I was annoyed enough to find alternative means of transport. My first attempt was with hitchhiking. I'd stand in the street with my thumb out and it never took too long to get a ride. This came to an end when my ride asked, rather mannerly, if I minded if he could "masturbate while I drive." It disturbed me when people smoked or tuned the radio; definitely there would be no masturbating while driving.

I bought a five-speed Raleigh bicycle which weighed as much as a medium-sized basset hound. Riding to work would be easy, straight down Beacon St. This worked well until I did a Marilyn Monroe-ish "subway-gush-of-air-skirt-blowing-up thing." I was riding my bike wearing a full pleated skirt when a car passed me. The skirt flew up over my head, exposing my panties. Since I couldn't see where I was going I hit a parked car. After that, the bicycle wasn't useful for work, but Sundays were spent riding it through Boston neighborhoods, stopping in Cambridge Square for ice cream or shopping in the Haymarket for bananas and fish.

My first job wasn't very interesting. I sold expensive shoes in a Newbury Street store. The ease and boredom of the job let me explore the city. Tuesday nights were free at the Museum of Fine Art and I was there nearly every Tuesday. Monet's, Renoir's, Manet's—I spent hours eating them with my eyes. Boston had other attractions. Classical ballet, four concerts for twelve dollars. The Boston Symphony had special rush tickets as low as two, three dollars. At the theaters I could volunteer as an usher and see the show for free. I was young and energetic and interested in everything. La dolce vita.

My first drug-dealing boyfriend. He was no small time dealer. He dealt cocaine in the big department store bags. He enjoyed spending the money and he spent it on me; dinners, dresses, jewelry. It was fun, flattering and glamorous. One night he threw a party, the kind with ice sculptures, tuxedoed waiters, canapés, good scotch and good drugs.

The party was winding down towards dawn. I was telling a story that I can't even remember. Suddenly he came from behind, grabbed me and put a gun to my head.

"Shut the fuck up." He said.

But I was in the middle of a story and I didn't shut the fuck up. I was in the middle of telling a story and I kept telling it. As I finished the story, finished talking, I felt the cold at my head. Cold metal. Gun. Real gun. Real gun at my head. Seconds went by. He pushed me away and I kept going. I didn't look back; never saw him again.

What was I doing? What was I thinking? I wasn't scared at the time. I wasn't scared until much later.

When I remember it I'm surprised by what I don't remember. I don't remember his name—Steve? Greg? I don't remember his eyes, nose, face. I think he had a mustache and mousy brown hair, or maybe blonde. I remember that he was tall, broad and stocky; formidable. I remember his presence in a room, how large he was. I remember his gold Mercedes-Benz that he let me drive in Boston and I was not a good driver and he didn't care. I remember seeing the bags of cocaine and thinking that it was a large quantity. I had seen small baggies. I had tried a lot of drugs. This was the seventies and though there were a lot of drugs there was no problem. The problems came later.

I remember myself a little. Very tall and very slender; long dark hair and dark eyes. I wore a long white dress. I noticed that people noticed me and that surprised me. I am nineteen and not accustomed to attention.

Words are like insects. Some are like ants and carry twice their weight. Some are like butterflies and float into nothing. Words don't have gravity; they may have energy, but they don't transform gravity to energy in the instance of their birth.

The story starts in my mind as a random selection of images—"white dress," "arm across my shoulder, around my neck," then "gun."

They will start to line up.

First there is the image of the night, the party. People mingle. Then I am grabbed. But I'm talking, telling a story and it's important. The image freezes. A long pause. How long? I don't know. In the image I am still talking. I still need to talk. Then "gun." The thoughts will circle around my mind, slowly, then faster and faster. Sometimes they follow the same order. Sometimes they are random. "Gun." "GUN." "Cold." "Cold metal." "White dress." "Ice sculpture." "Walk away." Just walk away.

Time goes by. The words organize. They follow a pattern and come out of my mouth. The timing is strange. I tell the story at another party.

I tell the story to impress someone. I tell the same story or I forget parts. I never remember the story I was telling. I never remember the words coming out of my mouth while a gun was held to my head. I remember struggling with the words to order them, to clarify what happened. The experience becoming more significant, yet a memory muted by time.

Now it is decades later and I think about it, but not as a turning point in my life. I was as reckless three months and three years later as I had been then. It was an incident in my life. The experience got thrown into a file of experiences. The time I got sick from eating too much...the time I got lost from...the time I went to the wrong address, etc. etc. etc.

Sometimes, in a moment, an experience explains itself. The part it plays in your life becomes clear. It is an epiphany. Now I know the experience of having a gun held to my head and why I kept telling the story. I know what it means to me.

Scheherazade.

It means Scheherazade. Run her name through a search engine and over two million hits will turn up. She's been linked with music and dance; she is even a software program. But more than anything she is fictional, truly fictional. She is the teller of *One Thousand and One Arabian Nights*. She spun the story of *Aladdin and His Magic Lamp*. She recounted *Ali Baba and the Forty Thieves*. She directed *Sinbad the Sailor* in his voyages.

Scheherazade is a mysterious woman. She seems to come out of Persia in the seventh or eighth century. Her story begins with a king, Shahyar. He was disillusioned with women and marriage after his wife's infidelity. He takes to marrying a virgin every night and beheading her in the morning. Until...enter Scheherazade. She knows what she is doing. She puts her life on the line. One night she marries King Shahyar and starts to tell a story. As the day breaks the story is not over. The King must wait and he keeps waiting, for one thousand and one nights as Scheherazade keeps the stories going. In the end it must be a comedy, because he does not kill her, he marries her.

That's what we do, we humans. We tell stories. I had a gun held to my head, but I was telling a story. The gun was not the story at all, but surviving to tell the story was the story. I continue to tell stories...

***

What's in a name? Lightfield is mine, but it isn't just what is on my driver's license. It is my way of making sense of the world. I paint. I am a painter of things in a landscape, although I never considered myself a landscape artist. It is not my intent to convey the outside world. Rather I'm concerned with what is inside my being and the overlap between inside and outside. The objects are outside, the meaning is inside. I don't use photographs or sketches. I don't work outside. I use the idea of the journey—the story unfolding in time and space.

The paintings start like a story starts, as a series of undefined images. Maybe a series of undulating lines that appear as mountains would appear. Maybe there is a small clearing with a copse of trees. Maybe there is a path leading into the distance. On a good day the paint just flows and no sooner than I imagine the place, there it is. On a bad day I am lost, utterly and completely lost. The world drains away in a mix of drab and disturbing blotches and I have to ask myself, "Why keep coming back?"

But I do and there is the difference. A mix of drab and disturbing blotches becomes a Rorschach picture. Maybe something in this mess can be salvaged...now I see a mist and there are clouds and a light comes shining through.

This is my story. This is my life. This is my art.

One's art goes as far and as deep as one's love goes. Andrew Wyeth

BIOGRAPHY

JUDI LIGHTFIELD

"Judi Lightfield is a gifted landscape artist and a hilarious master of black comedy—she has many stories to tell, including some that involve her dark childhood of pain and misery and more that reveal her fair share of heartache and loss as an adult. She tells stories that will grab you and vibrate you between laughter and tears, as you marvel at how all of it could have happened to one person who became such a gifted artist. She is one of the funniest melancholy people I have ever met...her art is a lovely and complete reflection of who she is, and along with her descriptions of the meaning behind each painting, her images will break your heart." A quote from a friend.

***

"Lightfield is as she paints: a woman who has emerged from many layers after a life-time working in the arts. She initially studied Environmental Design at the University of Massachusetts but transferred after two years to the University of Oregon. After receiving a Bachelor of Science in Fine Art, she moved to Colorado. Working at the Denver Art Museum surrounded her with many influences; contemporary, Western and Oriental. Her education was completed with a Masters of Arts degree from Regis University, emphasizing education. Lightfield has taught at Red Rocks Community College and is a freelance designer, planning educational and art exhibitions. Currently she teaches painting, art appreciation and art history at the college level as well as other selected classes." Excerpted from www.zensocrates.com.

Articles about Lightfield have been featured in many publications including Westword, Denver Rocky Mountain News, Denver Post, and Southwest Art Magazine.

***

"Sifting through layers to find her own voice, Lightfield borrows a technique of the old masters, sfumato, or very thin layers of paint applied as glazes. The

layers of paint capture light, reflecting it back to give the work an ethereal glow. The landscape emerges slowly from these layers. "The image is unconsciously sought," she says. Dark tones overlap pale ones. Strokes of color intertwine until a horizon line develops and the journey begins. It is an imagery journey, across mountains of obstacles, valleys of grace, through trees filled with life. Never a specific place or time; it is a journey of changing dreams, memories, and the feel of space. Maybe you've been there, the lost and undiscovered place that brings you closer to yourself and the sense of wonder in the world." Excerpted from www. zensocrates.com

Judi says, "Teaching is how I earn my living. Writing is new to me and taking some time.

Sometimes, in a moment, an experience explains itself. The part it plays in your life becomes clear. It is an epiphany. In my case it was the need to tell the story."

Judi is currently showing her art privately by appointment.

Visit: www.epiphanysfriends.com to see a sampling of her work.

CHAPTER TWELVE

AN ELEGANT SOLUTION
Jerald Lepinski

A completely irrational situation! Why should most of our adults be illiterate in their favorite art? Why should so many of our most capable and accomplished people believe that music is one of the difficult subjects?

What the reader will visit here is a paradigm shift, which will ask for patience and imagination. To comprehend the fundamental change at hand, musicians and laymen alike must allow that the traditional practice of reading and writing music might have been so mistaken that it made reasonable music education impossible and prevented what should be music's major contribution to learning in general. Everyone has his own concept of the role of music and its possibilities, based on the old system exclusively, with nothing for comparison.

To imagine that the accomplishments of Beethoven and Yitzak Perlman refute this point is to assume that they wouldn't have been as well or better off if they had inherited a better system, or even dealt with two systems. It might also assume that society as a whole should accept illiteracy as a norm in an easy and beloved subject area.

Why should most of the college freshmen who want to major in music arrive as ill-prepared as English majors would be, who didn't know a noun from a verb? Why do most of today's professional music performers, in the tradition of Paul McCartney, not read music?

Why do so few piano teachers read piano music? If "read" means the way you read a book, most can't. Those who can are given the special label of "sight readers." The rest of them know how to convert the information on the page to music, but the process is one of analyze—realize—memorize. To be fair, pianists have the hardest job. They have more notes to play than other musicians who mostly play one at a time.

Their two hands read two different languages, and they have to be "the whole orchestra," playing rhythms against themselves.

Why can't we teach the literacy of this very basic art to young children as they learn other literacy?

Now we can!

As I began to struggle with this dilemma, it seemed clear from the outset that the entire problem was the way music has been written for the last several centuries. The monks who began music notation a millennium ago did exactly the right thing for their purposes, and they are not to be blamed for our problem. They defined pitch *relatively*, like an informal group that moves a song up or down to find a comfortable range and then sings it in tune in that key.

The mistake that eliminated most people from the world of music literacy came when instrumental music evolved and required fixed pitch. Our ancestors, understandably, could not imagine replacing the old system, only adapting it by adding sharps and flats to accommodate the other five pitches. If they had been able to conceptualize a "chromatic" system (see below) at that time, everyone today would read music.

Terms: "**Chromatic**," of course, means colorful. It comes to music through the print shop, because music which uses eight to twelve pitches at once adds sharps and flats (ink) to the page. So we call a system that accommodates all pitches a "chromatic" system, even though it does so by providing twelve different note positions and without adding symbols. "**Diatonic**," describes the traditional system, because it means music that uses only the seven notes needed for any particular scale.

History: Making music without writing it down is the longest tradition. We had important and sophisticated music for fifteen hundred years before the monks began drawing lines just one thousand years ago. The power of oral tradition is demonstrated by what they first wrote down—the Gregorian chant they had maintained through those recent centuries. I submit that, if we had waited until now to decide on a notation system nobody would elect the system we've had. It has all the tradition behind it, but little justification otherwise. Of course, tradition is all powerful.

Before turning to the solution, here's a critical view of the old enemy. The traditional diatonic system is absolutely abstract, to no purpose or gain. So it compares quite poorly to a chromatic system, which naturally correlates to the keyboard, its only previous manifestation. The keyboard can be called the only true "picture" of music.

The old system correlates to nothing at all. It exaggerates complexity and is the primary reason for attrition from music studies, especially among piano students. That fact is potent, because at some stage everyone should be a piano student. The system is un-teachable in the primary grades and still very difficult to learn after that, when it is already remedial, because the basic elements should have been learned earlier.

Of course there is much tradition for early and thorough accomplishment in music by traditional means, but only through extraordinary dedication of time and effort; the kind of regimen that produces child star violinists and Olympic figure skaters. That approach is completely impractical and undesirable when applied to society as a whole. The practical approach to be pursued here is to make all doctors, lawyers and plumbers literate in music, having all options to pursue whatever they like. It will also make musicians better.

Credentials: When musicians hear that someone has a new music notation system, they rather automatically assume that he is an amateur kook, so the reader should know that while I might be a kook, I am a professional one. My degrees are from the Juilliard School and my career has been one of both musical and intellectual leadership, conducting orchestras and choirs in the most important venues and series in my part of the country and teaching college music. The work described below has enjoyed contracts with the U.S. Department of Education and been endorsed by the largest association of professional musicians in my state.

I had concluded over the years that just about any problem we face could be solved with adequate application of human brain power, and the inventions that keep coming, decade after decade, seem to prove that. Now, could I solve this one, for which I must be as well prepared as anybody?

So it all began with pondering whether through the centuries there could have been a better system than the one we inherited. More importantly, whether there could be one that would solve our problems now. It seemed that a better system should certainly be feasible. Whether it could succeed in today's world was the larger question.

The design should only make necessary changes, because it must be readable by traditionally trained musicians, keeping a horizontal staff where we read pitch up and down and reading the passage of time from left to right. Recognize that music notation is actually two systems, one for pitch and one for rhythm, and that the rhythm system does not need changing. The pitch system must accommodate twelve pitches without additional symbols.

A true chromatic system cannot have sharps and flats. That means that the note between G and A, and all the other black keys, will need letternames of their own. Some inventors use letters from their own names, but I discovered the best source, the name of the monk, Guido d'Arezzo (ca 990-1050). He was a music theorist a millennium ago, when monks had begun to draw horizontal lines to give a graphic illustration to the melodies they were maintaining in aural tradition, giving their music a more dependable system for study.

Guido's name is one that comes up on the first day of any music history course, because he was at least a "patron saint" in the cause of music notation. Certainly, his adaptation of the staff other monks had begun was one from which the five line staff that served posterity could evolve. It is interesting to note, in the context of this chapter, that he was dismissed from two monasteries for the work that we would applaud today. Finally, of course, everyone followed his lead.

In the name of Guido d'Arezzo there are just five letters that we weren't already using for pitch names, and five were all we needed. I proclaimed that to be a sign from providence and went forward. The two consonants, Z and R were assigned to the pair of black keys in ascending order. We learned to call Z "Zed," because that is the international name for that letter and because it isn't confused with "C" in the classroom—very important.

The three vowels I assigned to the three black keys in ascending order, I—O—U. That's handy in the classroom.

The twelve pitches have always been seven that have their own letternames, A through G, and five that borrow their neighbors' names. "A flat" ($\flat$) means don't play this note; play the pitch a half step lower (the black note to the left). "A sharp" (#) means play the one to the right.

All twelve pitches are equally important, but they can't be visually "equal." For example, a keyboard with all white keys would be unusable.

So in the new system let one group be on the lines (with lines running through their noteheads) and the other in the spaces. Five lines are a more practical idea than seven, so the seven can be assigned to the spaces. That means five lines per "octave" group (one set of twelve notes, before the letternames begin to repeat). Let there be a larger space between certain lines to accommodate both E and F and both B and C.

Lo and behold, the result is a keyboard "tablature," which means a notation system that looks like the instrument. Designing it after the keyboard was so far from my intention that I literally awoke with a start in the middle of the night to realize that I had, in effect, simply redrawn the keyboard. There is a lesson there: a chromatic system can be designed so that it doesn't correlate to the keyboard, but that isn't easy and it makes no sense at all. A lot of would-be inventors have done it that way; apparently they feel a compulsion to keep music notation abstract, simply because it has always been abstract.

In fact, there have been many attempts to design a chromatic system. The earliest I know was by Chopin. One keyboard expert wrote a paper about this system to conjecture that Bach would have used it if it had been available to him. One book was produced to show about a hundred systems that had been invented. Most of them were abstract from force of habit, and a few took the right basic approach, but none of their creators took their own work seriously enough to follow up with further development—materials, training programs, etc. In short, they seemed not to think that their inventions were even worth testing.

So I start here—the lines are the black keys and the spaces are the white keys but there is a problem. If we just have five lines with one space larger than the others and we apply conventional notes where all of the lines and spaces have new meanings, the musician simply can not read those new meanings in that context.

Here followed a number of design elements meant to make the staff both more attractive and more functional. One value in each difference was the difference itself, because function would begin with the musician's ability to avoid reading any note as if it belonged to the traditional staff.

There will be more lines in the new system, coming in alternating sets of two and three. Making the lines in sets of three be heavier and the pairs be light helps locate the eye.

A series of twelve pitches ascending the staff should take no more vertical space than seven used to. As the noteheads diminish in vertical dimension they should grow horizontally, so that they become different but not smaller.

Another useful difference is to have the noteheads on lines be diamond-shaped and those in spaces be horizontal blobs of one kind or another. Since E and F share a space, as do B and C, something should reinforce the difference between them, beyond the fact that one is in the top of the space and the other in the bottom. If E is shaped like a drop of standing water and F is made somewhat concave, retreating into the bottom heavy line, that should help. If C is shaped like E but upside down, and if B is an upside-down F, we've begun a system of individualized noteheads to maximize recognition of pitches.

In traditional notation every pitch looks different in every octave; any note that's on a line in one octave must be in a space in the next. The chromatic system lets us make every pitch look the same in every octave. By continuing the scheme of two light lines and three heavy ones when we need leger lines (those lines added above or below the staff) we eliminate another misery of traditional notation—counting leger lines. They need never be counted because their individual character is easy to read, no matter how many are stacked up beyond the staff.

I gave the system the name, Meloz® Music Tablature, borrowing and adapting the Greek word "melos" which means music, melody, etc.

Now it was time to test it. Could musicians easily learn to read the new system? Could laymen now read music who had never read it previously? Before we could search that out we had to create materials for them to read—a lot of materials! New music that nobody had heard before and couldn't bluff through if they couldn't read the new system, pieces converted from the output of great composers, teaching materials; these and many more had to be ready for the first demonstration sessions, so that no one would be left to guess what any of them would look like.

Responses were good from the very beginning, but the meaning of "paradigm shift" came to take center stage. We learned to refuse short demonstrations for anyone. The common reaction was to be skeptical after twenty or thirty minutes and enthusiastic after ninety minutes.

Each octave looks exactly like this, and each note looks exactly the same in each octave where it appears.

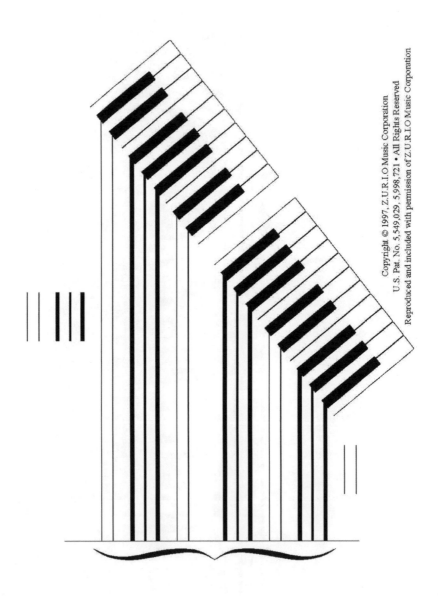

America

My coun - try 'tis of thee, Sweet land of lib - er - ty,

of thee I sing; Land where my fa - thers died, Land of the

Pil - grims' pride. From ev ___ 'ry ___ moun - tain side, let ___ free - dom ring!

One progressive composer, very mindful of the criticism of traditional notation in avant-garde circles, said almost angrily, "Why would you create a new notation system for two hundred year-old music?" I insisted that it was for all music of all times. I felt it was exactly what the avant-garde needed and was also the perfect way for everyone who had missed out on learning to read music to have a chance to catch up and fill that painful void.

A couple days later that composer called for an appointment. Then he opened that meeting with, "I don't think you realize what you've done here!" He's a very bright professional, but it took some time for the idea to come to full bloom in his mind. I tried to assure him that I saw the system as serving every aspect of music—those aspects that had occurred to him in the last two days and more. Eventually he came to work with us and created some very good materials.

Several groups sent by one professor were a mix of classroom teachers and music teachers, and early in those sessions the music teachers complained that the system was easier for the laymen, who weren't fighting the old system while trying to read the new one. They were right. The laymen jumped out ahead in the race to comprehension, but in each case, after thirty minutes more, the musicians had left the laymen in the dust.

From that time until now everyone who has studied the system has approved of it and agreed with us that it would transform society's relationship to music when it is fully implemented. So it would seem that this journey of an idea was destined for the land of happy endings. Publishers would rush to convert music to a system with twenty to forty times as many customers. Laymen who lamented having missed the boat of literate participation would rush to repair their lives. School districts would see the opportunity to upgrade education and rush to take the lead.

In fact publishers are foxes in charge of the chicken coup. As a rule they don't even read music, and they see educating the public as someone else's job, unable to see that they would become primary beneficiaries. Laymen can't find teachers to help them or even musician/friends who will forgive them for using another system. School districts, like bureaucratic industries, are headed by musical laymen who put all responsibility on middle administrators who understand that they must not make waves. So what began then was an extraordinary education in human foibles— barriers to our cause. When people have asked me whether I would write a book, my answer has been, "If I do it won't be about music; it will be about human psychology." Here goes!

There are many models for study of what happens when an important idea is rejected before is it accepted. The Xerox machine is a good one. With its adaptations it became the photocopy machine, the fax machine, and the laser printer—without which business and education could not carry on for a day. But an eight-hour documentary on that invention had to be entitled, "The Invention Nobody Wanted."

It became increasingly clear that my model should be Galileo (1564-1642). When you know that you are right and all your critics are wrong, it's comforting to study a famous and parallel case. I became a minor expert on Galileo.

With his new telescope he confirmed the writings of the previous century by Copernicus (1473-1543) that the earth revolved around the sun, contradicting the universal belief in the concept of Ptolemy, that the earth was the center. Copernicus had anticipated the kind of trouble Galileo later got into. As he handed over his own writings he instructed that they be published after he was gone, even though he had done his work at the behest of the Vatican. The purpose was to "straighten out astronomy" which he said was prerequisite to their request that he straighten out the calendar.

After several years of living with my dilemma I happened to re-watch the old great PBS series, "The Ascent of Man" with Jacob Bronowski. It was as if a private message was being sent to me. Discussing the lamentable end of Galileo's career, he pointed out his two serious mistakes. The second and "fatal error" was to leave the protective environment of anti-clerical Venice, in the belief that he could convince the Vatican of the truth. But the first error was, "like most scientists, to be naive about other people's motives." In this mission, of course, I actually play the role of a scientist, not a musician. I am, in effect, an educational psychologist, however amateur, and as the scientist I am searching for the truth, whatever that may be. As Ben Franklin said, "The truth waits patiently for you."

But where is the parallel to my case? One success which is vital to the survival of my mission is the schools, and while most readers will find it difficult to believe, an attitude that is common among public school music teachers is to not want a world where everyone can read music. Would you say that is a contradiction in terms? You would be right, but it's a fact. Consider their world: the improvements we project have never been possible and are not expected. That means that knowing how to have kids learn songs by rote and enjoy music while acquiring no literacy whatsoever is an honorable profession. An attack on that is an attack on what you are!

In our early years a musical curriculum writer told me of a friend who was qualified to teach both art and music in elementary school. "She has taught art for the last several years and is now going back to music. She has decided that musicians get more respect. I wonder if that is the problem you're having?" At the time I didn't even understand what she meant—that musicians get some prestige from being able to read traditional notation, and they fear losing that prestige. I couldn't believe that would lead to the next episode.

A few weeks later my friend had lunch with that same teacher. She turned over a paper place mat and drew lines to demonstrate the system we were teaching. She was dismayed at her friend's reaction. "She went ballistic! She snarled, 'That should not be allowed!'"

"But it demystifies music."

"Music *should* be a mystery! It should be very difficult! They should have to work very hard for music!" And finally, leaning close for a confidential but vehement whisper, she said, *"I don't want a lot of people in music!"*

Later I met that "teacher" at a demonstration of our program without knowing who she was. When she was finally identified for me I realized that she was the one who had confessed quite confidentially, "I'm really an art teacher." From then on our slogan became, "Beware the weak musicians!" (And remember that there are a lot of them.)

There are also a lot of strong musicians, and it's always heartening to see how those with exemplary self-confidence rave about the system as they discover it, but there is still a barrier. Music is a communicative art, and it matters little how positive a teacher and his young student feel about the system if all other teachers and students shun both the system and its users. It would seem that the only prerequisite to getting the first thousand people to use it is to already have a thousand people using it. I think they call that "inertia." Now we think we know the way but first, the arguments.

Most musicians and laymen assume a negative bias against any such innovation as this. They even assume that a negative bias is the responsible reaction. Before judging them for that, everyone should ask, "How many times have I seen an ad that told me 'You can learn to play the piano in eight lessons!' or something like that?" I'm sure I've seen a hundred of those. The more striking the "innovation" the less credible it seems.

The actual truth that everyone discovers when the system is put to work is that nobody can suggest any reason not to use it. There is everything to gain and nothing to lose, in spite of traditional reactions, such as..."**It would be confusing!**" In fact, it is mind-clearing. For most people it is easier to learn two systems than it has ever been to learn one, because the new system is the best way there has ever been to explain the old one.

"**How could you get everyone to change?**" Nobody has to change. Certainly symphony orchestras will continue to read from traditional notation at least until new generations populate their ranks, or maybe even forever. It is important to note that almost everybody has nothing to change *from*! We must keep in mind: "Almost everybody in the field of music" means almost nobody in society as a whole.

"**How could you ever replace all that music?**" Throughout the last two centuries of searches for an alternative system, that argument was the killer, because for all the centuries of printed music the process was engraving. The computer has now eliminated engravers because an engraver today would get forty dollars per hour and produce in two days what a computer operator does in two hours at fifteen dollars. Truly, a serious production schedule could convert all of the world's important music in one year, and have an army of customers increasing rapidly from two per cent of our people to closer to one hundred per cent.

But the most exciting facts to report are the educational discoveries. We had contracts with the US Department of Education for two and a half years. While we were not allowed in "typical" education, we were welcome in the world of learning disabilities. We were able to establish (or at least to present convincing arguments) that all children with learning disabilities function as well as others in music class where they are allowed chromatic notation. As a matter of fact, the specialists we were dealing with eventually agreed with us that "The general public's problem with music is that traditional notation creates the effect of learning disabilities in normal learners." Those with experience in the "LD" field are not hard to convince.

During projects in rehabilitation for stroke survivors there were wonderful revelations. Stroke survivors learned to read music who had never read it before. Since most people haven't learned to read music and everyone can learn to read Meloz®, that was satisfying but not astounding.

In those same studies professional musicians who had lost the ability to read music for several years after their strokes regained it after a few weeks of reading our more logical system. That was a bit of a thrill. But best of all, some survivors who had lost the ability to read text—books and newspapers (for years) regained it after a few weeks of reading music. The reason was contained in a basic element which is not always fully appreciated as a barrier to be mastered—tracking words is a hump to get over, whether you are learning to read or re-learning to read. Tracking is tracking, and it is the first element to explore when a stroke survivor can't read anymore. Tracking notes is an easy place to begin. Imagine the value for young beginning readers.

It is important to understand the essence of the difficulty that traditional notation brings to music. I like to start with the reaction of one music supervisor. She was inspired by the end of a two-hour demonstration. Holding a book open and pointing at the pages she said, "What I like is the rhythm!…the rhythm!"

Can you guess what was on her mind, since we have done nothing to change the rhythm system? We knew exactly what she meant. Her point was that, since the pitch notation doesn't need to be translated or interpolated, one has time to think about the rhythm. The average member of a high school band doesn't learn to read rhythm because he is too busy calculating pitch. He emerges from three or four years of high school band still "faking it" and still unable to read.

In contrast to that, with chromatic notation, we see everybody become independent in reading pitch and able to study rhythm effectively. Six-year-olds read new pieces at keyboards without help. After a couple years they know how to transpose simple tunes from one key to another and then another. Adults in keyboard class have essentially no difficulties, except to discover that the hands take more training than the brain, and that we haven't put practice out of style.

My epiphany did not come with the decision to search for a better system. It didn't come with the various points of design or the enthusiastic acceptance of key musicians. And it didn't come with seeing the system succeed much better with students than the traditional one. It came after fourteen year's work, when a courageous elementary school principal studied the matter, saw that teachers were apprehensive and announced, "I'm going to teach this!" That was our very first opportunity to try a program where it should always have begun—in kindergarten. That was when the lights and bells went on. I came to realize that we could accomplish far more than we had planned in the beginning.

This resource could create a new level of literacy and awareness that has never existed in early education—a level that could not ever be accomplished with traditional resources. Kindergarteners could easily learn more than their schools had ever dreamed of asking of them. It wouldn't be just a two or three-year gain because what they could learn routinely in the first couple years would surpass what is being learned in elementary school. There is no question in the minds of those who have studied the matter that if we can give all kindergarteners a functional concept of pitch notation, the keyboard, and rhythm, that would produce a new caliber of first graders. That would be a transformational improvement for all age groups in our society because it would transform the music curriculum of all the grades that follow. In terms of music literacy that transformation can be said to be from nothing to something and more. All children emerging from elementary school would be truly literate in music, at least at that level I've called "analyze—realize—memorize."

In many aspects of this subject we find meetings of minds, where experienced and imaginative professionals *know and agree* that certain results will follow. They don't need proof but realize others will. Bureaucracy demands data—conclusive evidence—as if it were easy to get a half million dollars and two years to produce those things. That makes the bureaucrat's life much simpler; he's not required to exercise his imagination or be courageous. But let us go at this that first way, the imaginative way.

First allow me one more comparison to my hero. No matter how terribly Galileo was treated, his message was unstoppable, even though the Vatican did take nearly three centuries to forgive him for being right. Certainly the huge majority of our citizens will eventually demand common sense from musicians and educators. It might be difficult to imagine the results of a limited adoption of chromatic notation, but I can tell you what will happen if it is fully embraced.

Come dream with me! Let's begin with those who have waited the longest; the seniors (my age group). We're living longer and better, and now a musical hobby is a real practicality. Seeing people who have spent an evening or afternoon making music with a small group at keyboards for the first time in their lives makes my struggle a little easier. For one reason or another many people who have never made music will not change, but it's easy to imagine half of our seniors discovering what they've missed. Then will come more and more, and this is exactly the kind of mental challenge that keeps the brain growing, if the study is intense, and why not?

Not-so-senior adults now become just as likely candidates. If they have difficulty finding the time in the frantic scramble to make a living, they might also find the kind of balm in music that relieves stress and adds years to life. Shouldn't this be as much a part of life as golf, playing cards, and reading books? It's more than just passing the time if it's done right, and why not?

Parents of children who study music make a great contribution by learning alongside their children, especially in the earlier years when it's easy to keep up. It's just not possible to be as supportive if you don't know up from down in what your child is doing. With chromatic notation we see parents of young children, who had no background, become truly literate in music in the process.

Of course, making music with their children at home (let's not call it "practice") adds magic to the process. We can have an end to that world where parents, teachers and other adults fall short in role modeling. If they can answer the question, "Is twenty-three minus seven sixteen?" or the question "Why can't I say, 'I don't have no money,'" they should have an answer for, "What are the notes in an A major scale?" That's at least as easy as those other two questions. All parents can be more complete role models when they discover that music is not rocket science, and once they have gone this far they'll go farther and farther. For those who are accustomed to thinking of music literacy at the periphery of daily thinking, it's probably important to note that the reading of one's own language was seen much that way for centuries. Finally, when more people learned to read, it became important for everybody.

Let this at least start some dialogue, and don't let musicians reject the ideas without some serious study and/or open discussion. Most strong musicians will want dialogue, and nothing could be better for this subject than to become very controversial. Its opponents have held it back by denying dialogue. If there is open debate we will win!

This would seem to be the greatest single educational improvement in our time. That might seem to be a foolish boast, but nobody has ever suggested another improvement to compare with it. I believe that nobody can debate me on the subject of music notation. The good musicians I know wind up on my side of the argument. We have very satisfying answers, and we haven't heard a new question in years.

For graphics and maybe even dialogue, visit: www.Meloz.com.

BIOGRAPHY

JERALD LEPINSKI

Jerald Lepinski's career has always been a combination of singer, voice teacher, choral conductor (plus orchestra) and music theorist. That has made him a strange animal because singers are not, traditionally, very good musicians, let alone conductors and music theorists.

Born and raised in Omaha, he began conducting choirs when he was eighteen. ("It didn't pay a lot, but I probably should have paid them.")

Jerald served in the Korean War, then returned to the university, followed by the Juilliard School for two degrees. At the age of twenty-eight he left for Denver to teach college and get out of debt, with every intention of returning to New York after two years to fight his way to the upper levels of the singing profession; strictly classical of course.

At the end of the two years the name Jerald Lepinski was established as conductor of Denver's Classic Chorale, and he had met the girl he would eventually marry, so he stayed another year...and another year... and so forth for forty-seven years at last count.

After a dozen years of college teaching he went to conducting full time, conducting the Classic Chorale for twenty-five years. All that time it was a special experiment in the field, because members received private voice lessons from Lepinski. "The sound of amateur choirs has to do with the fact that their conductors are mostly amateurs in the field of voice or at least in the field of voice teaching, and the singers are left to invent their own vocal technique, which is just about as bad as having violinists play without training."

The Classic Chorale functioned as a professional chorus because of that approach, performing many events with the Denver Symphony and in the Aspen Festival. Lepinski hosted a lecture series on classical music radio and in general held important positions of prestige for many years.

"Now I've progressed to kindergarten!" says Jerald, because of the work this chapter is about—the development of a common sense music system and exploration of how and where to apply it in order to correct centuries of failure in music education. "Never mind that some people have always done well with the old system;" he cautions, "the way that almost everybody has needlessly failed is the more important matter here."

Lepinski hopes this chapter might be some small contribution to a very important revolution in education and the general public's relationship with music, which he insists is a very manageable subject and our people's favorite art.

CHAPTER THIRTEEN

THE LUCKY
Shannon Paige Schneider

I remember being told I was lucky.

I remember not feeling lucky. I remember feeling angry.

I remember being: twenty-one, newly married, vegetarian, non-drinker, non-smoker with my whole life ahead of me. I remember my strong body, strong will, and strong plans for the future as a doctor. And then:

Cancer.

Cancer.

Cancer.

The day I found out Cancer had taken up residence in my abdomen, on my cervix and in my plans, was a day I slipped into a withdrawal from life that was more secretive and numbing than I can almost stand to recall.

I told no one. I hid.

I deleted voicemails from the doctor's office imploring me to call, to make a plan, to take action of some sort towards saving my life. I sat withdrawn into the seat of myself, the space of routines, as if that Monday were the same as any other. Classes, lab, errands, work, homework, housework, horses fed, and sleep.

Tuesday, I woke up and made it the same.

Wednesday, the same.

Thursday, same.

Same.

Same.

Same.

Two weeks passed, secrets intact.

No doctor's calls were returned. I oddly felt that if I perhaps refused it all, refused it as real, it would dissolve itself into the power of my plans.

One night, while cleaning the barn and massaging all the many needs of the horses to be put up for the night, the phone rang. I closed Daisy's stall door behind me and stepped through the dim light to the dusty barn phone.

Upon saying hello, my mother blurted out, "Oh, thank God!"

"Mom? Are you alright?"

"Shannon, I had a dream. Oh, thank God! I had a dream that you... You...You were very ill and, well...You died."

I was stunned into an awkward silence. The once familiar, comforting smells of the barn, the hay, the grain, the musky horse scent itself, all started to assault my senses to the point of nausea.

The word, "died" pierced the bubble of my secrecy and suddenly the word "Cancer" stepped from the bubble into the real and demanded my attention like a screaming child. I felt the embodiment of fear and at that moment knew I needed my mommy. Mom called me back from the long pause, which to her must have been insanely awkward and terrifying.

I responded to her, "Mom, I have Cancer."

My mom fell silent. No gasp. No tears. She simply fell into my silence that held those words finally spoken. I have no idea how long we sat there, hundreds of miles apart.

I was not alone in the barn that evening. In the intense quiet that sat between my mother and me on the phone, my husband swiftly finished his chores. He never looked up. He slid from Dolly's stall, latched it thoughtfully, neatly stacked a couple feed buckets, peeled off his gloves and left them palm to palm four feet from me on the ledge by the barn door. He stepped out into the night and shut the stable door behind him, closing forever any mistaken air of intimacy between us.

My mom was the first to speak. I cannot recall the first several words as they seemed to be lost in this fog of my mind; then followed a series of questions from my mom and limited answers from myself. The fog in my head began to part with every word I uttered out loud.

No, I did not have a plan.

No, I had no idea what stage of Cancer.

No, I did not know how I got it.

No, I did not know the prognosis.

No, I had not even returned the nurse's frantic calls.

No. No. No.

"This cannot be actually happening," I murmured through the settling dust of barn's dim light.

"Well, it seems as if yes, it is happening. You need to deal with what life deals you or whatever is dealt to you eventually deals with you. She spoke so sagely, so calmly, so confidently. I knew though, she would get off the phone and curl up in her own darkness, a mother's worst fear of losing her child, now a possibility. I knew her tears would fill the entire night's air. Hearing the first choke in her voice, she stated, "Now, go talk to your husband. Call the doctor in the morning. Go get some information. Call me the second you know anything and create a plan."

I hung up the phone knowing two things: one, I already had a plan; and, two, this piece was not part of it.

I walked over to Daisy's stall. She turned from her hay and spun her enormous body around to face me. She nuzzled her nose from pocket to pocket seeing if I was bearing gifts of sugar or carrots. She nuzzled my hands and moderately disappointed, raised herself to look me straight in the eye. I wondered if she understood, perhaps knew all along. I looked into those eyes of fantastic compassion and longed for a fraction of her wisdom. She blinked. She intoned a low goodbye and stepped back to her hay. Apparently, her plan still intact, she munched.

I dragged the heels of my worn boots slowly across the old barn floor to the stable door. I looked back across the precisely piled hay, the rows of stacked grain buckets and neatly ordered tack. I exhaled at the straightforwardness of it all, then clipped off the lights and stepped from the order into a chaotic cold future I was sure I did not want.

The night was icy and crisp and I felt it harden a part of my soul as I walked the hundred yard stretch between barn and house, alone. Alone, I walked into the house. Alone, I found my husband watching television.

The pair of us sat together, yet oddly separate, and held the fragile space between the flashes from the television screen and the rush of words from his show. I did not interrupt. I could not ascertain the jumble of his possible feelings from my own. I sat on the edge of the couch and waited. There was so much to say.

Miles seemed to stretch between us.

How could I even begin to apologize for holding this horror back as a secret for me alone to bear? I needed to start with an "I am sorry for not sharing the horror that was insisting its way into our newly established life together," but the words would not come. Before I could explain these or any of my feelings of fear that were strangling my ability to deal with the rational decisions that must be made towards my survival, before I could even take off my coat and find myself wrapped in his arms, he spoke.

"I do not want to talk about this again. You'll be fine." With that, he snapped off the television and walked from the room. I heard him slip from his clothes and climb into bed.

I sat there, in the dark, alone.

Alone, I went to the first appointment and alone I went to all those that followed. Alone I had to ask the doctor, "Are you serious?"

Are? You? Serious??

I kept saying the words over and over again wondering if this kind old doctor could really be telling me that at twenty-one years old I could die.

"Yes."

No, my heart countered, I could not die. I had too many plans! How could I be sick? I remember cataloging the reasons why I could not be sick: I did not look sick, I did not feel sick, I did not act sick, I did not go to class everyday like I was sick, I did not care for my horses like I was sick, I did not pedal my bike miles and miles a week like I was sick, I did not swim like I was sick, I did not run like I was sick, I did not bartend like I was sick, and I did not dream like I was sick. In fact, I was described by those who knew me as "with it," "radiant," "strong," and "most likely to succeed." Adding all of those things together, I continued to ask whether or not there could be a mistake.

I mean, sure, I was tired, but what American girl working her way through college en route to medical school is not tired?

The doctor remained stoic and painfully serious. He spouted off my condition, my prognosis, and my very uncreative treatment options as if he were ordering his usual sandwich for lunch.

Shit. Shit. Shit.

Cut. Cut. Cut.

Was not the Doctor's oath, "First, do no harm?"

He wanted my pound of flesh: my ovaries, my uterus, my woman-ness OUT. Into the space left behind, he wanted to pump noxious chemicals and radiation. Following this plan, he stated coldly, I "should" be fine.

Oh, and then he said, "You are lucky."

If I was "lucky," would not I have skated through all of life Cancer free?

I was not lucky. I was angry.

An enormous question of the most significant obvious proportions bubbled up within me and spat through the stoic discourse he was replaying over and over again for my benefit. Since I clearly was a classic case of denial, "No uterus means no kids, right?"

"Correct." How he did not roll his eyes at the obvious question of a pre-med candidate, I will never know. Perhaps it was from delivering this news on a frequent basis and dealing with shock at similar repetition.

"You can always adopt."

Let me be clear: I never wanted kids. I had too many plans to want kids. A Peace Corp doctor does not have kids; she changes the world in other ways. I wanted to leave my mark in those ways. I wanted to travel and travel and travel and a child in tow would have compromised that freedom. So, I married a man who did not want kids. In the blueprint of my future, I had clearly, already, and completely ruled children out of the plan.

So, why this? Why now? Why this unbelievable line of questioning crossing my brain, my heart, and my lips? Why all these weighty emotions dragging down my determination for survival? Should I not hand them over my uterus and a thank you card for securing a "birth control free" future for me?

In that moment, life got very hard. Everything I thought I had planned to the "T" came into question. Everything I was sure of just a month ago was now cataclysmically unsure.

Do I just want what I cannot have? Am I just mourning the loss of my feminine powers with the loss of my womb? I questioned my soul. She did not answer. Perhaps she could not answer. I think she was as stunned as I.

The plans I had spent an entire life dreaming into order shattered around me, within me and beneath me. I began to **feel** sick. I began to **feel** fear. Questions were growing inside me at the same rate as the tumor.

"What are my other options?"

"There are no other options, Miss. I am not here to negotiate your options. I am here to state your plan to optimize your survival." He stared me down. I felt smaller and smaller with every breath I could not breathe.

I scheduled the surgery only to cancel it from home hours later.

I begrudgingly did some research and found another doctor. He was nice enough. He was gentle enough. But most importantly, he was creative enough to buy me some time with my uterus. He agreed to some options the other doctor had not offered. There were several marginal surgeries, not recommended, but potentially effective enough: take the tumor off and leave the uterus, and follow it with an aggressive chemotherapy, an experimental drug. I might end up sterile anyway, but at least it was a gamble of sorts. He even suggested that perhaps my boldness could save other women and their unborn children for years to come. He agreed to let me keep the uterus I was unsure I ever had any plans of using.

It seemed as though the day after the first surgery, the rain came. I remember that spring being the grayest spring I had ever seen. It just would not stop. Every day was a more dismal shade of gray.

Several rainy weeks and painful surgeries later, a shower drain full of the hair that was once on my head, and a growing intolerance for anything I once considered food, I began to feel my bitterness growing against each gray dawn that followed the night.

Still, I got myself up and out of bed every morning and made myself choke down some toast and peppermint tea. I would sit and watch television and cry until I had to head into the clinic for a treatment or go make a feeble attempt to sit through a class or two. I would cry for lives on television that seemed so simple. For every emotional situation that arose, every illness, every loss, the story seemed to wrap itself up thoughtfully in thirty, sixty, or ninety minutes. I longed to wake up from this dream and find out my life was really a sitcom and I had just missed some lines.

I cried for hours throughout the morning. I cried for the pain in my body, the loneliness in my heart, and the seemingly cold silence in my soul.

I cried for the marriage that was slowly dissolving itself into memory, as he avoided me and I avoided me. There was less and less "we" to even avoid.

I cried for the energy I used to feel driving me in the direction of my dreams.

I cried for all of that energy rerouted in order to fake smiles to my husband, muster cheery voices to ensure my family I was on the mend, and convince everyone that, indeed, I was surely "lucky."

I wondered if I would cry forever.

At the end of that rainy, tear-stained spring, I found myself sitting like a shadow in the doctor's office; nauseated and limp; I awaited my fate.

"Well, it is not working. Our options have ceased to present themselves as viable. We need to schedule a full hysterectomy and follow with a course of radiation." The doctor stated this as he filtered through some papers on his desk. He did not even look at me while he delivered the news. I felt like an after-thought's after-thought.

"No," I muttered, "There must be another way."

"I am sorry," he looked up from the papers and into my eyes, "We'll give you all of the pain killers in the world little girl, but you are not going to make it unless the uterus comes out. If you refuse this surgery, you will die."

Vomit boiled up inside of me. The foul volume of anger, fear, and frustration rose within my being and then angrily found its way out of my system, spraying across his desk, his papers, and his plans.

"You're fired," I spat. The nurse fought back laughter, as she collected me and my things to steady me on my way out the door. She walked me to the ladies room and cleaned me up. She stayed with me and held me while I cried and cried and cried.

Upon leaving that office for the last time, I felt a surge of desperation flow through me. I needed my mommy. Upon returning home, urgently wanting connection with her, I returned to the scene of the crime. I walked into the barn and called her.

I told her of my loneliness and my hopelessness and the words the doctors all shared. She helped me gather my feelings and then she spoke, "We're going to see the Pope."

"HUH??" I thought.

It was not a completely random statement. My minor was in Roman art and archeology. Perhaps she was trying to get me to a place of inspiration so that I would continue to fight. Further, my mother was a former Catholic and was perhaps turning towards a God she once felt as a strong presence in her life. Granted, she was kicked out of the Church over twenty years prior for divorcing a man who refused to uphold the sanctity of their marriage. Maybe she wanted to pick that bone in person and knew that I would gladly go to battle for her. Or, perhaps, the desperation to try anything to save her daughter's life was softening her anger at God and the Church.

The next several weeks were a blur of preparations and growing excitement. It was the first time I had felt inspired in months. Though the chemo's nauseating effects were still prominent in my system, I packed, I planned again, and I hoped.

My mother's growing faith and generosity held me in my fragile state. She drained her savings along with her fear in the hope that this Pope could work a miracle. I saw her step from fear into belief as we walked from the plane into a power space of antiquity. Perhaps my mother was right. Perhaps a holy place could bring about a miracle. Perhaps I would be healed.

We toured Rome for ten days. We saw into every corner of the place. We saw every sight and statue and column. We laughed and ate pizza and sipped wine in amazing alley restaurants we could not find again the next day.

Wednesday finally came and we loaded ourselves onto a bus for the Vatican. Wednesday is the day that the Pope blesses the world. I was thrilled to learn that if you are a devoted Catholic, the world starts over at noon on Wednesdays. We walked across black obsidian cobblestones. We gazed up at all of the looming statues that lined the buildings binding Saint Peter's square, with eyes wide in disbelief at the magnitude of beauty around us. The square is enormous and can hold tens of thousands of people. One building had a long red banner hanging down from a window that clearly indicated that this would be the spot from which the Pope would address those gathered.

"Where do you want to stand?" My mother asked me.

I looked around at the entire square and the sheer number of buses pouring people into the space. My eyes fell upon a group of young Polish nuns who were clearly giddy with excitement at seeing the Pope. I guess the Pope to them is like Sting to me. They were abuzz with the anticipation of fans at a rock concert. I expected them to light candles and do the wave.

"There! If he is going to see anyone, he will see them!" I grabbed my mother's hand and we walked towards them. We set up our little camp and waited. The sun began to heat the marble beneath our feet and the people began to fill in all the spaces that were once air around us.

Noon struck. The Pope came to the window and waved. He spoke and blessed in nine different languages. When he spoke in Polish, he acknowledged the women to our left and they went crazy, jumping up and down and waving at him. He spoke of love and peace and kindness. He spoke for about an hour and then made his farewells and slid from the window back inside. It was over.

My mother spun me towards her and questioned me deeply, "How do you feel?"

She was not worried about the heat, she was inquiring into how one feels when one has been bestowed the grace of divine, miraculous healing.

I did not feel any different. I felt the same. Apparently nothing happened.

Her strength of newly reclaimed faith was about to be shattered, when the world around me began to spin. The world within me began to spin. I grew dizzy from my feet to my face. I crumbled beneath myself and headed to the earth. My fall was stopped by an older nun. She knelt on the ground with me and held me across her lap as my mother scrambled towards me with her water bottle. I was half in and half out of the world.

The nun smiled gently, stared into my eyes with hers, glowing with compassion.

"Dobra," she spoke as she traced the sign of the cross on my forehead. She passed me thoughtfully over to my kneeling and sobbing mother who held me close to her.

In an instant, the flurry of people exiting the square and the heat swelled around us. Several young nuns helped walk us toward our bus, steadying me on my legs. My mother and I looked and looked around and could not see the older woman who had caught me from my fall. She had vanished.

Sitting on the bus, sipping water, my mother spoke, "Dobra means 'good' in Polish." How interesting that my mother, though a woman of Polish descent, knows very few Polish words. But she knew this one.

"Good." I wondered what she meant. I did not feel good. I did not look good. The situation of collapsing in a crowd is not generally a good thing. What did she mean? We flew home a few short days later.

As I made room for my Roman treasures in the house, I moved some mail that came while I was away. Several of the packages were books from friends and family. It is amazing how many books on abnormal cell growth there are in the world. There are stories upon stories of miraculous healing from eating nothing but organic greens to drinking one's own urine. It is even more amazing still how many of those books an individual dealing with Cancer can be given.

I always smiled in gratitude when a loved one, for lack of a vocabulary to pull from, (as Cancer had stripped them of the ability to say anything they normally would say to a friend, a sister, or a daughter) would hand me yet another book of abnormal cell growth victories.

I never cracked one of them.

Instead I just cracked deeper into myself and continued to feel more and more withdrawn. The energy of answering the basic "How are you?" and watching a person's face fall when I answered them honestly took its toll in such a way that I initially started lying. I would respond with a quick "Great, really feeling on the mend," "stronger every day," "the chemo is working!" You believe they want these words. So you give them. You believe that Cancer should not have them as a victim too. They take these words and smile and with pity, look past your swollen eyes and do not believe a word of it.

After a while, you feel as though the lies are not serving them. You stop answering the phone. Eventually, those closest to you stop asking and start holding your hand, silently screaming for help from a God they simultaneously question for his cruelty.

In the worst of it, before Rome, I went to a support group for individuals living with Cancer. I met some of the most amazing and inspirational beings on the planet. They would speak, with bald heads a-shining, about how Cancer had changed their lives and how they no longer sweat the small stuff. They would very clearly describe how everyday is a gift. They would talk about how "lucky" they were. No matter how bad things got for them, they held grace in a moment they referred to as "Now."

The larger part of me wanted to scream "BULLSHIT" at the top of my lungs and point out the injustice they had been dealt. The smaller part of me hid in the back, cried, and was unwilling to engage in conversation. I returned to the group only a handful of times more. The smaller part of me was stronger. I contemplated for hours how these people could cheerlead for Cancer in their lives. Cancer shattered my sense of self. Cancer shattered the "me" I knew so clearly and the "me" I knew I wanted to become. Cancer was even challenging the child I never knew I might somehow possibly want.

I recounted this in the initial meeting I had with the new Grandma-type, Birkenstock-wearing, Boulder oncologist that agreed to take my case. I believe that this goddess, with a flowing gray mane, *saved my life in this first meeting.* She saved my life not by pulling out a vial of magic potion locked up in her top drawer, reserved for only the most depressed and pitiful of Cancer patients, or by drawing out of another drawer, a secret scalpel to cut out my fear, or by drawing out of yet another secret drawer, an inspired new treatment plan.

Instead, she saved my life with her ears. She listened to me.

She listened well past the amount of time I am sure she had scheduled for me. Once I found myself talking to her and delving into the silence of my soul, I could not stop. My soul sprang forth and it had a lot to say. My soul and I had a lot of tears to cry. After I was out of tears and words and Kleenex, she spoke and her words blanketed me in comfort.

"Life never goes as planned. Twenty-year olds learn this lesson the hard way, and do you know what they are called when they have learned this about life? Thirty. Let's get you to thirty. First, before we discuss any medical plan, we need to get you to stop feeling so sorry for yourself. We need to connect your heart and mind back to your body."

"And yes, Cancer sucks; however, I feel strongly that this life needs you to be of service to someone other than your anger and fear."

I swallowed hard.

"Medically, your previous treatments show you to be in remission. As renegade as those treatments were and against protocol, congratulations! The danger is, with Cancer, no one can really tell you why one cell suddenly shifts its memory and decides not to die and becomes Cancer. Oddly, too, we have no clear answer as to how we turn that cell's memory around. I do know, however, that for us to keep you in remission, we have work to do."

She stepped from behind her desk and padded her well worn cork soles over to a file cabinet. She pulled an amazingly overstuffed file from a drawer. She planted it steadily on the desk and pronounced, "You are going to start volunteering and you are going to take yoga."

I flipped through the fat file she slid in front of me and marveled at how many brochures for saving the world this woman had collected. She had everything, from organizations that were actively saving the world to actively saving the water and the animals and people in the world. I was drawn to an organization's pamphlet that had a child on a horse, grinning from ear to ear, with the horse led by two proud adults on either side. The organization was local and it focused on teaching children with disabilities how to horseback ride. By learning to ride, these children connected deeper into a joy of self and an integration of mind, body, and spirit not previously available to them.

"Those kids will change your life," she said as she observed me reading the inside of the colorful flyer.

I looked up meekly and smiled weakly.

She walked me to the door and handed me a card and a schedule to a local yoga studio. The business card was for a surgeon, "just in case." She was direct, but not too direct. I liked her.

I found myself awake the next morning at least hopeful that the heaviness of the depression would be absent. No such luck; I found the gray weight of fear and anger and sadness still intact. I made a deal with myself to call the organization for which I would be volunteering and schedule my orientation. I further made a deal with myself to check out this recommended yoga thing.

Over my tea, I perused the yoga class schedule and list of class descriptions. I have always been very athletically inclined. I played sports as child, I took dance and gymnastics in school, rode horses my whole life and raced my bike as an adult, so when looking at a yoga schedule, I passed right over the "beginning" classes and the "level one" classes and headed straight to the "level two" and "intermediate" offerings. How hard could they be, right?

I dragged myself into the car and headed to the studio. Once there and in the door, I noticed that people were all filing into the studio around me carrying their own mats. I did not have a mat. I saw this immediately as a great reason to go home, right? The instructor saw me and offered me hers. She helped me get signed in and placed my mat on the floor.

She gave a brief introduction with a philosophical flare about the ending really being the beginning and a connection of all things to all things. She then instructed us to lie down on our mats and close our eyes. I felt a wave of connectivity and relaxation roll over and through me and I fell instantly and deeply asleep. I awoke to a rhythmic collection of thuds and looked around to some gentle smiles. Everyone was flowing one posture to the next on their mats in a fluid precise dance of arms, legs, and breath. I scrambled to my feet and attempted to follow along.

Easy, it was not. The postures were complex and the postures linking one to the next were very difficult to coordinate to the breath. I was exhausted as we lay down again for the final resting pose, although I made a deal with myself to stay awake this time. This rest was inspiring; I felt the moving of my cells inside in concert, doing their jobs with vibrancy and grace. I had not felt vibrant and graceful in months and months. Emerging from the rest posture many moments later, I acknowledged that I felt refreshed. I walked from the studio straight on a search to buy my own yoga mat.

Every day I went to yoga and people began to smile at me. I began to smile back. No one smiled past my eyes with pity. Here I was regarded as well rather than sick. Here I was becoming more and more well. Sickness was becoming a memory.

I enjoyed seeing my new doctor for tests and follow ups and discussions. I enjoyed telling her about my volunteer work walking the horses while the children with autism rode and thrived. I enjoyed telling her about my first yoga class when I arrived to a level two class prepared to be bored out of my skull and was instead challenged beyond belief! I realized that her prescription was beginning to work; I was beginning to "enjoy" again.

Her smile at the end of my tales gently turned into the most compassionate pause in time. I knew something was about to be said that was not what I wanted to hear. However, I felt strangely prepared. I felt strangely centered. I felt my soul reach forward and hold my hand.

"It appears as though the Cancer is fairly determined. Let's talk." She did not drop her eyes from mine. I nodded and held her gaze.

"Yes, let's talk."

We talked for a long time about the effects of the surgery and what our limited options were for removing the uterus given the nature of the Cancer's return. We spoke at length about the options of this drug over that drug and what radiation might feel like. At the close of the meeting, we had woven a plan. From the back of my day planner, I drew the card of the surgeon she had handed me, "just in case." This man was now the one who would hold the delicacy of our newly woven plan. I felt ready to trust.

I sat before his desk the following afternoon. Nice desk. I made a mental note to myself to not throw up on it. I saw many smiling faces of women and children shining back at me from the numerous pictures he had adorning the walls of his office. Interesting, I thought to myself, this is where I remember degrees and accolades had been posted for other doctors; he was clearly inspiring a different type of confidence.

He stepped into the office and I melted my gaze from the photos slightly embarrassed as if I may have been invading his doctoral privacy. He just smiled at me in the same steadiness that the women and children in the photos smiled at us both. I felt held in a collective smile.

He was young. He was very young. He wore a CU sweatshirt and scrubs and carried an enormous latte. He did not sit behind the desk across from me, but rather sat on the edge of the desk immediately in front of me.

We talked easily about many things: school, my hopes, my dreams, and finally my fears.

"What are you *really* afraid of?" He asked me this in response to the laundry list of fears I had just shared with him.

From concealment into full revelation, the answer came forward from my lips, "I do not know, maybe everything."

"Do you think that is why you have been so determined to keep your uterus? With the uterus gone, you are more likely to live a long, healthy life not knowing."

I answered back, "Well, what about love? What about loving and letting others love me and not knowing if I will live or die?"

He looked through my eyes and spoke, "What about love? Love as hard as you can."

From this, we talked about kids and possible adoption and my volunteer work at the riding center. He was right, if I really loved children and it really was my calling, I would find a way. A uterus, does not a mother make. We talked about yoga and this growing connection I was feeling between my heart, my mind, and my body.

As we talked, I began to merge my past forward into my future. I felt suspended on the fabric of NOW and I began to want to live in a space of not knowing. I began to feel the nameless fear fall silent into the pencil thin shadows cast by the light of this revelation. I began to breathe a deeper breath.

I left his office with a surgery scheduled as an appointment I would keep. I sat in the car in his parking lot and thought and thought. I think I sat for hours. I thought about the person I was before the diagnosis, the person I became through the process of fighting the disease, and the person I could choose to become once I became committed to participating in my own survival. The bitterness melted, as the heat of the sunshine warmed the car and my awareness warmed my heart.

I drove to my yoga class and began to move. I creatively moved between one pose and the next as the breath led the way. A sense of calm rolled through me as the next breath came and the next and the next.

I felt "lucky."

I have been Cancer free now for years and years. I left the pre-med track and began wholeheartedly to study yoga, comparative religions and their art and I find myself studying still. I delved from yoga teacher training to yoga teacher training and I continue to practice, study, and teach every day. I feel blessed to have met some of the most amazing life explorers on a completely different path than I ever thought I would walk.

I felt the strength to say goodbye to one marriage and hello to another. The man I drew into my heart of not knowing is a man whom I love everyday as hard as I can. I have no idea what tomorrow will hold, but today is pretty incredible.

A couple of years ago, my sweet husband and I sat together, hand in hand, on our yoga studio floor before our philosophy teacher, and the topic of miracles arose. My ears perked up at the sheer mention of miracles and the questioning of miracles. What did happen to me in the square of Saint Peter? My mother found her faith strongly that day. She was as certain as the day is long that there was an unseen force that knew to plop a nun, or an angel, right next to me to catch me as I fell and remind me of my intrinsic goodness. She believed in a miracle that resulted in the word, "remission," upon my return to the United States.

I wondered. No one was ever able to tell me what plunged me into remission when the doctor was so convinced he could hear my death rattle before I decorated his desk with my breakfast. Was it luck that I am still alive? Was I really just lucky? Similarly, after meeting the most compassionate doctor that set me on the path to self-love and wellness, no one could ever tell me why I started to come out of remission. Was it luck? Was I really just lucky?

I wondered. If the nun was luck, or rather a miracle, do miracles have time limits? And if so, when will mine expire? Did I do something to unseat luck or piss it off to initially get Cancer? What would happen if there were no certainties in the world at all and every time you lit a match, it was not fire you got, but a random miracle: sometimes fire, sometimes rain, sometimes bananas, sometimes monkeys, and sometimes glue. I bet we would eventually stop lighting matches.

I wondered. Perhaps there is no plan, no design, just luck. However, the wondering in me no longer raised fear, but rather an ever more interesting level of faith. I did not know. I found that I was strangely comforted by not knowing, but instead believing in the good and feeling a warming to effort in the direction of the good.

Shook from my mental wanderings, our professor began to speak, and to discuss "miracles." He began a story:

"There was a television interview with a Belgian bike racer in the Tour de France. The racer was not favored to place or to win. He had some horrid days of hanging on and flattening a tire here and there and then out of the blue he had a day of exceptional performance. He won the stage and amazed the on-lookers. Everything seemed to go his way. The very next day he flattened and lost time, in fact, he lost a lot of time; however, he did not give up and came across the finish line dead last. The reporter questioned him on his inconsistency. He asked if it was a miracle the day prior. The racer looked at him and shook his head.

'No, sometimes you just have *the lucky* and sometimes you don't. You still have to pedal. Yesterday, I had *the lucky*. Tomorrow, I hope I have *the lucky*.'"

That I ever got Cancer in the first place was certainly not good luck. I could not praise it; what an awful and terrible disease. However, it radically changed the direction of my life. Cancer made me want to quit and lie down and melt into the memory of my dreams. It shook me off my plan and opened me to the possibilities of more than one plan. It opened me to the creative evolution of the revolution of all the time I might have on this planet.

In that moment, on that studio floor, an epiphany was born to me that drew my life deeper into itself: today, I have *the lucky.* Life is a creative and organic dance of *the lucky.* I am so blessed. I have one more day. I have the ability to love as hard as I can and direct my life in the direction of my dreams, as long as I do not give up. I have no idea what may happen to me and those I love as time flows through itself; however, I am not afraid. It was not a child that I needed to bear, it was not a doctor that I needed to become, it was a life purpose that was fighting its way from the source of me to the surface. A love of life bubbled from inside of me into experience and into existence. Life, through me, wanted to prove how strongly it desires to live. I am grateful. I am engaged in the daily experience even more so than before. Perhaps through the lives I now touch, I can inspire this insight. Today, now, I have *the lucky.*

BIOGRAPHY

SHANNON PAIGE SCHNEIDER

Shan, as she is known to her students and friends, is the founder and muse of "om time yoga centers" located in Denver and Boulder, Colorado. She is an activist, an author, an eternal optimist, and a lover of the flow of grace within everyone. She is truly here to be part of the collective flow that is "changing the world one downward dog at a time."

Shannon was selected as a charter member of Zobha's Circle of Grace, an inspiring collective of women who support fundraising and programming that uplifts the active practice of LIFE. She has been featured in *Alternative Health Magazine* and *Yoga International.* She presents for Yoga Journal Conferences and leads weekly classes in Boulder and Denver, as well as workshops, intensives, teacher trainings and transformational retreats nationally and internationally. Shannon writes for the *Denver Magazine* and om time's online inspirational e-letter.

Crediting the power of yoga to her survival of Cancer, Shannon founded the vision of om time yoga centers. She has aligned some of the nation's most beloved teachers to develop programs, daily classes, inspiring workshops, and transformational trainings to serve the community. Om time yoga is locally and nationally highly regarded as a place to begin yoga, deepen one's continuing practice, and take one's practice to an advanced level. Recognizing that yoga can be intimidating from the onset, the company boasts an array of non-threatening entry level programs, easy and fun non-yoga programming, and worldly goods boutique where yoga questions can be easily asked by the novice and answered by an "om-y" in a safe and meaningful way.

In addition to directing om time yoga centers in Colorado, Shannon tours teaching yoga and showering inspiration.

To reach those who wish to let the breath lead the way in a manner of strength and verve, Shannon guides powerfully inspirational vinyasa classes taught to radically affirming music and an uplifting message. Students of all levels are empowered to experience prana, their own "life force" as the navigating source of yoga practice and vital living. She is also a dedicated assistant and mentor of Prana Vinyasa Flow, an energetic, creative full-spectrum approach to embodying the flow of yoga for master teacher and founder of Prana Vinyasa Flow, Shiva Rea.

To meet the needs of those who need to lie down and heal rather than flowing through powerful asana, Shannon developed and teaches Anjali Restorative Yoga, a deeply restful and healing yoga practice. The practitioner is guided through meditations and thoughtful visualizations, while the body is held and supported by bolsters, pillows, and blankets. By resting deeply, the body engages its natural ability to heal and reset. The effect is profoundly nurturing, thoughtful, and balancing.

As proof of yoga's healing power, Shannon lives Cancer free. She believes in and practices all that she teaches. Her smile, her laughter, and her enthusiasm for living are happily contagious. Her courage and compassion breathe energy, as well as being an inspiration for potential to all her students.

Visit: www.omtime.com

CHAPTER FOURTEEN

HARLEYS AND OLD LACE
Richard "Ross" Rossiter
with his sister

*T*o *the outside world we all grow old. But not to brothers and sisters. We know each other as we always were. We know each other's hearts. We share private family jokes. We remember family feuds and secrets, family griefs and joys. We live outside the touch of time.* Clara Ortega

Visiting my two crazy brothers (I use that term affectionately, they are not in asylums) is a study in commonality and contrast; that is part of what makes it so much fun. One is this way; the other that way—both do this, neither does that—you know how it goes in families. We compare genetic traits and mannerisms; we see our parents in each other. No matter where we are in life or what we have done, we are linked to our siblings in ways that go unaltered through decades of time.

I made a trip recently—first visiting the older brother, Fred, on the west Florida coast in Cape Coral and then younger brother, nicknamed "Ross," on the east Florida coast in Ft. Lauderdale. It is probably more than just a coincidence that they both prefer to live in gorgeous, sun-drenched, hot flamingo pink and cool turquoise tropical Florida where the fish are plentiful and the weather is usually fine and the day is never too short for some type of outdoor adventure. It was fascinating to see these two exotic specimens up close and personal in their lush native habitats separated only by a brief drive across the state through alligator alley. While visiting these "rare bird" brothers of mine, I was able to hear their characteristic warblings, observe their eating habits and see their intricate nests as they went about their daily routines. They are indeed colorful, rambunctious and hard to tame...*Still Crazy After All These Years* in the immortal words of Paul Simon.

Just like the two coasts of their natural environment, my brothers are alike and they are equally different. They have similar physical features. They are each handsome. Charming. Mischievous. They are cut of the same stone but the sculptures are unique. They have tastes that dovetail but each emphasizes different strengths. They both demonstrate a tremendous lust for life and they appreciate the finer things. You know the old saying—"you can tell the age of the boys by the size of their toys"—well it fits. There are lots of toys between the two of them, sometimes strewn all across Florida. They have wonderful families and long marriages. Beautiful homes. Great hobbies.

Are the two brothers competing? Hell no—they didn't even *know eachother* until they were into their forties and fifties! They are half-brothers...but sometimes I forget who is the half and who is the whole, so that term is meaningless to me. I proudly claim them both as whole.

You see my brother and sister and I had a baby brother, Ross, born in 1958 to our father and his second wife, into a family we saw only on weekends and for just a few brief years. When our father's second marriage ended, we kids, including his new wife's two children by her previous marriage and the new baby boy (of course our half-brother), Ross, they had together, were all launched quickly and without much discussion to the far frontiers of the rest of our lives. In a generation when children were to be seen and not heard; nothing much was said to us and we were expected to accept these changes without question. The ties of that second marriage (loose ties to begin with) had unraveled so completely and so quickly that we kids were suddenly on the fringes of a former family for the second time in our lives. This happened just a few short years after the ending of the long marriage of dad and our mom. Talk about confusion—it was the kind of memory you might be successful in pushing aside during the day but that keeps you awake at night.

I do remember, however, that at the age of about eighteen months, baby Ross's right eye was put out and he was permanently blinded on that side through the intentional, probably jealous "popgun" shot by his older half-brother from his mother's first marriage. At age seventeen or so I was devastated by that news, for Ross of course, and it made me forever protective of my eyes since my interests all revolved around the visual arts.

Ross says: *"Christmas morning, 1959. I was eighteen months old. But still, as young as I was, there are parts of it that I remember very well. I don't remember any pain, but I do remember running down the hall screaming. This was caused by a toy pistol that was sold as a "cap gun" that my brother got for Christmas. You saw them all the time in the catalogs; a miniature gun that said on the packaging "Big Bang, Small Gun! My next memory was sitting on Uncle Doug's lap, then having to stay in a crib at the hospital. I remember that the crib was right next to the window. When I looked through the glass at people walking up and down the halls, the glass had little squares in it—Safety Glass. I saw that glass again in the doors in elementary school and it brought back bad memories. They removed my eye because that's what they did back then. I remember the cotton paper eye patch that would tickle my nose and around my eye. And the feeling when they pulled off the tape that kept the patch in place. Things like that you never forget. They were afraid that infection would set in. So they removed it. They never found the piece that entered my eye. I have a huge problem with needles because of this whole thing. My mom took me to be fitted with an artificial eye. My first one was brown—I have blue eyes…This was really traumatic for me, because I would have to go to downtown Dayton to the eye doctor. Scary for a little guy like me. The doctor would pry the eye out with a wooden Q-tip which hurt like hell and made me cry. My uncle Harold would tell the doctor that if he made me cry again he would punch him in the nose. I didn't want the doctor to get punched…Much later my mom sued Rikes Department Store for selling what was known as an "un-blocked barrel" for a toy gun. Blocking the barrel would have prevented any projectile. We went to New York to meet the lawyers. They asked me questions, like how all the furniture had been positioned in the room, where I was standing at the time, etc. They had the cap gun there and showed mom how it shot half-way through a phone book! When it was all said and done, and I turned eighteen, I was awarded about thirty-eight thousand dollars. This was not good for a poor kid turning eighteen, living on Hilton Head Island. Mom said, "You have suffered all your life with one eye, so you can go buy yourself a car." I bought a used Corvette. And I bought her a used Jaguar. On Hilton Head Island, in 1974, she was looking for investments for me before I blew all this money. We went over to Defuskie Island. A book was written about Defuskie called The River is Wide. A movie was produced called "Conrad" about a bunch of superstitious black people that were still into voodoo and whichcraft there. They were settlers from Africa who could not swim and Conrad introduced them to the 20th Century. Anyway, we took a boat over to this island to see what property was available. It was all under-developed pine woods. Later I found out that I* *could have bought half of that island for $30,000 dollars. And now it's one of the most exclusive golf courses in South Carolina. Having nothing to show for my little nest egg, this was very depressing."*

Shortly after that horrific "accident" the three of us lost touch with Ross completely. Until, that is, about 1997 or 1998, when my curiosity got the best of me, and I decided to track down our no-longer a baby, baby brother. When Ross was born I was just entering the best time of high school—learning to drive and having boyfriends—so of course I had other things on my mind. I remembered him only as an adorable baby boy—but I had no idea what kind of person he had grown up to be. I just knew that I missed him as if he were an appendage of me and that I could not let my life go by without trying to contact him.

It took me just three phone calls. Nearly forty years later, it took just three uncomplicated calls. I was astonished when I had his phone number in less than a half-hour of research at my desk on one normal afternoon. I discovered where he lived, amazingly, and I was about to make the fourth call to the actual home of our long-lost brother when I decided to give that number and that first call to my brother Fred as a gift. A gift of having the brother he had always wanted. So I let him do the honors.

My sister and I each received a dozen roses from Ross, within days of that series of calls, thanking us and saying it was to celebrate all the birthdays he had missed. Now there was a big clue about what a fine person he was, in case we had any doubts. It was a unique and powerful experience to find our brother after so much time had passed. I was ashamed I had never made the effort in all of those years. When people say that life is short, believe them.

We all spoke with Ross and he told us that he had always wanted to find us and know us as his family. We loved him immediately. He visited brother Fred and I in Denver; he flew out west from Florida, and he brought meat—yes, meat. He was, at that point in time, in the business of importing exotic meats from around the world for restaurants. He had meat packed with dry ice when we met him at the airport. Every kind of expensive meat. He cooked for us—we learned that he had attended the Navy affiliated (at that time) Johnson & Whales School of Culinary Arts in Charleston, South Carolina and he was a trained chef! How perfect for a family who lives to eat, always inquiring what and when the next meal will be. We all made a trip to the market for vegetables and side dishes that afternoon, and we had a feast. He certainly knew his way around the kitchen. It was an amazing reunion. The wine and the stories flowed and he was a fascinating addition to the western branch of the family tree. He was truly one of us.

The other reason he flew west was that coincidentally, I was making plans for a move from Denver to Scottsdale where my sister Vicki lives— I was to stay with Vicki and her husband Tom until I got settled. Ross offered without hesitation, on the phone from Florida, never having seen me since we were all kids and he was a baby—*to drive my rented truck full of my furniture and prized possessions to Scottsdale for me* as I followed along in my car. A ROAD TRIP was to be the perfect chance to get to know eachother. Vicki would be waiting at the Scottsdale end of the trip to see him for the first time after nearly a lifetime of not knowing him. Then, more cooking—more celebration! I thought that was the most wonderful offer and I was overwhelmed with the generosity of my newly discovered brother.

The morning after the big meat feast Ross and I set out well before sunrise and we drove like bats out of hell, I am ashamed to say—we knew we could make it to Scottsdale in about fourteen hours in a car; driving straight south from Denver on I-25 and hanging a right in Albuquerque was simple enough. I had done it more than a dozen times. But with the big truck and a driver who had never been west or driven through such stunning scenery before, who knew how long it would take? Well I think we made it in fourteen and a half hours, no problem. It was a happy, exciting, white-knuckle trip for me, watching Ross on the road ahead of me, barreling along and sometimes making impulsive, crazy, last-second right turns into dusty parking areas of Indian souvenir stands to look at the silver jewelry and rubber rattlesnakes as possible take-home gifts for Pam and the kids. He had quite an introduction to the west—sagebrush flats and distant mesas flying by in a blur as he kept the truck on the road. I kept telling myself, as I watched all this from behind him in my little red car, that he was so much like me and that we had a lot in common—impulsiveness and enthusiasm for life certainly being two.

When we finally arrived, sweaty, sticky faces powdered with the red dirt of the desert, and we were standing safely in Vicki's kitchen I said to him, "My God you are a fast driver—I can't believe we're here already—*how do you do that with only one eye?*"

He said, "Yeah I only have one eye but that one eye is a real MUTHAH!"

Thus my adventure of knowing Ross again began.

Ross is a highly creative person. He is most creative simply in the way he has chosen to live his life—a sort of "free-form, grab for the gusto and have a lot of fun" type of pattern has been his life history so far. Creativity, generally speaking and by actual definition, includes being a bit of a risk taker. Impulsive. Unpredictable in a good way. Accepting the challenge of the moment. Living in the NOW. In a family of risk-taking characters, some of whom have become legends in their own time and in their own minds as well, Ross holds his own quite well. He is in his own class, actually, raising the bar to new heights. He is now a devoted and responsible family man, with three carefully parented, outstanding children and a wonderful wife of warmth and beauty of whom he speaks lovingly. But he came to that family-oriented chapter of his life after he had most definitely gotten his "wiggles" out, as I like to say.

Before the current chapter of his life began, about 1986-88, Ross traveled to South America—Argentina, his favorite location—for the love of a hot-tempered "Selma Hayek type" Latin woman, of course. After a time there, he talked himself out of marrying her and he came home. But he got to South America in the first place by selling his cherished collection of expensive, fine wine in order to finance the trip...

Ross says: *"I actually met 'Sandra from Argentina', in Charleston, South Carolina; she was visiting her brother who was going to a Catholic school in Charleston. We hit it off right away, except for the language barrier—the English. We really struggled with her English. I guess that was part of the romance. I showed her around Charleston and the beach. She was sweet and weighed about ninety-five pounds but she had a body that would stop traffic—I saw it happen. She stayed a total of a couple of weeks, I guess. Her voice when she spoke Spanish was amazing. She sounded more Italian then South American. So here was this drop-dead gorgeous girl that showed a huge interest in me, to put it delicately, and I felt the same about her. Everything to her was new and beautiful, including me I guess. She said that often; that I was a beautiful man. This was a FIRST for me, having a woman in such heavy pursuit of me. She went home to South America and we wrote back and forth. She wanted me to move to Argentina to be with her. I thought about that over the summer, while the letters kept coming and coming. Every single one expressed how she loved me and missed me and wanted to spend the rest of her life with me in Argentina. Well I had enough of Charleston and was looking for a change anyway. I had had my heart broken more than once by Daphne, a girl that after ten years of dating left me for an older guy with lots of money, and then Beth. Beth had been my bartender at Silks Restaurant when I was the manager. She ran off for New York to continue her art career. So I was alone and lonely in Charleston and getting restless.*

By the end of the summer I decided to sell all the wine in my prized collection and move to Buenos Aries, Argentina. I had acquired over one thousand bottles of fine wine from Silks Restaurant when they sold to the new owner. We had the finest collection of California reds and whites in Charleston—maybe in all of South Carolina at that point in time. Ranging from fifteen dollars to over four hundred dollars for some of our Cabs and averaging three hundred dollars for our champagne was not uncommon. Once a year Robert Mondavi himself would come and introduce his newest annual reserve at a dinner that Silks hosted for the Charleston Wine Society.

OK, funny but not funny. Nobody was going to pay anything close to what these bottles were worth. Two-hundred-dollar bottles of Cabernet could only bring thirty to forty dollars a bottle. But in the end, I still made enough money for a plane ticket and a little extra. So after calling Mom one last time from Miami, still not believing that I was going sort of against my better judgment; hating this whole idea and yet loving the girl, I left. Mom had watched a show on TV about all the kidnapping that was going on by the local policia in Buenos Aries. They were stealing children in the middle of the night for child labor or prostitution. This was also around the time of the Falkland Islands War against the Britt's and Argentina. But this still didn't stop me, and on November 19th, 1986, I started my trip. When I landed in Miami from Charleston, I thought I was pretty cool having to show my first Passport. Kind of shocked that the agent wasn't as excited as I was, I handed my Passport to the agent and then she weighed my luggage bag.

'Your bag is overweight; you owe one hundred and ten dollars.'

Now, I had over three-thousand dollars in tens and twenties rapped with a rubber band hanging below my balls inside my underwear. My Mom had gotten me so worked up about how dangerous Argentina was that this was the only place on me that I thought was safe. Seeing how she was a lady agent and there were a dozen people behind me, this was a problem. I didn't want to go into my pants right there at the counter. I asked her to hold that thought and told her I would be right back. Off to the bathroom...I quickly stripped down and got my wad of money. This was fine because I was starting to get chaffed with a couple of paper cuts on my sack.

I had no idea how long the entire flight was, but the first flight to Caracas,Venezuela was short. I walked through the airport to my next flight to Brazil. It was the first time I had ever seen the military in a public airport with real machine guns. That should have been my first tip-off that I was really out of my element. Then from Caracas to Brazil was a really long flight. We were served several breakfasts and lunches during the flight; I sat next to a little old lady that spoke no English at all. But I made friends with her by handing her my flatware after each meal. (I realized after breakfast that she was wiping off her fork, spoon and knife with a napkin and sneaking them into her purse.) We had a total of three meals during that flight, times two, so it was a pretty good haul for her. I also noticed that every time we landed anywhere people would applaud and whistle like we had just done something really special. Finally we landed in Argentina and you'd have thought a miracle had just happened with all the celebration on that plane, but then by the time we had flown over the mountains in terrible turbulence, I was cheering and applauding too. The flight was scary as hell and I still had hours to go before we landed in Buenos Aries.

We finally landed in B.A. and I walked through the airport and there she was. Sandra along with her whole family. We greeted eachother and all five of us headed for the car which was the smallest car I had ever seen. We were shoulder to shoulder in the back and in B.A. you really didn't get your own lane to drive in all by yourself. At that time, we shared the equivalent of a normal sized U.S. highway lane with three other cars darting in and out, sharing just this one lane. I was always proud of my driving, and although I always drove fast, I was never out of control and nothing much ever really bothered me. But on the way back from the airport I screamed with silent terror under my breath.

Also, in B.A. they have a different kind of stoplight. The light will be red, then yellow (you start going forward) then green. Exactly backwards from the U.S. It's OK to start moving through the intersection on yellow from a stop, and by green you are half-way through the intersection. Here's the problem—from the opposite direction or from a ninety degree angle the light goes from green to yellow to red. So everyone meets in the middle on yellow! Whoever is deepest into the middle of the intersection gets the right of way. This will cause to you to piss your pants the first time you experience it. And of course my wad of money was stored in my pants…"

Even before that, Ross and his mom had been the founder of the first bakery on Hilton Head Island, called The Gingerbread House. He made what seemed like a million croissants, muffins and such before the sun came up…improvising every delicacy that he did not have an exact recipe for and making a great success of it all.

Ross says: *"We started the Gingerbread House, the first bakery on Hilton Head Island. Mom and I moved there in 1974 and we started the bakery around 1978. We were a scratch bakery, which means everything was made from scratch; all bread doughs, all sweet doughs and all cookie doughs and donut doughs. We were open twenty-four freakin' hours a day and there were just two bakers—my brother-in-law and me. Famous people would show up at 3:00 in the morning, staggering and drunk, after all the bars where closed. Funny seeing famous, really famous people drunk or hung over trying to order pastries."*

I see mannerisms in him that are my Dad—that are my other brother—that are my sister and me. He looks like Dad from the cheekbones up but did not get Dad's large nose—he has a mouth like mine only wider and what comes out of it is way funnier, and even saltier. He can tell a great story—he can have you rolling in the aisles. He knows the dead-pan look to give as you are laughing yourself silly. He is *of us* and he is *with us* and he is *in us*—we are family. The DNA cannot be denied. He is an entertainer through and through—as we all are in the Rossiter family. We are frustrated, stand-up comedians with only eachother in the audience. There are enough stories inside the family to last us as long as we are able to tell them. Telling a great story is an art—there is a skill to it—and Ross is just the best. He is highly creative in that regard as well.

***

I was looking forward to visiting him and his family on this recent trip. He and other brother Fred are not the only "rare birds" it turns out. While visiting Ross's family these days you can't help but notice that they have a feather-less bird of some exotic variety that was so very nervous during a Florida hurricane a few years ago that he picked out all of his beautifully colored feathers during the scary time when the house was boarded up. He was terrified of the wind and the vibrations and the dark. He plucked out all of his feathers, one by one, during that traumatic time and has never permitted them to grow back. He has been on anti-depressant bird medication since then but he is still not happy enough to let his feathers grow back. All day he searches and inspects and keeps checking, checking, checking to make sure there is no sign of a feather growing back. And he looks like a rubber chicken sitting on his perch, with the goose-bumps sticking out in high resolution where the feathers were and blue veins showing through his transparent grayish skin. He yells "HEY ROSS" all the time. Lucy the dog runs into the family room at the first hint of music from a dog food commercial so she can see the dogs on TV—barking and jumping up and down in a straight vertical motion with wild enthusiasm.

Near the family room is a home theater addition that Ross finished where the family watches films together. This is a joyful house—the kids are active in many directions, the pets are all characters, the rooms are painted brave colors of Big Bird yellow, sunset orange, ocean teal and rusty red and the mood is like confetti—happily chaotic. Creativity oozes out of the woodwork.

On a coffee table in the living room is a magnificent alabaster sculpture of a sea turtle on a pedestal—done by Ross after seeing some of our Dad's sculptures and convincing himself—*actually just knowing*—that he also had that art gene and that he could sculpt. It is beautifully proportioned. It is a potential "A" in some college sculpture class, but instead it was done on a whim just a couple years ago at home.

In the garage are *three* Harleys; what Ross would describe as assurances of his manhood, awarded by himself to himself in fleeting moments of male insecurity. Because he is a great appreciator of fine china and four-hundred thread count Egyptian cotton sheets, linen and lace, he needs to feed his soul great gulps of testosterone once in awhile to compensate. Like after he has made a "girly" purchase such as the colorful dishes he bought in Hawaii; the ones with the hot coral hibiscus flowers and the hula girls that seemed so perfect at the time, for BBQ's at home in Florida. Oh and that brings us to the outdoor kitchen—the vast expanse of living space that must have doubled the size of the house, for the purpose of outdoor entertaining and cooking. Martha Stewart should visit—she should do a show from Ross's outdoor kitchen! I can just see her there with Ross, seasoning some New Zealand lamb chops and tossing them on the grill. I think to myself how wonderful it is to live in an era when men are pleased to choose china and linens and show off their cooking skills and throw the most notorious neighborhood gatherings. Our father's party genes live on.

If you are thinking that the toys are the "thing" right about now in the story, you have flat missed the point. There is more to the story than the toys. Ross is the kind of warm-hearted guy who will do anything for you—the kind of guy who says, "Love you; mean it," every time he talks to you or emails. The kind of guy who truly loves the company of women, children, dogs, naked birds and aims to please everyone. The kind of guy who listens when you talk; who chooses to take you on a walk in the woods for quiet conversation before a spectacular, sparkling afternoon cruise on the inner coastal waterways. The kind of guy who *knows about food* and will order from the menu for you at the fancy restaurant by the coastal waterway, selecting not one, but two entrees since you can't make up your mind. Then adding three appetizers and many mojitos. This is a sincere and loving kind of guy; who is funny as hell. He laughs a lot. He "gets" life—he knows it is not permanent and we are here to make each other happy. He spreads fun.

His epiphany came a couple years ago when he read my first book—*Epiphany and Her Friends, Intuitive Realizations That Have Changed Women's Lives*. In Chapter Eighteen, I wrote about my life's unfolding—my family DNA—my artistic, interior design and literary genes that were so strongly beeping and flashing at me from such an early age that I could not deny their presence. I talked about my love of our family furniture store, where the fabrics and the art and the accessories and the furniture awakened a passion in me that has never waned, only strengthened through the years. When my sister Vicki and I first learned that our great-grandfather had sold fine linens and lace in England, we both said in unison, "Well that certainly explains a lot!" *We knew who we were.* We had the history of us at every turn of the head. We were Rossiters through and through.

Ross never had access to any of us during that period of time—he had no frame of reference, growing up. My other brother Fred and my sister and I had each other of course—Ross had only his Dad as an example of the family characteristics, and seldom did he see his Dad.

Ross says that when he read my chapter he had an epiphany. It explained to him for the very first time who he really was and how he had become the man he is. He understood for the first time where his creativity originated, how his love of the finer things in life had been born, and he understood that it was as natural to the definition of him as were his loves of Harleys and guns and boats and all the toys he accumulated as extra proof of his masculinity. He felt instantly whole in the knowing of that. He called me on the phone after reading my chapter, which is actually his chapter too, and greeted me with, "Jo, this is freakin'AWESOME! I understand myself now!" The light bulb in his head was turned on and brought understanding. It was one of those instantaneous epiphanies that delivers complete, instant gratification, satisfaction and huge discovery! The kind of epiphany that clears all the fog, opens the windows of your mind and offers you illumination and a fresh perspective you never had before; and then makes you happy as a bonus.

The information Ross had needed to better understand his creative side had never been provided to him. There was a void where his siblings should have been. He thanked me for revealing the missing parts of his life to him. He thanked me for showing him who he really is. He appreciates furniture, home accessories, cooking equipment, dishes, linens, and an artistic, eclectic home, along with the Harleys, boats, cars, trucks, and women. He was astonished to find that he is a typical Rossiter family male in all the best creative ways. He is a Renaissance man in the true sense of the word and you can't fake that—it is either in your genes or it is not. Ross is the real deal. His creativity is genuine and he comes by it naturally—instead of questioning its complexities he just needed to understand the origin. He needed a *context* in which to place himself. After he understood his roots, he simply eased back into his lovely life and enjoyed the ride, being comfortable at last in who he really is. He found his soul's home sweet home.

Ross says, "One of my biggest gifts that I can give to my boys and my daughter, is to be sensitive to others. Listen to what people say when they are talking to you. Watch the cursing, and get a grip on your egos. And they do just that. I always thought the perfect TV father was Andy Griffith. The way he could talk to Opie without raising his voice was amazing. No four-letter words, no screaming, just, "I am disappointed in you Opie," was all that it took. That is the kind of relationship that I wanted with my kids. And so that's the way I try to speak to my kids. Always finish on a good note. But here's the thing; they are great kids with good morals and plenty of love to give. They all make A's and B's and keep on the honor roll. This is all Pam's doing. They all excel in sports. But what I am most proud of is how they love and interact with people; grandparents and their cousins and everyone. When we all get together it is card games all weekend long. My mother-in-law taught all my kids to play poker and every other card game, from "Screw Your Neighbor" to "Cards and Marbles." Now for me growing up as a kid, and being hauled up to my grandmother's house for the weekend in Kettering, Ohio was not fun. I missed playing with my friends and riding my bike, and catching frogs and snakes down by the creek. I was not into seeing and hanging out with adults. But my kids love it, and even look forward to it. Listen, I am used to getting things—cars and motorcycles—with instruction manuals on how to get the best performance out of your new purchase. But with kids, there are no manuals or instructions for maintenance; you just fill their little tanks every morning with love and support and hope they make it through the day.

And I know for a fact that I have the best wife you could ask for, and the second I forget, I am reminded by either my neighbors or my family. On any given day Pam can be a Biker's Wife and understand when I want to head off for the evening. Or a Baseball Mom who has vowed to herself to never miss a game. Or a Party Mom who loves to entertain family and friends. Or the best lover a man could want. This is Pam, my true love…. And my family is everything to me— for any one of them I would give my last eye to keep them out of harm's way."

These days, as always, we find Ross attending to his family—watching Susie ride her horse and the boys play ball—and helping Pam at the bookstore when he is not busy with his position with Strauss Veal and Lamb International. That company is initiating a new **GREEN** approach to raising veal that will change the industry much for the betterment of the animal's quality of life and the people who consume the meat.

And he is thinking about getting a boat…

Life is good.

BIOGRAPHY

RICHARD "ROSS" ROSSITER

Ross was born in Southern Ohio, later moving to South Carolina to what was to become the future Hilton Head Island resort area, before it was completely developed. There he opened The Gingerbread House Bakery with his mother and made it a success. While in S. Carolina he attended the Navy affiliated (at that time) Johnson & Whales School of Culinary Arts in Charleston, South Carolina and trained as a chef.

Ross has been in the exotic meats import business for many years. He is currently with Strauss Veal and Lamb International and travels the entire Eastern portion of the United States as a sales rep and an expert chef in the preparation of lamb and veal. You might cross his path at Madison Square Garden at a food show or at any number of other food events where cooking is being done.

Ross and his family currently live in the Ft. Lauderdale area of Florida, in a lovely area where tall oaks and gorgeous green stretches of protected land are enjoyed. He is married to Pam, who owns a local bookstore, and they have three beloved and accomplished children, Tyler, Corey and Susie, in addition to assorted pets.

CHAPTER FIFTEEN

AWAKENING
Ria Moran

A s I sit down to write this piece, I take a breath, close my eyes, and shift my attention to a quiet, receptive space in the back of my head. Within moments, a flow of words sends my fingers scurrying over the keyboard. It's an odd feeling, as if someone else is putting the words together and I'm taking dictation. I don't often talk about this aspect of my creative process, because I don't know how to explain it. Words aren't the only messages I receive from this indefinable source. I'm also a painter, a graphic designer, and a jeweler, and whenever I want to design something, I tune in and watch a slide show.

I haven't always been so comfortable inside my head. For the first few decades of my life I was gloomy and depressed, and television was my drug of choice. When I was a kid, I ate my meals in front of the TV, did my homework in front of the TV, and on weekends, I would stay glued to the couch all night long watching a lineup of movies on the Late Show, the Late Late Show Number One, and the Late Late Show Number Two. The intro for the movies started with a black and white graphic of the New York City skyline all lit up; as it got later and later, more and more lights would turn off, and by the end of the Late Late Show Number Two, only one lonely light shone in Manhattan. That solitary light comforted me. It made me feel that a kindred spirit was out there, a soul as alone and as lost as I was who felt most comfortable when everybody else was asleep.

I have never fit in. For as long as I can remember, I felt separate, and different. As a little girl, I would look up at the stars with inexplicable longing and wonder which one I came from. Since my earliest memories, I have been haunted by what poet John O'Donohue calls the "longing to belong," a vague, intense yearning in the heart. When the Beatles hit, my longing found a target, and I was one of those prepubescent girls who were thrown into fits of agonized ecstasy. Then I grew up, and transferred my longing to men. But I found that no matter how much I loved a man, my longing was never quenched, and somewhere along my journey I discovered that making things took the edge off my disquietude. My sister gave me a frame loom when I was twenty, and I started to weave. I sold handwoven scarves and purses at street fairs. If I wasn't weaving, I was making god's eyes with twigs and yarn or knotting cord into macramé wall hangings. My hands were always busy.

But that feeling, that longing, wasn't satisfied; I felt pushed by a visceral force to dig deeper, to search further. I was already a "Make Love, Not War," idealist, a war-protesting, headband-wearing, anti-establishment hippie in patch-worked, bell-bottomed jeans. But my political activism didn't do the trick either. I kept searching, but nothing was ever exactly right, nothing was ever enough. Then I found a guru, and it was like throwing a steak to a hungry lion. For the first time, I knew I was on the right track. After devouring its meal, my longing curled up and purred.

For about two years, I was part of a spiritual community in Denver, Colorado. It was a period of free love, open trust, sisterhood and brotherhood. A few thousand of us traveled around the world in blissed-out love caravans, meditating under our blankets and following our guru from city to city for programs and festivals. But after about two years, the magic glow wore off and the lion woke up and roared, "Enough of this baloney! Find me another steak!"

I left my guru, and another teacher appeared. She was a voluptuous ex-Avon lady with curly blonde hair, long, painted fingernails and piercing, ebony eyes. Smart, funny, charismatic and shockingly psychic, she taught raja yoga classes with the intensity of a no-nonsense schoolmarm. When I wasn't diligently studying Vedic scriptures, I was making art and selling it through galleries. I moved to the New Age capital of Boulder, Colorado and married a kindred ex-guru follower. The lion was getting regular meals. But was it content? No way. It looked me straight in the eye and growled. That old, familiar feeling was still there, that drive to find something, to do something that would scratch my persistent itch. And deep down, I had problems. I wasn't satisfied with myself or with my life. I had married a guy with visionary ideas and a fiery kundalini, an Irish charmer who loved to drink and party. He liked people, craved attention, and put on a great show, and for a long time, I was content to hide in the background while he cajoled, juggled, and performed on the stage of life. But when he started to spin wildly out of control, I looked the other way. I felt numbed-out and powerless, and I was trying to ignore my inner demons: my fragile health, my chronic depression, my unresolved grief over my brother's tragic death, my childhood with alcoholic parents, my co-dependence with my alcoholic husband, my fear that I couldn't take care of myself if I were alone, and my feelings of alienation. In reality, I was frozen like a deer in the headlights, too frightened to say or do anything as my life began to crumble around me.

When my marriage finally exploded, my world was hit by a hurricane. I lost my home, my money, and my car. I was emotionally blown out, and my entire being felt like a raw, exposed nerve. There was nowhere for me to hide, and no way to pretend I was okay. Some kind friends offered me a place to stay while I attempted to put my life back together. I cooked them lots of soups—split pea soup, lentil soup, minestrone soup—and fought to control my tears as I chopped veggies and tossed them into a steaming pot. Penniless, I found some odd jobs to supplement my sporadic, meager income from the art galleries. My solace was that only a few months before, I had rented a dream art studio in the heart of downtown Boulder, a roomy loft with twelve-foot ceilings and a huge skylight. The place was utterly charming. After climbing a tall flight of rickety stairs and stepping into a long, poorly lit hallway, I'd hear haunting strains of violin as Dave the violin maker tested out his newest creation. Then a flock of giggling girls in tutus would spill out of the ballet studio after their lesson and race each other to the dressing room at the end of the hall. As I waded through the ballerinas, I'd poke my head into the art studio next to mine and say hi to my best friend, Sherry. But after I stepped inside my own studio and shut the door, I was left alone with my inner demons.

One day I looked around at my work, slouched into a chair, and sighed. The raw emotion that I felt inside didn't match the decorative, pretty, lightweight art that surrounded me. The voice was back, and it said, "Throw all this stuff in the trash. Start over, and go deeper." I held my head in my hands and cried. The artwork I'd been selling was hamburger, and the lion wanted steak.

My friend Sherry was a godsend. We had been through a lot together, we told each other everything, and we supported each other through our mutual dramas. When I told her that I was stuck in a dead place with my artwork, she assured me that my creative flow would return, and that the one thing we can count on in life is change. Sherry was another of my kindred ex-guru followers. Although we had outgrown our guru phase, we still shared a passion for spiritual studies. She joined my raja yoga classes, and every Monday morning we drove to a funky little metaphysical bookstore in a bad neighborhood in Denver to learn about the secrets of the universe. Our teacher, Dee, was a fascinating woman. Intuitive since childhood, her psychic abilities expanded exponentially after a fall down a flight of stairs broke open her kundalini, the storehouse of spiritual energy at the base of the spine. When she came to, the world looked blindingly radiant. Her ajna center, also called the third eye, was wide open, and she couldn't distinguish between the physical world and the spirit world. With everyday tasks like driving and working suddenly impossible, she enlisted the help of a Tibetan Buddhist monk who was able to teach her how to turn her clairvoyant ability on or off at will. Dee used her powerful abilities to help people understand the patterns of their soul; she helped me to see myself more clearly, to believe in myself, and to wake up from my ex-husband's spell.

One of the things she told me was that I was capable of an enormous creative flow. She said that I hadn't found the key to open it yet, but I would. And when I asked the inevitable question, "How do I find the key?" she said that was up to me to figure out.

Well, I certainly hadn't figured it out yet. Although I had always engaged in one creative project or another, my ideas didn't come easily, and my artistic process had always been a struggle. But things were changing. After my marriage blew up, I felt different inside. All my years of numbing out and running away from my feelings were over. Although I felt sad, lonely, grief-stricken, angry, betrayed and devastated, I *felt*. My senses had come alive and I was more permeable to the experience of each moment. On most days that still meant tears and heartache, but I had good moments, too.

One day I went into my studio and puttered around for a while on nothing in particular. A bit tired, I lay on my beat-up couch and closed my eyes for a nap. But instead of falling asleep, I had a waking dream, a visceral experience of a weighty, rock-like form that was shaped like a curved slice. I could feel the heavy, grounded serenity of it in my body, and it reminded me of the sculpted rock outcroppings that were scattered along the Boulder foothills. I opened my eyes and sat up. This felt like a significant event in my life. Along with the awakening of my inner senses, I felt a powerful drive to make this massive thing.

I made the sculpture. In fact, I made a whole family of large, archetypal sculptures that embodied the power of the Great Mother, and one of them was shown at the National Museum for Women in the Arts in Washington D.C. The lion never roared at me again, because I finally found what it was urging me toward. My intense longing had been to find my true home, my inner fountain of soul. All those years that I had searched for the perfect man, the perfect teacher, the perfect place, the perfect work of art, the perfect world, I was searching in the wrong direction. My epiphany was that the treasure I was looking for was inside my own self the whole time. When my marriage failed and the shockwaves of my divorce awakened my numbed senses, I was suddenly able to commune with my inner source for the first time. The castle walls that I had unconsciously built with bricks of denial, illusion and repression had crumbled around me, and in the rubble, I had found the precious jewel of my soul.

Dee was right. Since the day that my portal to soul opened and I saw the image of my first sculpture, I have been blessed with a prolific flow of creativity. When I commune with soul, I experience swells of expanded awareness and deep connectedness to the inbreath and outbreath of creation. Soul is my secret energizer bunny, my wellspring of inspiration, inner knowing, creativity, and life direction. It's the source of my belief in myself because it pierces through my fears, doubts, pride, and perfectionism and shows me clear, humbling truth. Soul connects us into the One Mind. When we open to soul, we become like the Zen archer who places an arrow in its mark from sixty feet away with his eyes closed because he, the arrows, and the target have become one.

When I forget to draw my awareness into my center and commune with soul, I sometimes wrestle with the dark swirls in the cosmic parfait of life. Rebellious against a Divine Power that refuses to edit out the dark side, I jut out my chin and kick rocks like a stubborn twelve-year-old, mad at the whole world because bad things happen. Then I remember something I heard Ram Dass say: "We have to be willing to let our heart be broken every day." That's soul talking, and I let its truth and beauty pierce my anger, which has been trying to protect my broken heart; and when I allow myself to feel my broken heart, my heart breaks open, infusing me with compassionate acceptance for this crazy, wonderful gift of life.

BIOGRAPHY

RIA MORAN

I was born in Long Island, New York, attended college at Boston University, and moved to Boulder, Colorado in 1977. My two passions in life have been visual art and psycho-spiritual studies.

Chosen as a "Significant Colorado Woman Artist" in 1988 for a series of large sculptures that symbolize the Divine Feminine, my artistic career has also encompassed clothing design, painting, wall treatments, and jewelry design.

My recent series of paintings on the Cosmic Egg that reflects the archetypal union of matter and spirit was exhibited at Naropa University, and I am developing a line of silver and gold amulets that symbolize spiritual transformation.

In 1986, I became certified as a Gestalt psychotherapist, and in 1990, I became certified in the Hakomi method of body-centered psychotherapy.

I am currently writing a book on the transformation of suffering into compassion.

CHAPTER SIXTEEN

sym-bol-ism
T. McKinsey Morgan

Webster's defines symbolism as the practice of representing things by symbols or of investing things with symbolic meaning or character. Symbols can also represent or indicate what lies beneath the surface or just beyond our reach. I've come to use symbols in my artwork as a tool to help work through some of life's most difficult journeys.

I was married to a non-verbal alcoholic for twenty-seven years. During the last part of our marriage in particular, we both had difficulty communicating with one another. My oldest daughter once remarked that the silence in the house was deafening. The "elephant in the living room" held a prominent place in our home. We walked around the elephant and never discussed his presence. Just as my mother had denied that my father was an alcoholic, I refused to acknowledge that my husband was also one. Although I didn't know the term at the time, I had become an enabler. As I found his bottles of vodka, I poured them down the drain; I didn't realize my children were doing the same thing. None of us wanted to hurt one another with the ugly truth. Whenever he fell out of his chair at night, one of us woke him up and walked him to his bedroom. During the last few years of our marriage, he had moved downstairs to a guest room to be closer to his office and to his drinking. (My oldest daughter once reminded me that an alcoholic and his alcohol are not far removed from one another.) Most of the time I really didn't care whether or not he slept in his chair, on the floor, or in his bed. We had become strangers; I hated him for what he had done to himself and to us.

In addition to his drinking problem, he ignored me and our four children throughout most of our marriage and throughout most of their childhoods. My former husband gave new meaning to the term, "absentee father." Upon his return home from teaching school each evening, he would immediately retreat to his office in the basement. It was there he graded homework or sorted the photographs he had taken of students or families. He worked part-time as a photographer. He seemed to think this gave him permission to take the summers completely off. As I drove to work each and every morning during the summer months, he would still be in bed snoring. I never knew when he finally climbed out of bed. His days were filled with "errands" and watching television. It didn't matter what sporting events were on television; he watched them all. The children grew up; he didn't.

Obviously, he never took the time to sit down and talk with his family. He joined us for dinner and then immediately excused himself to retreat to his office. Once at a sporting event, one of his students was introduced to my oldest son. He told my son how much fun his father was in the classroom and went on to say that he was really lucky; it must be great to live in a house with such a neat father. My son was stunned and had nothing to say. Later, my son told me that the comments made him very angry with his father. He said it hurt him to know that other kids experienced a side of his father that was never given to him. Whenever my former husband made it to my oldest son's soccer games, he went armed with crossword puzzles and magazines. At one game when my son made an exceptional goal, he looked up expecting his father to be smiling at him, but instead saw him reading a magazine. He never asked him to go to another soccer game. These are the moments that children remember for a lifetime.

What goes around does indeed come around. After the divorce, my former husband quickly moved away to another state to live near his brother. Lately, he has expressed an interest in wanting to be a part of his children's lives. He has been disappointed to find, however, that after lying to his children for so many years, this re-entry option is no longer available. Over the years, he's promised each of them that he would stop drinking, that he would start going to AA meetings, and that he would get his act together. After loaning him money and driving him to the emergency room several times (each visit due to injuries from drinking), his own brother has finally given up on him.

Getting my former husband to do chores around the house was next to impossible. If I asked him what plans he had for the weekend, he would respond with, "Why, what do you need?" Resentment became the word of the day—and every day thereafter. Days turned into years.

Why did I stay in an unhappy marriage? I had already survived one failed marriage. I left my first marriage (coincidentally? to an alcoholic...) when my oldest son was barely two years old. I hesitated to consider another failure. Truthfully, I felt it was easier to stay in an unhappy marriage rather than to be out on my own with my children. I kept telling myself that it wasn't "that bad" or that it would "get better." Denial. We all do it. Sadly, as my children graduated from high school and then college, I was still clinging to the image of "happily ever after." I wasn't ready to admit that I had failed once again. It was my youngest daughter who gave me the strength I needed to move forward. She told me that none of my children expected me to stay married to their father. The burden of guilt was immediately lifted from my shoulders after I had convinced myself for so long that I was staying married for the sake of the children. My children had absolved me of my wedding vows, as well as freeing me from my original Catholic guilt. As I finally made the decision to get a divorce, I knew it was the right decision for all of us.

At the time, I didn't realize that the transition from my divorce to the present time would result in a journey to a brand new identity— mine. I was no longer a wife and no longer comfortable with my last name. I wanted my new name to symbolize my character and the person I had become. In the process, I dropped my first name and used only an initial. I thought it was a coincidence that I chose McKinsey as a middle name. I couldn't explain why that particular name kept coming back to me. A year or so later, I was going through a family history book when I discovered a name that I knew had been there all the time. Without realizing it, I had adopted my great grandmother's maiden name. The name was also given to my mother's brother, as a middle name. There are few coincidences in this life. Finally, I chose a strong common name to bring new meaning to myself. Thus began the journey to find my new identity by redefining my art and then myself. Along the way, I've discovered that, as the saying goes, happiness is a journey, not a destination. *This journey was the beginning of my epiphany*

I've been an artist all my life. For the past thirty years, I've taught drawing and painting classes to all ages, including college students, as well as seniors in adult education. Even though I continued to teach evening classes, there was always something holding me back from pursuing art as a full-time career. At first, I was a working mother with four small children. When the children were grown, I continued to work to help with their college expenses. I thought of my interest in painting and photography more as creative outlets rather than professions. Because I also had a full-time job, I classified myself as a "Sunday painter." But the freedom and strength I derived from the divorce gave me the nudge I needed. I redefined myself through the help of my artistic interests.

To quote someone that I only know by the last name of Souza: *"For a long time it seemed to me that life was about to begin—real life, but there was always some obstacle in the way, something to be gotten through first, some unfinished business, time still to be served, a debt to be paid. At last it dawned on me that these obstacles were my life. This perspective has helped me to see there is no way to happiness. Happiness is the way. So treasure every moment that you have and remember that time waits for no one."*

The divorce symbolized a pivotal time in my life. I hadn't taken the time to become involved in my painting or my photography. Once I committed to an art exhibit in the local area, I was inspired by the timeliness and subject matter of the project. I used a series of symbols in my paintings to represent my journey. This was the perfect creative avenue I needed in order to work through all the issues I had stored up in my mind and in my heart. I used symbolism to represent and reveal the suppressed images or issues I needed to address. My art became, as they say, the window to my soul.

Once I started to paint, I realized I had so much time to make up for and so many thoughts to express and expel. Images spilled out onto the large canvases in my own particular symbols to represent anger, hurt, anxiety, fear, frustration, and finally happiness. Reactivity took control of my thoughts and transfixed images onto the naked canvases.

All art is a kind of confession, more or less oblique. All artists, if they are to survive, are forced at last, to tell the whole story; to vomit the anguish up. James Baldwin.

On the top portions of each of the paintings, I painted massive eyes, which symbolized my looking out at the world through a mantle of wet lashes—through new eyes. This was the beginning of an awakening. The symbolism in my art indeed mirrored my soul. The eyes were my eyes—always filled with tears of hope. There was no need to recreate myself on the canvases in figure form. I could see the world just fine using my new eyes.

My first painting represented my life from my childhood up to the present time. Sunflowers in shades of yellow ochre, raw umber and burnt sienna symbolized these four different stages of my life. A brown wicker picnic basket with a bottle of wine, wine glasses, a loaf of bread, and a wheel of Brie cheese created a seemingly pleasant scene. The blue and white-checkered blanket symbolized a magic carpet; however, one edge of the blanket seemed to be slowly sinking into the quick sand. Scattered around the picnic scene were oozing tubes of acrylic paint. The bright colors symbolized my passion for painting. A khaki colored camera bag and several cameras symbolized my interest in photography. A musty colored calendar with only the date of my divorce was discarded under an old oak tree. The large oak tree stood on the edge of a cliff with her roots exposed. A misshapen Dali-esque clock in shades of muted blue-green hung limply over one tree branch. The clock, devoid of hands, symbolized the absence of time. It sounded an alarm that "time waits for no one." The elegant pine trees (in various sizes) signified the strength and support of my four children. A mountain range in shades of alizarin crimson and ultramarine blue provided a background that symbolized the bosom of a mother's love. In a far corner of the painting, an overflowing rusty trash can symbolized discarded emotional garbage.

Someone once said that art isn't always pretty. As I started another painting of a large brown high-heeled shoe gouging into the hood of my ex-husband's cherry red Trans Am, I had to agree. I used the high-heeled shoe as an instrument of destruction of the male ego. The red sports car symbolized the end of a twenty-seven year old marriage to an alcoholic, as well as a symbol of his mid-life crisis. As the shoe gouged the car, a shocking pink phallic symbol (yes, that's correct, a penis) shot straight out of the engine into the air. The car was speeding down a wooden pier headed into the swirling water below. A hand (my hand) rose out of the water in a last attempt to stop the speeding car. Fragments of my divorce decree, together with empty vodka bottles, drifted silently in the murky turquoise water. Particles of a wedding veil and wedding beads danced quietly among the fish images. As the marriage ended, images of crying eyes filled the sky above, symbolizing that I love thee not. The clear turquoise waters softly caressed the sandy beaches of the beautiful tropical isle where I escaped. Swaying palm trees, sailboats, and all things beautiful decorated the seashore. It was here I celebrated the beginning of my new life. This series of paintings became known simply as "The Penis Paintings."

The long, hard journey women make in high-heeled shoes was symbolized in another painting. No one expects less of us, including ourselves. As women, we continue to set high standards and sometimes unrealistic goals for ourselves. We strive for perfection in everything we do, even if we have to sacrifice ourselves in the process. We want it all, and we have convinced ourselves that we can have it all. Who says we can? *We do.* We are the epitome of the Superwoman. Hear us roar. Hear us cry.

Shoes marched across the top of another painting, some backwards, some forward, all going nowhere. Iconic images of Marilyn Monroe, Elvis, and Dorothy's shiny bright red slippers danced across the canvas. Fragments of vinyl records indicated happier days. This painting symbolized the end of an era, a part of my life. This life happened so many years ago that I barely recognized myself. Yet, this is still a fragment of who and what I am today. These symbols serve as reminders that the Superwoman ideology and the Barbie Doll mentality have done much to hamper the journey to our own identities.

An image of a yellow brick road divided another painting in half. It symbolized the fact that something lies beyond the end of every road. I painted a field of misshapen mushrooms literally devoid of color. They were painted as symbolized line drawings onto the canvas with the underlying beige color coming through. Upon closer examination, the mushrooms could be interpreted as a field of phallic symbols. None of the mushrooms stood erect. They all leaned limply to one side and were pitiful in size. On the other side of the road, a field of brilliant bright red and yellow poppies symbolized femininity and provided a sharp contrast to the bleakness of the stylized phallic symbols. Massive tearful eyes rose high above the two fields. Painted in shades of Payne's gray, their presence enhanced the menacing skies. On the signpost, the words were written backwards. It suggested that the journey to the end of the road is not that far away. We are reminded that when one road ends, another begins.

In addition to the paintings, I also used a series of landscape photographs to symbolize transition. The title of the exhibit, "The End of the Road," was taken from one of my photographs of the same name.

On the way home one night, I stopped to take two photographs in the drizzling rain. One of the photographs, entitled "Mountain Shadows," was an image of a Colorado mountain range near Pikes Peak. Although taken with color film, the rain and the time of day changed the color into subtle gray/violet tones. The other photograph was literally taken at the end of the road near my home. The muted gray/violet tones were especially symbolic in this photograph. They represented the end of the marriage, the end of our lives together as a family, and the real possibility of selling the family home.

In sharp contrast to the subdued photographs, I paired two brightly colored photographs of sand and sea. The water in the Caribbean is several different shades of green, as well as aquamarine blue. The sand is almost white. It reminded me of powdered sugar. After my divorce was filed, I captured these two "Isla Mujeres" (which translates to "Island of Women") photographs on a small island (of the same name) near Cancun. These photographs symbolized the transition to my new life and happiness.

Photographs of high-heeled shoes symbolized the strength involved in a woman's journey. Photographs of multi-colored high-heeled shoes filled the gallery walls. Some high-heeled shoes were pictured lying among discarded wine bottles and black trash bags. Other high-heeled shoes bulged from wicker laundry baskets. And still other silver and gold bejeweled high-heeled shoes hung aimlessly and foolishly from room dividers. To further illustrate a woman's journey, I lined the walls of the gallery with countless pairs of my own four-inch high-heeled shoes. The shoes were facing forward and backward, all going nowhere. The night of the opening, my two sons attended the Gallery Talk, which I was asked to present. I was both thrilled and terrified at the prospect of speaking to a room full of strangers. Someone called me "so brave" for being able to paint "so many penises" and to display them in a gallery setting. Someone else asked if I had a script in hand or had rehearsed anything in my mind. I'd done neither. I waited for the fear to creep in and paralyze me. I caught a glimpse of my sons smiling at me and I knew they were proud of me in spite of the subject matter.

Somehow, with the aid of a glass of wine and the support of family and friends, I was able to express my epiphany, which led to the exhibit. Using creativity and symbolism as a means to heal myself, I was able to get on with my new life, without the cumbersome high-heeled shoes.

Someone once said she'd come to terms with the fact that there is no Prince Charming or Cinderella. In the real word, there aren't always fairy tale endings or beginnings; any guarantee of "happily ever after" usually occurs in fiction. The Cinderella Complex isn't for everyone. One size doesn't fit all and that's okay. Looking into the mirror and coming to terms with the fact that we may never be a size five or a perfect ten is better than the alternative. When we stop competing with the image inside our heads and quit agonizing over how we've "stacked up," we can gain a sense of serenity that is born out of acceptance. That's when we can finally accept the fact that we're not perfect and that not everyone will always love, appreciate, or approve of who or what we are. And that's really okay.

A time came in my own life when I finally "got it." In the midst of all the fears, tears and total insanity, I stopped dead in my tracks. Somewhere inside my head, a voice screamed out—ENOUGH. Enough crying and fighting and struggling to hold on to something that really didn't exist. Like a child quieting down after another blinding tantrum, my sobs began to subside. Shuddering once or twice and blinking back tears, I began to look at the world through new eyes.

In the process, I dumped my collection of self-help books right along with the Superwoman ideology and accepted the fact that I'm a Raggedy Ann in a Barbie world. I learned to accept myself for who I am and for what I want to become. I'm not fearful of being alone or making it on my own. I realized that being alone does not mean lonely. I enjoy taking responsibility for everything I have earned and learned in this life. Finally, I've decided to take my art and myself seriously on and off the job.

In making the journey to my own identity, I found these words comforting. An unknown author defined the difference between being a strong woman and being a woman of strength:

"A strong woman wears the look of confidence on her face, but a woman of strength wears grace. A strong woman makes mistakes and avoids the same in the future. A woman of strength realizes life's mistakes can also be unexpected blessings and capitalizes on them. A strong woman won't let anyone get the best of her, but a woman of strength gives the best of herself to everyone. A strong woman isn't afraid of anything, but a woman of strength shows courage in the midst of her fear. A strong woman works out every day to keep her body in shape, but a

woman of strength builds relationships to keep her soul in shape. A strong woman has faith that she is strong enough for the journey, but a woman of strength has faith that it is in the journey that she will become strong."

As women, we all walk down similar paths in life wearing symbolic shoes. Let's get real; four-inch heels are not all that comfortable for long distance running. So, pack up your pride, unload your guilt, love yourself, and wear your sensible shoes. When you understand the symbolism, you'll enjoy the journey.

BIOGRAPHY

T. MCKINSEY MORGAN

I was born in Denver, Colorado, but I grew up in Wyoming. I attended the University of Wyoming, majoring in art education. After marrying at a young age, I moved to California during the colorful sixties-seventies lifestyle of sex, drugs, and rock and roll. The transition from "small town USA" to "larger than life LA" resulted in culture shock, equivalent to a never-ending roller coaster ride. Suffice it to say, I have a multitude of real-life stories that would permanently curl your hair or make it all fall out.

For the past twenty-seven years, I've lived in Colorado on five acres in the middle of a forest. I own and operate a bed and breakfast out of my home. I host artist and yoga retreats, as well as renting rooms to guests, who sometimes rent for six months at a time. When I retire, I hope to run the bed and breakfast full-time, as well as continue to work and teach out of my home art studio.

I have four dynamic children. My eldest son is an aerospace engineer. I refer to him as a rocket scientist. My eldest daughter established, manages, and teaches restorative yoga in her yoga studios. She also hosts yoga conferences locally, as well as internationally. My youngest daughter is a well-known artist (painter) in the local area. My youngest son is also an artist. He is quite literally the Michelangelo of glass blowers. Both of my talented young artists recently participated in a local art exhibit in Denver Colorado.

During the day, I work as an administrative assistant in a multi-layered, military facility known as the United States Air Force Academy. In order to balance this left-brained environment with my right-brained creative side, at night I teach "Drawing on the Right Side of the Brain" and acrylic painting classes through an adult education program. I also work part-time as an editor, editing numerous articles and manuscripts for publication. I've recently written a children's book (still to be illustrated and published). I'm currently working on a book detailing my life; mostly for my children's benefit. I've also turned one of my hobbies, designing and creating dichroic art glass jewelry, into a small business venture.

Over the course of my career, I've worked as an illustrator in the graphics industry. I've also taught photography, television production, studio art, and art history to the future leaders of tomorrow in the classrooms of USAFA.

A dozen of my original illustrations were published in Perry Luckett's book, *Charles A. Lindbergh, A Bio-Bibliography*. Some of my articles and photographs have been published locally. I've also provided photographs for book jacket covers.

I enjoy teaching drawing and painting classes to enthusiastic students, reading books, practicing restorative yoga, walking through the forest, traveling, writing my books, listening to music, and drinking Earl Grey tea in front of the fireplace on cold, snowy nights.

In the process of creating my paintings, I've gone through many different phases. While I like the clean-cut look of illustration, I seem to be leaning more in the direction of abstraction. Building up the surface of a painting with modeling paste adds new depth and dimension. After the paint is applied, hidden meaning or symbolism many times emerges from the depths of the painting. I've exhibited my paintings in restaurants and galleries, both locally and in Denver Colorado.

CHAPTER SEVENTEEN

TURNING IT AROUND
Adolfo H. Muñoz

The Call

On a warm and lazy Sunday afternoon in May, 2000 at our house in California, the phone rang, interrupting a nice glass of white wine that I was enjoying. It was Andrea, a colleague of mine who worked for a non-profit that operated a large federally-funded program. She called to ask if I was interested in applying for the position of CEO/Executive Director of that agency. After taking a hard swallow of my wine, my first question was, "What happened to the new CEO?"

Back in 1997 I had left my job as Vice President of a fairly large management and governmental consulting firm, to venture on my own into the organizational development and change management consulting field. One of my first clients was an agency that was in the midst of some heavy turbulence, and in danger of losing a thirty-two million dollar federal grant. The telephone call was from that same agency.

That agency had hired me as a consultant in the Spring of 1998 to help them resolve internal management, governance and communication issues that had brought them to a precipitous edge. So with my consulting tool belt that included many years of management consulting, an academic background in Organizational Psychology and experience in working with federal funding agencies, I helped the agency craft a quality improvement plan and they eventually hired a new Executive Director, restructured their Governing Board and had the deficiency status removed. In that process, some of the senior managers, who had been the architects of the agency's dysfunction, appeared to be threatened by my recommendations and advice, and once my initial consulting contract was over, made sure that it would not be renewed. So getting a call a year later asking if I was interested in being the new CEO was to say the least, ironic.

That phone call triggered an avalanche of changes in my personal and business life, opening a wonderfully challenging and creative, but also at times painful chapter in my very young fifty-five years. Saul Steinberg once said that the life of the creative man is led, directed and controlled by boredom. Avoiding boredom is one of our important purposes, he concluded. And for the next six years after that call, there would be little room for boredom.

Mental health experts say that three of the major stressors in life are separation/divorce, moving to a new city and starting a new job. Just one of these can trigger a clinical depression. I had not read anything reporting what happens to people who go through more than one of these stressors. Now I was considering taking on all three of these stressors mano a mano. My wife and I had only recently separated when the job offer came around. We were both in the painful early stages of the separation. Taking the new job in a different county meant being away from our four adult children as well. On top of all that, I would be taking on my first "real" job as the Executive Director of a thirty-two million dollar non-profit enterprise, one of the largest in the county. It was a difficult decision to make, but after discussing it with my wife, and some of our children, I decided to jump on the opportunity in spite of my dread and fear.

I packed up my Jeep Cherokee with everything I could squeeze into the vehicle, and cruised along Highway 5 on a clear Friday morning in early June, 2000. My soul hurt as I left my home. There was no question that this would be a life-changing moment that I needed to embrace and trust. There is a reason that jets do not have rear-view mirrors; you can't turn back. It was one of those rare moments when I truly felt like having a good cry. But I did not—traffic was too heavy.

I also needed to trust my talent and ability to succeed in a new and very challenging environment that was full of unknowns, uncertainties and potential political land-mines. But I felt confident that my twenty years experience as a senior executive in the management and public policy consulting industry, and many years of consulting for federal education programs, prepared me for this "test." I had survived other tests in my life, so this one was not that big a thing.

Mr. Genius here decided to drive to my destination on a Friday afternoon. I very slowly navigated through the traffic mess and tried to re-adapt to the Macho with a capital M, lane-changing style so typical in California. In the middle of all the crazy traffic, and my life-changing migration, my cell phone rang. It was my dear daughter, Mercedes, who was obviously unaware that I was going through a *heavy duty Epiphany.* "Hi Dada, it's me, Cedes. I wanted to know, can you help me buy a new car? I need to get one before school starts in September." At first the question stunned me; it was so alien to the context of this diaspora. Then I thought it was terribly funny. It was a true reality check in the midst of a man's major life transition. Some things in life simply do not change. But a few weeks later, she bought a new car with her own credit and all was well.

As a child, I had not been so fortunate.

The Stick

A few weeks before graduating from High School in 1962, a well-dressed gentleman paid a visit to our classroom to describe a brand new summer employment program being launched by the Texas Employment Department that would have us working in Wisconsin. The state official told us that we would be taken to Wisconsin, by Greyhound bus, to work for the Del Monte company in the city of Fond du Lac, for about three months and with the prospect of earning several thousand dollars. The deal was too good to pass up, so several of my friends and I (after persuading our parents that it was an excellent opportunity) decided to sign-up for that adventure.

So here we are, four Mexican American teenagers who had never been out of Texas, waiting for the Greyhound bus to pick us up at the local state employment department. It was around 6am, we were a bit groggy, but anxious to get started on our journey. Del Monte was picking up our travel expenses, and would also provide housing and meals throughout our internship in Wisconsin, according again to our friend from the state employment department.

My Dad and I were surprised to see a very big truck, with wooden siding and a brown tarp covering the truck bed, pull up the driveway. It was definitely not a Greyhound bus. A burly Mexican (I don't think he was Mexican American) stepped out of the truck cab, said something in Spanish, and began herding the twenty-five or so new employees into the back of the truck. I kissed my Dad good-bye and tried to ignore the very worried look on his face, but he managed to smile, took a big puff from his cigarette and waved adios.

All twenty-five of us, young and old, were in back of that truck for the three-day trip to Fond du Lac, Wisconsin. It was a tight space, so we took turns standing, sitting and lying down on the truck bed. Here I was sixteen years old, leaving my family back in Laredo, and being hauled in the back of a truck to God knows where. I could not precisely tell if I was feeling emancipated or incarcerated. Probably a bit of both.

We were a diverse group, as sociologists like to say. Mostly male, young and old, with a few just recently released from prison for some major crime, including as we discovered during the journey, homicide. Plus four high school graduates from Laredo.

We got to the Del Monte farm-worker camp in the middle of the night, and were assigned to the company barracks. The barracks each had two bunk beds. One of the gentlemen with the homicide conviction, nicknamed El Arabe was one of our roommates. He could barely read or write, was big as a closet, had a shaved head, and stood about six foot five inches. And he looked like an Arab.

While I was only sixteen, I observed several things that would be important to my survival in that new environment. First, it was a rough crowd, not unlike what one would find in a prison culture. Most of these guys were dirt poor, uneducated and often mean-spirited. Fortunately, most were Mejicanos, which helped me forge some level of rapport. Fist fights, and a few knife fights, were common most every evening, either in the dining hall or outside. I was not very big, but was in good shape from playing sports in high school. If anything, I could out-run most of the colleagues in a pinch. But a superior solution came about over the next several weeks.

After helping my roomie, El Arabe, write letters to his dear mother in Mexico, along with money orders, as well as handling other administrative details, an invisible, but very effective, protective shield was created. I achieved the status of "untouchable"—that is to say El Arabe was both my roomie and now my friend and bodyguard, so no one in the camp messed with me or my Laredo friends. Which was a great relief.

Picking peas is hard work. After a few weeks of hard labor in the fields, I was transferred to the Del Monty factory. Indoor work! It felt like a promotion. My job was to pull freshly sealed cans of peas off a conveyor belt into a large steel barrel that later found its way to another part of the processing chain. We had to work fast and at a constant pace. My keen eye then noticed that the Mejicanos were doing the heavy lifting, while our Anglo counterparts (Fond du Lac high school grads) had a much easier job that, we discovered later, paid more. The

Fond du Lac grads' job was to tap the conveyor belt with a long wooden stick when the cans got jammed. Period. One evening I strolled over to the Supervisor, a very large man of definite Germanic stock, and politely asked how I could apply to be a "stick" man. To my surprise, the Supervisor broke out in laughter saying something to the effect of "boy, those jobs are not for you Mexicans." That was one of the first times in my young life that I had ever felt the blunt blow of discrimination. It was, in retrospect, a painful but empowering epiphany. My sense of self, and who I thought I was, was sharply re-defined, slamming into reality and life in Wisconsin.

My first impulse after hearing that bit of racist trash, was to sic El Arabe on this Del Monte minion. Beat the guy to a pulp with the damn wooden stick. Fortunately, for the German guy, the factory bell broke the silence, marking the end of our twelve-hour shift. So I jumped on the truck that would take us back to the Del Monte camp, wondering which two amigos would be in tonight's featured boxing match.

In retrospect, it was during my time in Wisconsin that my being different, or at least defined as different by the larger society, primarily based on my appearance and surname, would be a life-long label. Ethnic and racial labels, I now understand, are an enduring element in our American society. Although there is no biological basis for the racial classifications (this fact surprises a lot of my colleagues and friends), racial and ethnic labels persist and unfortunately tend to further stereotype people.

I was always curious why in Laredo, my hometown, the European/Anglos were generally referred to by my family and other Latinos, as Los Americanos, literally meaning "the Americans." My grandparents had been born in Texas, so our lineage and Americanism spans several generations. It was as if those of Mexican or Spanish heritage were systematically denied the privilege of being called "Americanos." That practice persists even now. I have friends who are descendants of Irish, British, French or German families, and they typically enjoy being referred as Americans. However, if one is Black or Latino, or Asian, then the mandatory hyphenation steps in, as if we had dual citizenship and dual loyalties.

This for me has always been just a fact of life. It bothers me less now than it used to, but it still grates. A few months ago, in talking about these ethnic labels, I asked some friends how long does a Latino or Latina have to be in the United States to be called just an American? No answer was forthcoming, probably because we all knew the answer.

My Epiphany in Wisconsin was clear and powerful. For the rest of my life I would be first defined by my appearance, accent and name. Period. Thereafter, employers and colleagues would maybe learn more about me as an individual, and deal with me on that basis. It was at this stage in my young life, which represented the first time I had left the safety of Laredo, that I came to understand what it would take for me to succeed both socially and professionally. It was a skill and practice that many of my counterparts had learned in school, but it was nameless, more of an unconscious response, like breathing.

Later I learned that social psychologists refer to this phenomenon as "code switching." In very simple terms, it means that I behave, act, respond, think and speak in one code that is associated with my essential cultural self, and may include inter-changing Spanish and English, a certain type of humor, and even bodily kinesthetics. In contrast, my language and communication style, and behavioral style are distinctly different when I am in a business or social situation with mostly "Americans." We have learned literally to quickly switch-codes. It's a cognitive, linguistic and behavioral adaptive mechanism that allows us to effectively switch between two worlds, and gain access and acceptance in the larger US society. That takes a lot of work, consumes a considerable amount of emotional energy, and requires years of practice to perfect. We often do it so well that our American colleagues are surprised to hear us speak or sing in Spanish, and talk about enjoying authentic Mexican food other than a burrito. It's like a signal that the absolute acculturation somehow came up short. And that I am different.

Thoracic Surgery

When I was about eighteen years old, in my second year at St. Mary's University, the lower lobe in my right lung was surgically removed. Though the post-surgical recovery was extremely painful, that experience connected to three very important elements in my life.

For one, the idea that I would not survive the thoracic surgery never crossed my mind. I could see my Dad and family members were worried. Later I found out that the surgeon had given me a fifty-fifty chance of coming through that surgery. Coming to the edge, that thin line between living and dying, was empowering and transformational. It imbued in me a very deep sense of optimism about life and the future, and my ability to navigate around barriers and roadblocks, to succeed where others might not.

Second, after getting over the surgery it was too late to enroll back in college, so with the help of the thoracic surgeon, I got a job as an Orderly at Santa Rosa

Hospital in downtown San Antonio. As I strolled around the hospital attending to my very important duties (changing bedpans and the like) I saw the most beautiful girl I had ever seen. She was a high school volunteer who helped patients during the weekends. Every time I saw her my heart started pounding. On weekends, I made sure to wear my best Orderly Uniform, crisply starched. For some reason, this young lady would not give me the time of day. I tried charming her with my jokes, ignoring her in the hallway, inviting her to share a snack. Nada! The point of all this is that because of this awful surgery my path connected with that beautiful young girl in the hospital. I was optimistic we would one day get married. In fact I mentioned that feeling to her, and she was not a happy camper, claiming I was arrogant and self-centered. In retrospect, I believe my declaration that we would someday get married was a genuine revelation, at some higher cognitive dimension, that for me was as real as the air I was breathing. No question mark. It was a fact, for me at least.

So with persistence and blind optimism, things eventually turned around and we were married in 1969, some five years after our paths had crossed at Santa Rosa Hospital.

And the third element associated with the thoracic surgery, is that it probably saved my life, again. In 1968 I was drafted and would have been deployed to Viet Nam. Having gone through officer training at St. Mary's University made me a prime candidate for artillery or infantry assignments. But after multiple physical exams, the Army finally concluded that I was not fit for military duty given that I was missing a big chunk of my right lung, and I was granted a medical deferral. They did not know I was also a very bad shot, so it was a sound decision to keep me out.

Having survived the thoracic surgery I was grateful and sensed at some level that perhaps I had been spared by a higher power to carry out some special purpose in life.

Interestingly, I was about seventeen years old when I went through this surgery, and thereafter I suspected that my life would be short, say until thirty-five or so. That did not bother me, it was sort of an internal fact that I carried. Now some twenty-eight years later, I discovered that perception was inaccurate, and for that I am also grateful. I suppose that going through that kind of "loss" tends to make one feel incomplete and vulnerable.

I also understood the sacrifice made by my Dad in first agreeing that I should undergo a risky surgical procedure, and then also agreeing to pay for the surgery out of his pocket. For some reason our health insurance policy at that time did not cover the entire cost of the procedure, and I recall seeing my Dad hand a check to the surgeon the morning of the surgery. That is an act of sacrifice and generosity that I will not forget.

Intuition

My Dad passed away on June 9, 2006 in Laredo, Texas. He spent all of his life in Laredo. He was a courageous and heroic parent to me and my four siblings. When I was about thirteen years old, our Mother left the family and never came back. So my father, with lots of help from his parents, raised the five us in Laredo and never once complained about the hardships and pain that he was going through.

Being abandoned by one's mother leaves a huge void in your life and psyche. Growing up, our world was incomplete, missing that important second partner in raising and nurturing a family. Somehow, my Dad managed to give us lots of love, generous support and attention. At times when I was growing up he seemed distant and distracted, probably still grieving the loss of his wife, who I believe he dearly loved while burdened with raising five children. When my mother left, my youngest brother was still in his crib. My other brother was about three years old, and the youngest sister not more than five. And the oldest sister was five years younger than me, so I was about thirteen years old at the time that our family disintegrated. We are all now grown up, have our own families, and I am in close touch with my brothers and sisters.

Unfortunately, after our father passed away, the connection with my sisters and brothers became strained because of personal disagreements. Someone once observed that religion teaches us enough to hate one another, but not enough to forgive. I am not a very religious person, but if more Christians practiced that philosophy of forgiveness our world would be a much better place. Forgiveness often comes much too slow, and often too late. Fortunately, over time our relationships healed and got stronger as we each learned to let go of the past.

As I drove along in heavy traffic on this Friday afternoon in 2008, I knew that my Great Grandfather, Fabian Liendo, had died this hot morning many years ago in Laredo, Texas when I was about eight years old. This awareness of his death, like a warm wave, wrapped around me and I just knew Papa Fabian had passed away as we sat in Our Lady of Guadalupe Church. No one else knew at that time. My Grandmother, Elvira, and Grandfather, Adolfo, had been taking care of him at their home for several months. When we got back from Church that Sunday morning, Mama Elvira cried, deeply saddened by the passing of her dear father. When I became aware of Papa Fabian's passing while I sat in Church, it was with a definitive clarity that I did not question or evaluate. I just knew that he had died.

In retrospect, that gift of intuition did run in our family. Papa Fabian's father, Jesus Liendo, a Spaniard who settled in Texas, was well known for this healing powers and extra-sensory capacities. My great-grandfather Jesus died when I was about two years old, so I have no recollection of him. Mama Elvira, who was his grand-daughter, shared wonderful stories with me, recounting times when Papa Jesus was called to tend to the sick Mexican families who lived in the dusty ranchitos in Southern Texas. It is said that by laying his hands on the person, Papa Jesus had the power to heal, and for that he was famous and in large demand. I may have perhaps inherited a small grain of his gifts.

On my Grandfather Adolfo's side, his sister-in-law, also named Elvira, was a practitioner of the healing arts as well, but more on the side of folk medicine (curanderismo) rather than the para-psychological gifts of Fabian Liendo. At about the age of ten, I was privileged to be treated by Tia Elvira for "susto," which literally means an emotionally traumatic experience. My parents took me to Tia Elvira's house on a summer afternoon (in Laredo it seemed like it was always summer) to be treated for "susto" which I had recently experienced when I saw my Mom being taken away by an ambulance. She was OK afterwards, but it was a very disturbing and scary thing for me to watch.

Tia Elvira asked to me to recline on a small bed and she gently swept my body with a small wooden broom, which made me giggle. She had a bowl with hot water perched on a nearby table. I think it may have been boiling. Tia Elvira spoke, saying, "Donde estas Fito?" which means, "where are you?" (Fito was my nickname). So I responded, "Here I am!" Tia Elvira gave me a stern look, indicating that I should be quiet. She asked the same question two or three times, and it elicited the same response from me, which eventually frustrated Tia Elvira to the point that she gave up on the therapy.

Unfortunately, for me, the "susto" therapy did not take hold and a few years later I was inflicted with a severe and debilitating stutter that lasted well into my early professional life. I suppose I should have let her do her work and kept my mouth shut. But as a child I just loved to talk—ironically the stutter snatched that joy away for many years.

The New Job, May, 2000

My first day on the job was on June 4, 2000 and I was warmly greeted by some of the managers in the lobby of the building. I felt both welcomed and valued in that moment.

I was quickly escorted to the Director's office (which I had been in before as a consultant for meetings and the like), and told that we would be having an all-staff meeting in a few minutes. My heart was pounding; it was scary and exciting. Like a first day at school, surrounded by friendly nuns.

The agency was housed in a four-story office building, smack in the middle of a tough neighborhood in the old part of this California city, which had seen better days some thirty years ago. Taking the elevator required a profound act of faith. Staff was scattered throughout the four floors, in small private offices, like one hundred little silos.

The Director's office looked like a cozy cave, located in the far corner of the third floor, protected by two foyers that served as a gate for staff and visitors. It was very secluded. I noticed there was a computer by the desk—but no internet connection, which seemed odd.

There were about eighty people at the all-staff meeting, employees who worked in the agency's main office. The remaining four-hundred or so employees were deployed across forty education centers scattered across the county. The Board Chair introduced me, then one of the senior managers who had been with the agency for some thirty years, broke into "The Company Song," which sort of caught me off guard, since most meetings that I attended did not include a musical interlude. So folks were singing, waving their arms and legs, full of enthusiasm in what I sensed to be a genuine love for their work. I felt like I had arrived at the right place for the right reasons, and my soul settled, still sad about leaving my family and home, but filled with the belief that I would make a difference in this organization.

During the first several weeks I spent a lot of time reading, meeting with managers and staff, consulting with board members, and basically "diagnosing" the organization's culture, processes and capacities.

Over the weeks it became evident that we had a lot of work to do, and not much time to do it. For one, the federal funding agency would be conducting its tri-ennial monitoring review (involving some thirty consultants/reviewers looking at all systems for a whole week) in

May, 2001. That meant that we had about eleven months to get ready. Given that this particular agency had been found "deficient" in the prior federal review in 1998, staff was naturally nervous and worried about the forthcoming assessment. I soon learned that worrying was an important part of the organization's culture. Needless to say, that worried me as well.

I decided that the pending federal review would give me some excellent leverage for introducing some key changes in structure, processes and mind-set. There was a definite sense of urgency to get ready for this review. To prepare, temporary teams were created to complete specific projects in preparation for the review, doing such things as auditing conditions at each of the education centers, reviewing program files, and organizing fiscal and program-related files. This approach required that staff move out of their comfort zones and silos, and work cooperatively with staff from other departments. By creating these temporary teams, we saw the beginning of informal inter-disciplinary teams, which would represent one of the substantive changes in later years.

Moreover, the agency was in dire need of modernization. There was one computer with internet access located in the fourth floor library, which was kept under lock and key. That was the extent of technology at that time. The Accounting Department was still using manual methods to track a thirty-two million dollar annual budget. I was in the Twilight Zone.

Control was a huge part of the current culture. Interestingly, on my first day at the office, I was being walked through the Human Resources Department on the first floor of the building when suddenly one of the women HR analysts popped her head out of her office and in a loud voice asked, "Adolfo, can we start wearing backless shoes?" After consulting with various managers, I did change the policy allowing female employees in the main office to wear backless shoes, with men having the option as well if they so chose. So that was my first act of "liberation" in a highly controlling managerial world.

A second act of "liberation" involved the male employees working in the Accounting Department. That department had been under the dominant thumb of a Finance Director, who resigned a few months before I arrived, who had not allowed computers, nor permit his staff to talk to each other in that office. And men had to wear shirt and tie to work.

Well, California gets dreadfully hot in the summer. In late June, 2000, a heat wave hit our area, knocking out power in the downtown area, and disabling our building's air conditioning system. I saw an opportunity there and issued a memo "relaxing" the dress code for male employees. Next day I wore one of my many Hawaiian shirts...bright and colorful. Within a few weeks, Hawaiian-style shirts became the norm in the Accounting Department, scandalizing a few of the senior managers, but otherwise bringing a bit of cheer to the place. Remarkably, the quality of the financial reports and accounting did not suffer, and in fact, the quality of the Hawaiian shirts improved over time, to the point that they became part of our agency's signature attire.

It became apparent after a few weeks on the job that the agency had many of the attributes and characteristics of an "addictive organization." Anne Wilson Schaef and Diane Fassel wrote in *The Addictive Organization:* "*An addiction is any process over which we are powerless. It takes control of us, causing us to do and think things that are inconsistent with our personal values and leading us to become progressively more compulsive and obsessive. A sure sign of an addiction is the sudden need to deceive ourselves and others to lie, deny, and cover up.*" These addictions were powerful and quite entrenched in our agency.

There were definite rituals and rules that reflected the addictive dynamics within the organization. There were some very clear rules in place designed to protect the status quo, control knowledge and information, preserve authority and power with the veteran managers, enforce strict dress codes, reward longevity and discourage joy and fun in the workplace. Penance and personal sacrifice were also on top of the list. Management meetings tended to be lengthy and mechanical, with few concrete outcomes; often continuing on for hours, sometimes consuming a whole day. Some of the senior managers worked long hours, came in on weekends to handle paperwork, and came back on Monday to re-visit that same paperwork.

One of my first management meetings lasted a mere one hour, which shocked some of the managers. I explained that if we can't resolve issues in a one-hour meeting, then those issues need to go back to staff or specialists for more analysis. That's committee work. With shorter management meetings, some of the managers found themselves with more time on their hands. A few even began to go home on time. Reluctantly, at first.

My main challenge, in the short-term, was to create a sense of pride among the agency's staff; to encourage them to think and act like winners and to be confident about change and our ability to grow and evolve. The turbulence and the 1998 federal deficiency designation had seriously damaged the agency's belief in "self." In 1998, the founder and executive director of that agency retired after twenty-five years of service. He had been pounded by the in-house rumor mill, and some say, was undermined by some of his senior managers. A new executive director was hired in 1999, but he left in early 2000. Understandably, the agency's governance leadership and employees felt vulnerable.

In addition, we needed to create and introduce improved business and operational processes, shift people to work on the basis of procedures rather than personal preference, and apply basic planning techniques to shape future structures and services. In a nutshell, we had to move the agency's managers, in particular, more in the direction of counter-intuitive ways of doing business. While intuition is a wonderful part of humanity, it is very difficult to administer a thirty-two million dollar enterprise exclusively on the basis of how things feel. In effective organizations there is ample room for both intuitive and counter-intuitive mental models. Finance and accounting are not good arenas for intuitive management styles, as an example.

Understandably, people that go into the early childhood educational field tend to be right-brain, and rely on intuitive resources in working with young children. And that is beautiful and exciting. This approach, in my view, had to be balanced with a left-brain style that operates on the basis of factual information, analysis of data and outcomes, and strategic thinking. Effective leaders typically are skillful in working at both levels, right-brain combined with left-brain perspectives.

By the end of 2000 we had implemented a new organizational structure and hired people from the outside to lead the recently created divisions that included Operations, Administration, Finance and Human Resources. These Division Directors brought fresh executive leadership, along with new talent that would help modernize the agency's systems.

The dreaded federal review was conducted in May of 2001 and the results were positive. Since my arrival at the agency in June of 2000, we had less than a year to install badly needed management and service delivery systems, and ensure that our program services were in compliance with the seventeen hundred and eighty regulations that came with the federal grant.

I had been very optimistic about this federal review, knowing that the agency's services were in good to very good shape. Not perfect, but certainly in compliance with the various regulations. In 1998, the federal reviewers had observed what they referred to as a "hostile work environment," and it was that finding that led to having the agency designated as deficient. I was hopeful that the changes and interventions that we had made in the past several months had been successful in healing those wounds. Generally, staff was in better spirits, more hopeful about the future, and certainly under my watch they were not being terrorized or intimidated by supervisors.

This relatively successful federal review in 2001 brought new energy into the agency and set a firmer foundation for future changes and initiatives. This positive outcome represented an important stage in re-building the agency's culture.

Hail Mary

About the time I started the sixth grade at St. Joseph's Academy in Laredo, I developed a severe stutter that would stay with me for many years; well into my professional life. Not understanding why this happened to me, I wondered if I should have been more cooperative with my Tia Elvira's folk treatment for Susto. Everything is somehow connected.

Being a stutterer in a Catholic school during the early 1960's was probably the worst place to be. Every single day of school I dreaded having to recite the Rosary out loud right after our lunch break. I dreaded gutturals. Guttural is a term used to describe any of several <u>consonantal</u> <u>speech sounds</u> whose primary <u>place of articulation</u> is near the back of the oral cavity. Those triggered an immediate blockage of speech for me. Just froze me. And just my luck, many a day when it was my turn to recite part of the Rosary, it was the "Glory Be to the Father." Bam! Hail Mary's were much easier. Our Father was OK...But that "Glory Be" was a killer. Even to this day I rarely start a sentence with a guttural.

My parents tried to help, and I am thankful. I remember sitting in the doctor's office with my mother. The good doctor handed me a Reader's Digest, opened it up and asked me to read one of the paragraphs out loud. I stuttered, stammered and spit, but could not get the words out. "Situational stress" it is called. My poor mother broke down and cried. I couldn't sense if it was pity or embarrassment. I think it was more like sadness. Our physician, in his medical wisdom, put me on Dexedrine or something in that family of drugs. With the magic pills I was running around like the Energizer Rabbit and my disfluency abated, at least for a few weeks. Then I went back to stuttering, and continued bouncing around school like a jack rabbit.

Unfortunately, at that time the teaching brothers had little if any training in special education, language development or speech disorders. Stuttering was viewed as more of a character defect, or so I felt.

In Spanish the term stutterer translates into "tartamudo," a very cruel term in my estimation. "Mudo" means dumb, as in unable to speak. And "tarta" probably refers to the repetition of certain sounds. Being labeled a "tartamudo" or referred to as such by family members and some friends, was demeaning and plummeted my sense of self- worth and brittle self-confidence to the lowest levels.

As a kid I loved to joke, and could crack up my schoolmates at the drop of hat. Which frequently landed me in Detention Class at St. Joseph's. But these were precious moments when the words would glide smoothly, and create wonderfully, delicious laughter. I could sing and not stutter. And I could joke with my close friends and not stutter as much. But my voice became trapped in stressful situations. Even making a simple telephone call was difficult and at times impossible. Reading out loud in class was terrifying. Introducing myself in a group (as when you go around and take turns) was paralyzing.

As I approached the time to enter college, I figured Journalism would be a good pathway since it relied on the written word. Around my sophomore year at St. Mary's University I changed my major to Psychology with sort of a vague idea of eventually going into Clinical Psychology and discovering a cure for stuttering.

Shortly after Susie and I were married in 1969, I was offered a job by the Leadership Institute for Community Development, based in Washington, D.C.; a brand new entity funded by the federal government to train leaders and executives in the War on Poverty. A stutterer going into the training profession, which relies 90% on public speaking talent, was analogous to a blind man signing up to fly jets. Not a good match, one would say.

That moment when Susie and I decided to take the offer and move to Washington D.C. was a life-changing moment. I figured either the stutter would dominate my life forever, or I could grab it by the neck, put up a good fight, and with some good luck come out speaking. From then on I engaged in a journey of "self- treatment," propelled by my wife's constant encouragement and support, picking me up from the canvas and nudging me back into the ring. That was around 1970.

Since that time I have been an executive in the management consulting industry, a professional trainer and facilitator, have been a keynote speaker for various professional conferences, done a couple of TV talk show interviews, facilitated management seminars and retreats; all with a profound sense of confidence and sheer joy at being able to get the words out. I have been relishing the power of my words to make people laugh a bit, enjoy learning and making a difference. One is not ever truly cured of stuttering. You are in a constant process of recovery.

In a famous analogy, Joseph Sheehan, a prominent researcher in the field, compared stuttering to an iceberg; with the overt aspects of stuttering above the waterline, and the larger mass of negative emotions invisible below the surface. Like that saying goes, if the stuff doesn't kill you it only makes you stronger. And so it was with my constant companion, Stutter. It eventually made me stronger.

The Unsettled Side

By early 2002 I realized that there was a side to the agency that had evolved and entrenched itself over many years, damaging many employees along the way. Although I heard stories from staff about this dynamic, it was not until about eighteen months into my tenure that the workings of the unsettled side became more apparent.

This unsettled side appeared to have players from within the agency, as well as from the outside. I had never encountered such a persistent and mean-spirited energy. This unsettled side expressed itself through tactics such as anonymous letters and vicious rumors. It had no face, and did its work under a mantle of secrecy. This unsettled side seemed to be well orchestrated and with a clear Mission: protect the status quo, create chaos and mistrust, and destabilize any new foundations we created. It was invisible and it was dangerous. It was part of the addictive syndrome I suppose.

A noted expert, Scott Peck, defined evil as the use of political power to destroy others *"for the purpose of defending or preserving the integrity of one's sick self."* Interestingly, the unsettled side, though certainly not intentionally evil, typically took action when a major change within the agency was being planned or about to be implemented.

Tom Heurman, an Organizational Psychologist, observed that, "... *the addictive system moves from crisis to crisis. Most people are kept too busy and too confused to challenge the system. Those who do challenge the behavior of an addictive organization are neutralized and marginalized. Change agents who challenge the status quo are often demonized and scape-goated."* A couple of times the unsettled group came directly at me through anonymous letters to the Board of Directors, or anonymous fax messages to agency employees charging the Executive Director (me) with favoritism and fraud. These were hard body blows that I suspect were meant to divert my energy and break my spirit and optimism. These attacks also served to create crises.

In the end, these assaults by the unsettled side subsided and we moved on, at least for a while. Fortunately, there was a small cadre of senior managers, some of them veteran employees, who recognized the unsettled side, and who were willing to help push the organization towards a healthier direction. Several years later, around 2005, I am told that a disgruntled employee (former), who had been a part of the unsettled side, was instrumental in launching a union organizing effort, which in the end changed the character and relationship between management and many employees forever.

The Good Years, 2002-2004

By 2002 the agency had entered into a period of transformation; key pieces were coming together, new executive leadership seemed to be gelling, with Board and executive staff humming along in a healthy alignment. This was an exciting time. Jim Collins in his book, *Good To Great: Why Some Companies Make The Leap and Others Don't,* describes the *Flywheel Effect*. Basically, the *Flywheel Effect* is what happens when companies stay focused on their core business, with all of the team members and stakeholders going in the same direction. Change efforts, projects and initiatives gain momentum. Like an engine, the constant rotation begins and the improvement processes begin to operate on their own.

In March of 2002, a magical year, my wife, Susie and I got back together after being separated for almost two years. I had flown into her local airport on a Friday afternoon to pick her up at her home and drive her back to the county where I worked the following day. Susie had her clothes and personal belongings neatly packed in suitcases and a few boxes in such a way that we could squeeze all of it into her SUV. After saying goodbye to her Mom, who joined us a few weeks later, Susie and I headed out on my old friend, Highway 5, for the trip to my one-bedroom apartment. We were both happy to be back together, but also sad that we were leaving our adult children who lived a distance away from where I worked.

My apartment was small but quite comfortable. One bedroom, a small living area and a tiny kitchen. We were so tight on closet space that if we bought new shoes or other clothing, we had to get rid of something to make room in the closet. We made many deposits at Goodwill. But it was worth it—I was happy to be back together with Susie. Naturally so were our children. Although we were separated by geography, the family was back together. We were excited about our future, eager to buy a house and enjoy the beautiful beaches in the area together. It was the period of wine and roses for us.

Starting in 2002, we started to build a very positive momentum, and the beginnings of the *Flywheel Effect*. Creating a sustainable change in the agency's culture required that we somehow "unfreeze" the present systems of addictions, relationships and practices. This was effectively done by moving out of the old county building.

In April, 2002, we moved the agency headquarters to a modern office building equipped with state-of-the-art computer technology, clean offices and functional cubicle areas for accounting, operations, human resources and executive leadership staff. In contrast to the former headquarters building that was spread over four floors, all ninety administrative staff were housed on the ground floor. That physical move was a dramatic milestone, at least in my mind, in the transformation of the agency. Not necessarily a popular one with some of the unsettled side's disciples, but an effective change. In fact, shortly after moving to our new headquarters, the agency was bombarded with anonymous fax messages sent to our headquarters and each of the education centers, alleging misuse of federal funds. The unsettled side was not happy. Over time employees adjusted to the new environment, and many even agreed that this was an improvement.

Around this same period we secured funding to construct some new education centers to replace older and dilapidated facilities. Thanks to a series of one-time grants from our federal funding source, our agency was able to build half a dozen brand new preschool sites with state-of-the-art designs and furnishings. This was indeed exciting given that many of the existing preschool centers were in old, poor condition. By 2004 these new centers were in place and provided the children and families that we served with first-class facilities, along with some of our best teachers and staff.

Over a period of two decades, the agency had evolved a practice of naming certain preschool centers after some of the senior managers. Many of these managers were still employees of the agency in 2004. I discontinued that practice, and suggested to the Board of Directors that in the future, preschool centers should more appropriately be named after deceased individuals who had left a legacy to the community, but who were definitely not current employees. The unsettled side rumbled a bit at this edict.

The next BIG federal audit was scheduled for May, 2004. Our agency went through several large-scale self-evaluation exercises that took a critical look at fiscal, management, educational and governance processes. Naturally when one drills that deeply into an organization's bowels, stuff is going to come up. And it did. But in my estimation these "findings" were more along the lines of widgets rather than an indication of deep, fatal flaws in our systems. These "findings" however became fodder for the pessimists who came to management meetings with the "sky is falling" mentality. They were fairly certain that the forthcoming May, 2004 federal review would discover a bunch of mortal sins and possibly sink the whole ship. Some people appeared to be addicted to bad news, crises and failure.

In May, 2004, a team of some thirty federal staff and consultants descended upon our agency on a Monday morning to kick-off the five day federal audit. I always had felt confident that we would do well in this audit, and that our basic systems and procedures were not necessarily excellent, but were in compliance with the federal regulations that governed our federal grant. I truly believed, and so did many of the senior managers, that the agency was healthy, working diligently to improve service quality, and on the road to re-inventing itself.

I had heard agency managers recount the story of the federal "exit conference" in 1998 where the agency was declared to be "deficient" and in danger of losing the entire thirty-two million dollar grant. Those painful memories still lingered among some staff as we went through the 2004 federal audit. This experience was cemented into the institutional memory. Nerves were on edge as we waited for the final results of the one-week audit.

By nature I am an optimistic person. This optimism has gotten me through a lot of challenges. My inclination is to visualize good endings and positive results, with an awareness of the problems at hand, but with my mind's eye focusing on optimistic outcomes. In prepping for the 2004 federal audit, some of the senior managers teased me about what they described as my "Pollyanna" tendencies. I had no real idea who this Pollyanna was, but the implication was clearly not positive.

Rumors floated that the Executive Director (me), would be bounced by the Board after this federal audit, if we were found to be deficient. One of the senior managers on my leadership team, I later learned, was grooming herself to be my replacement in that event. Sort of a self-anointed succession plan. Similarly, a few of our subcontractors who held multi-million contracts with our agency, were certain that the feds would recognize how unfairly these subcontractors were treated by our agency. In fact, these same subcontractors during their interview with the feds made outrageous and untrue charges, alleging every conceivable form of fraud and abuse on my part and the part of my leadership team. Ironically, the federal auditors, upon investigating the subcontractor's allegations, concluded that these were simply bald-face lies.

At last the 2004 federal audit was coming to an end on a Friday morning. The federal audit team convened an "exit conference" at the end of the week at a local hotel to announce the results of the 2004 audit. Some staff members, subcontractors and perhaps some of our Board members were much surprised when they heard the federal team leader announce that our agency was in good shape, with evidence of some exemplary practices. The federal team leader recited some of the "findings" which were relatively benign, and balanced that with an extensive acknowledgement of the progress made by the agency since the infamous 1998 review. I felt like crying. Some of my managers did cry out of relief and joy. In contrast, some of the disgruntled subcontractors stormed out of the hotel conference room full of indignation and full of themselves. They apparently did not like how the movie ended. I thought it was a perfectly ironic ending. Pessimistic expectations and reality clashed beautifully and the outcome was appropriate.

At an intuitive level, I was very confident that the federal audit would have a positive ending. Much like in sports, it is important to visualize the results one wants in a given situation. At the same time, to get the positive outcomes, one also needs to invest through preparation, planning and lots of hard work. Visualizing an end-result does not automatically guarantee success. I learned, however, that when coming into a situation confidently, particularly as a leader, a powerful energy is created as people hear and sense that the leadership has a deep belief in their success. This goes back in some ways to the so-called *Pygmalion Effect*, the theme of the movie *My Fair Lady*. Basically, people's behavior and job performance are affected by the expectations of the leadership. The same applies to children in relation to their parents.

2005: Stormy Period

Dark clouds descended upon our agency in 2005, signaling the coming storms. A convergence of unanticipated changes and external political pressures created heavy turbulence that would shake the agency's foundation.

Studies suggest that the life-expectancy of a CEO in the non-profit arena is about eighteen months. Unfortunately, no one told me that earlier. But when I started this new job I intuitively gave myself a five-year time frame. About the time it would take to re-invent the organization, and once that was accomplished the organization would likely require a different type and mix of leadership. Also I had learned that the board that hires you is not always around three to four years later, so the institutional memory and loyalties often evaporate. At a very intuitive level in June, 2000 I sensed that in five years it would be time for a change.

This turbulence was a result of several events including our attempt to hold subcontractors accountable and an aggressive campaign to unionize the agency's teachers and other employees. These two circumstances in turn produced unrelenting political pressure on the agency's management team as well as the Board.

In early 2005, the Board of Directors rightfully reaffirmed its position that we hold subcontractors to a high level of accountability, particularly in fiscal matters. The Board also affirmed its independence from outside political pressure.

One of our subcontractors had spent several thousand dollars purchasing new equipment for their organization—all this without my agency's prior approval which is required by federal regulation. My Board directed that it was time to draw the line in the sand with this subcontractor and hold him accountable for what appeared to be a blatant disregard of federal rules and the terms of our contract. My Board further directed that I move forward and advise the subcontractor that the equipment purchase expenditure was disallowed, and we would be deducting those dollars from their subcontract. Even the federal regional office upstate was on our side, and seemed to be enthusiastic about our diligence.

Needless to say, our attempt to recoup taxpayer's money created considerable resistance, got the subcontractor director into a hissing fit, or so I heard from reliable sources. Within a few days, I started getting calls and letters from elected officials demanding to look at our financial records, subcontractor records, and the like. Well my Board took a hard line and directed me to politely refuse the official's request for agency records. And I did.

We were subsequently threatened with a full-scale Governmental Inquiry. On top of that, the federal regional office, reacting to the political heat they were probably getting, called me most every day to learn how I planned to resolve this problem.

In January, 2005 some of our employees reported getting calls from unknown individuals claiming they were conducting a survey for a national association regarding early childhood education issues in the county. We were one of the few programs in California that was not unionized. Those days were numbered. By February, 2005 a local union launched a campaign to organize the agency's employees.

Heavy political pressure came to bear a few weeks before the union election. I shortly discovered that because unions have a bagful of political currency, particularly with elected officials who are in power, unions enjoy a certain degree of "protection" in exchange for the union's generosity with its money and union member votes.

Our agency had been in business for some thirty years, and was never on any union's radar screen, until 2005. And we were ill-prepared and ill-equipped to fend off the union organizing effort. Literally, the agency's hands were tied by federal law that prohibits federally-funded entities from preventing the organization of a union. Our budget was 100% federal funds. I told one of our Board members that I felt like I was going into the ring with both hands tied behind my back. And I was.

Finally, at that time I believed that the Board had recognized that we did not have the resources to effectively stave off the union. Federal regulations were very restrictive, and the corporation had zero non-federal dollars. My recollection was that the Board and I agreed that the union election would proceed; we would do our best to educate agency employees prior to the election, but that we would avoid polarizing our employees. In the end, 60% of the employees voted for the union, forcing the remaining 40% to join as well.

The unionization of our agency, and the perception by some Board members that I had somehow failed in this battle, was for me very discouraging and disappointing. I was further discouraged by having to back-pedal on holding our subcontractor accountable for unauthorized expenditures. Both the Board and the feds wanted this matter to go away.

Later in September, 2005, the fabric of my leadership team began to tear. The Director of Finance, whom I had hired in 2000, came into my office one morning and tearfully explained that she was going to have to resign her position in two weeks and rejoin her family in a different state. She left the agency and I assigned a recently hired Financial Analyst, who had a CPA and was a quick learner, as the interim Director of Finance. Rumor had it that one of the Board members was interested in temporarily leaving the Board to serve as the interim Director of Finance.

My annual performance review was typically conducted by the Board of Directors during the summer months, and formally presented to me in September for review and discussion. As planned, I met with some of the Board officers in the middle of September, 2005 and I received their feedback. It was a tense but civil meeting, not necessarily pleasant, but quite candid. A few days later Susie and I left for Kauai to enjoy a week-long vacation and have time to reflect on things.

Back in March, 2005, right in the midst of the union election, Susie and I were arriving at the Las Vegas Airport for a long weekend to celebrate my birthday. When we arrived, I felt quite discouraged and unhappy, and told Susie as we walked to collect our baggage that

I needed to find a new job. I loved the agency, loved the staff and loved helping make a difference in children's lives—but I was no longer able to devote my energy to the Mission of the agency. My time was taken up working with the Board, fending off the union, battling some of the subcontractors, and tap dancing around the political heat that often hit me and the agency. I knew in my heart at that moment in Las Vegas that it was time to make a change. How or when to make that change was another question.

Now it was the latter part of September, 2005, and I was back at work again after a vacation with Susie in Hawaii. I recalled that Steven Covey, in his series on the *Seven Habits Of Highly Effective Leaders*, observes that our ultimate freedom lies between the time of a specific event and our decision. That span of time, though it may feel like an instant, is where we have the freedom to make a choice. Life—in the end—is essentially the culmination of the choices we have made, both the good and bad ones.

A few days after returning from Hawaii I met with the Board Chair and Vice Chair on various matters, including my annual evaluation. It was a polite and brief meeting in my office. I noticed the Vice Chair was terribly nervous, and was having a hard time reading his notes. The Board Chair took over the discussion. I also had my notes prepared, and felt centered and comfortable in our back and forth on various items. We had a common objective. It was now a matter of the "how." Calm voices. Civil tones. Our meeting was concluded. We shook hands. They quietly left the building. Staff sensed something was happening.

A few months later, the agency's Winter, 2005 Newsletter had a very flattering front page article about me, and I felt good that others recognized some of the contributions I had made to the agency in that five and half year period. The Newsletter's front page also described the background of the interim executive director that came in a few weeks after I had resigned.

My last day on the job was Halloween of 2005. That date was coincidental, but my mischievous mind tempted me to dress up like Superman or a Mariachi on my last day on the job. That day was one of the saddest times in my life. A few hours before I was scheduled to leave the office, one of the senior managers hung a Hawaiian lei on my office door. Aloha means both hello and goodbye, and that afternoon I would be greeting a new chapter in my life, and bidding farewell to a very dear friend.

My wife Susie was my source of strength and faith during this transition. She kept reminding me that "everything happens for a reason", which I understand but it conflicted with my naïve belief that we control our destinies. One door closes and another opens. However, the time in between these two doors can seem like an eternity. Susie and I hoped that we could find a door that would takes us closer to our four adult children and our grandson, Evan.

I took a few weeks "off" to clear my head, reflect on the past five years, and go through some of the emotional and spiritual healing that comes with separation and change. I did some consulting work for a couple of clients; that was fun and it paid well. Several executive director jobs cropped up in other areas of California, as well as in the State of Washington and Nevada. I went through phone interviews at home, in my car and the Mall. Three jobs in California, for which I had applied remained on the radar screen for many months. One of the jobs called me back for five separate interviews, which required me to fly in to the area, rent a car, and pay for a hotel room each time. In the end, the Commission selected the Deputy Director for the job. Ironically, the agency is called the First Five Commission, which I suppose is why I had to go through the five interviews.

As I said before, my Dad passed away on June 9, 2006 in Laredo, Texas. I was unable to attend his funeral, which was very difficult. By a cruel coincidence I had been scheduled for a critically important final interview on the same day that my Dad was buried. Susie and my siblings all agreed that I should go ahead with the interview. The interview did not go well. I was sad and terribly distracted.

Life's Circles

Susie and I loaded our suitcases into the back of our Jeep Cherokee on a Friday, right before the long Labor Day weekend in 2006, and headed back onto Highway 5. Our beautiful condo had finally sold. The moving company had come by the day before, picked up all of our stuff and taken it to a local storage company for safe-keeping until such time as we settled into a new house.

We had put the condo up for sale just when the real estate bubble started to leak in California. Susie and I were fearful that we would have to take a giant loss in order to sell the condo. Susie, however, with her usual determination and faith, hired a realtor and over a period of several weeks, literally packed everything we had into boxes, while I was away starting the new job. As an added protection, she buried two statues of St. Joseph. One in the back yard and the other in the front yard, with the fervent belief that St. Joseph would intervene in the local real estate market dynamics and help get us a good price. Which he did.

Our drive was smooth. Traffic was thick, but moving at a steady pace. I had traveled this highway many times since moving back in 2000. The road was like the face of an old friend, with unique folds and wrinkles that gave it character and meaning. We reached a crest in the highway as we approached the rich agricultural green belt in the San Joaquin Valley.

Our lives are built on a delicate foundation woven with big and little circles, events and difficulties connected by the stream of choices that we have made. As a child, struggling with a severe stutter, I was somehow blessed with an abundance of optimism and a firm belief that I could accomplish most anything. This optimism is largely thanks to my being spoiled by my grandparents who made me feel like the center of the universe when I was growing up in Laredo. That optimistic view of life has carried me through scary journeys.

Some things in life are accidental, yet few things happen by accident.

Those five years in at the non-profit agency were a wonderful chapter in my life. And I miss it. By the same token, I now realize that it was also a journey that would have a beginning and an end. In between, those two points our agency team came together and collectively helped transform the organization, reshaping its character. Not perfectly. But I left with a deep sense of pride. My five years spent focusing on helping to turn around a wonderful agency are unforgettable. Ironically, these processes often do have a distinct starting point and a well-demarcated ending. Leadership is not about being tough. Most anyone can do that. Leadership is about making others feel stronger, because people are fundamentally good—even those on the unsettled side.

The circles of our lives were reconnected, merging into one. We were now going home, to reconnect with our children and friends. That is what life is about I suppose. Happiness and fulfillment in life seem to be about completing important circles. There is no distinct starting point or ending to these circles, but rather a stream of moments and opportunities, joined by the personal choices we make. I have been blessed with an ingrained optimism that has helped me navigate through hard and painful periods; completing important circles that connect our love, lives and destinies. Acknowledging that some circles are still incomplete, and may stay that way. Our life's circles intersect with those of others, producing new friendships, powerful relationships, creating new and uncharted pathways.

In life, I learned that one must trust the journey itself. Trust that some higher power, plus the energy and love of our family, will get us through those painful and difficult turns.

There are more circles in my life left to complete. So far life has been a good journey and will continue to be if we can just convert our weaknesses into strengths, and ensure that our strengths do not become our weaknesses.

As we approached the northern edge of the beautiful San Joaquin Valley, Susie held my hand, and both of us knew that this was a very special moment.

The circle was now complete. We were back home.

Imagine me and you, I do
I think about you day and night, it's only right
To think about the girl you love and hold her tight
So happy together.

If I should call you up, invest a dime
And you say you belong to me and ease my mind
Imagine how the world could be, so very fine
So happy together.

Song by The Turtles

BIOGRAPHY

ADOLFO H. MUÑOZ

Adolfo, born and raised in Laredo, Texas some sixty-three years ago, has had a multi-faceted career, the most memorable stint being a seasonal farmworker shortly after graduating from high school. When people insist on asking about his "ethnicity," he prefers to describe himself as a *Tejano*, noting that he has only been to Mexico five times and never stepped foot in Spain. But that is another story.

During the past thirty-five plus years, Adolfo and his lovely wife, Susie, have lived in many different parts of the United States including San Antonio, Washington, D.C., Los Angeles and Irvine, California, the San Francisco East Bay and the San Joaquin Valley. Adolfo and Susie, have four adult children that includes a set of triplets. Their oldest son, Adolfo IV, was born in Washington, D.C. and Jose, Miguel and Mercedes, the triplets, were born in San Antonio, Texas. All four adult children now live in the San Francisco Bay Area. Adolfo and Susie have one grandson, Evan Muñoz, who turned five in August, 2008, and who is carrying on the Muñoz family tradition of humor, love of sports and resistance to authority.

Adolfo enjoys cooking *Tejano* food, sharing odd jokes, strumming the guitar, playing tennis, traveling to Hawaii with his wife, and persistently trying to master the art of Texas Hold-Em.

On the more serious side, his career path has included being a senior executive with an international management consulting firm. Adolfo was Vice President of Development Associates, Inc., an international management and governmental consulting firm headquartered in the Washington, D.C. area for some twenty years. During his tenure with Development Associates he directed all marketing and business development efforts for the company in the West Coast region and led major training, research and evaluation consulting projects. Adolfo has worked in various parts of the globe and served as Chief of Party on numerous international assignments in countries such as Colombia, Peru, Bolivia, Cyprus, Nepal, Nicaragua, Tunisia, Kenya and Botswana.

Subsequent to his work in the management consulting industry, he jumped into the non-profit and governmental sectors serving as executive director of a large non-profit organization based in California. Adolfo and Susie later moved back to Northern California in 2006 where he is an administrator with a local county governmental entity.

He claims that he has more degrees than a thermometer with a BA in Psychology, Masters in Education, and a PhD in Organizational Psychology. Adolfo is an organizational psychologist specializing in change management consulting. He has concentrated on research in the areas of human motivation, interaction and performance. He has specialized in the identification and analysis of work and leadership behavioral styles, and the application of various behavioral science models in training programs focusing on organizational change, cross-cultural business practices, managing a diverse workforce, gender-based style differences and building high-performance work teams.

CHAPTER EIGHTEEN

THE LOVE OF MAKING ART
Jo Ann Brown-Scott

As a kid in Ohio, I remember my first attempts at drawing mountains that I had never seen or heard about except in books. Rows of tall pointy cone-shapes filled my paper, sometimes with stick-shaped pine trees clinging desperately to the steep slopes, slanted at forty-five degree angles instead of growing straight up. How does a pine tree grow on the side of a mountain anyway, I wondered? Next came horses and then fashion drawings of women in every conceivable mode of dress. At some later point I picked up speed and took a giant leap from realistic life-drawing to realistic landscapes to non-traditional watercolor landscapes to semi-abstracted watercolor landscapes using mixed media collage to abstract acrylic collage landscapes and then finally stuck pretty solidly for many years in contemporary mixed media collage landscapes in the style of abstract expressionism. I am surprised by what I am painting now—ethnically flavored African images and Indonesian fabric-collage abstractions. I have evolved another notch or two and it feels good.

For as long as I can remember art has been on my mind, consuming the hours when I am free to let my mind wander and even stealing many of the hours that should be spent on other practicalities. In the times when I am not actually physically painting, sometimes for months at a time, as I work on my writing (writing is so very similar to painting), I am still painting in my mind's eye. I continue to see images in my head and I store away the ideas for later—looking forward with anticipation to the day when I can pick up the brushes again, wondering what will happen on the canvas when I do. I see everything in color, texture and pattern. I am fascinated with layer upon layer of color, using acrylic paint sometimes thinned like watercolor wash and other times as thick as frosting, combined with prisma color pencils, inks, exotic papers, and fabric in the creation of some highly textured image on canvas where you can run your hand across it and feel its sculptural qualities in high relief. I love light against shadow; dark against light, black contrasted with white, as in new snow powdered against dark evergreen trees turning them into giant etchings. I am into faces now, of ethnic people who have wisdom in their eyes.

In all fairness and truth, art showed up on my mother's side of the family tree too. Mom's sister was a fine painter, and so I guess the gene came to me from both directions. But Dad was my favorite fine artist. He had a block of clay on a stand in the family room and after we went to bed at night he had mom lower her blouse so he could sculpt her likeness. He also re-finished furniture, he painted, he sketched and he was an interior designer. He was creatively gifted at so many things and he knew another artistic soul when he saw one. When he noticed I liked to draw, I was signed up at the Dayton Art Institute for Saturday morning classes in watercolor. I must have been seven or eight. I felt nervous; inadequate for the challenges of such an imposing, monumental establishment, perched on the banks of the river as I remember, with a wide formal staircase up to the arched doors—but in some ways it validated for me very early on that I was an artist, and I was different. None of my other friends attended—no one else was interested in spending their Saturday morning sleep-in time away in the city in art classes. During this time, when a public school art teacher questioned me for deviating from the natural color of something, I knew she was not a true artist at all; just a pretender, because any true artist would know about artistic license granting you the privilege for color changes if you thought they were aesthetically necessary for your image.

In high school I began to demonstrate brief glints of artistic eccentricity in my evolving personality and lifestyle. Orange was my favorite color for four years straight. This preference eventually mellowed and deepened to a lovely shade of bittersweet and then russet. But even in its subdued forms it was deviant enough, in the opinion of my mother, to be considered an overt indication of rebellion. Orange seemed a clear indication that I was going to do something exceedingly reckless and/or stupid. Like run off and get married way too soon, possibly even while pregnant, because in her mind those were the worst indications of rebellion she might ever have to endure as a parent—the absolute ultimate. (It was a simpler time—no drugs and barely any beer in high school.) I was constantly talked out of any clothing in my favorite color and pushed into something more practical, which equaled boring to me. I yearned for personality and style and instead I got gray or green or turquoise blue, her favorite color. She didn't know that at that point in time her fears for my irresponsibility were groundless. My serious stupidity surfaced much later when I favored Prussian blue for my last two years of college.

In college art classes during the sixties I wasn't yet sure myself if I was eccentric enough to be an artist of high achievement. I felt sort of confident I had the talent but I was sure I lacked the angst. I had "artists" on a high pedestal of worldliness and sophistication and I doubted my artistic gene. I felt counterfeit. I was just a little too practical for my own taste. And I was bland. My cheeks were not sunken—I longed for a more exotic and angular face, on top of longer legs and substantial, earth-mother breasts. I knew I would have to over-compensate in other areas to fill the weak void left by those juicier body parts. I refused to do drugs or smoke pot, however, in spite of the perfection of those choices in defining me as an artist of deep seriousness, so the two most available and stereotypical artistic traits of the times that nearly everyone else in the art department used and abused were out of the question for me. I feared the loss of control and I was sure that I would like them too much and slide off the deep end of life. So I was not being noble; I was being unadventurous, in my opinion. I thought about becoming a YPSL—a member of the campus Young People's Socialist League. But here was the biggest obstacle to all of my reckless ideas—I was a member of a reputable national sorority, with dress codes and scholastic standards and curfews, and I had responsibilities to that group, to myself and to my parents to be a good girl. Ahhh the contradictions of life. But isn't it true that we are more defined by the wishes that are not granted in life as by those that are?

My first-ever college level art class was Sculpture 101. I arrived eager and intimidated. In the spare, cold, bare-floored room with the tall windows, standing off to one side was a dirty-haired, barefoot, Bohemian looking woman smoking a cigarette. She had on a man's shirt that hung nearly to her knees. The shirt was not even buttoned, just pulled together and held that way by her crossed arms. I knew she was naked underneath and I was looking at my first live nude model. When the time came, she stepped up onto the model's platform, and without the slightest second of hesitation she dropped the shirt in one fast move into a pile on the floor at her feet and took a pose. We all saw that she was quite obviously pregnant. Those curves, those firmly packed round shapes; that confident attitude she assumed—I was instantly hooked—I was gone—I was into that class, heart and soul. There would be no turning back. That first class alone, lasting three hours, fed my desire for artistic grit and provided me with a nice jump-start toward artistic seriousness. To think that I got to attend class twice a week for the entire semester was like pure dope to me.

Later in life my real art genes kicked in a little more forcefully as I got more perspective on my lonely childhood, including my parents' divorce. Those memories, plus a weird and wonderful group of college art professors, introduced the arrival of intensity to my art that I had been searching and waiting for, and I was no longer quite so concerned with my apple pie face and figure. Gradually the character crept into my creative expression and I loosened up and let my guts hang out a little further onto the paper and canvas. Thank God for bizarre parents and a period of darkness in my otherwise sunny life. I needed all the help I could get in my journey toward depth. One of my best paintings during that time was a huge abstract piece, all craggy with collage paper and bold color in orange, indigo and white. I titled it *Fire and Rain.*

Much later, in my thirties, for a pivotal period of time I became lonely and less spirited in my enthusiasm for life in general and to fill the void, I painted with authentic passion, I thought. The more faintly dim my spirit grew, the lonelier I got, and the more intensely and brilliantly I painted. I was once told by a man who commissioned a custom piece of art from me that I was probably unable to paint at my best when I was unhappy, or experiencing drama in my life, because I was sensitive and easily bruised emotionally. Oh give me a break. Quite the opposite, you fool. I gave Oscar winning paper and canvas performances during the Viet Nam War when my husband was away for a year, again and again during the illnesses and deaths and divorces of various friends and family, and again after 9/11—and this ability to paint through my emotions and use them to my advantage is a trait that most artists and actors cherish. We have a tendency to categorize and store the emotions away and then pull them out to daylight again just when we know we need them. The soul is never empty of material for art.

In my mid-thirties as the ball began to roll with my artwork I did not at first even realize or believe that there was a ball at all, much less that it was moving. I saw every small success as a fluke—an isolated and quirky bit of luck, just enough to keep my spirits up. It took a creative epiphany to wake me up from the fog.

In my life that ran parallel to being a mom, a wife, a cook, a laundress, a gardener, and meticulous housekeeper, and even while holding a string of part-time jobs (in addition to everything else) that were art and design related, I was a maniac painter in my soul. I woke in the early morning seeing abstract compositions in the wrinkles of the sheets as I cracked open my eyes. I painted off and on all day long and then dreamed about paintings when I slept again. Nothing was wasted in the creative process. Listening to music inspired me. Cooking gave me color and textural ideas. I walked with my wise dog-guru, golden retriever mix and I remembered and re-used vistas we enjoyed in the great outdoors. I drove to the grocery and saw the familiar mountain horizons in a different light of day each time.

I had channeled my private loneliness into something constructive. I was not an alcoholic. I was not unfaithful. I did not have an eating disorder, or a sexual disorder, or any great need for compulsive exercise. I did wash my hands a lot but it was because they were always covered with paint. I didn't have the slightest need to experiment with sleeping pills or drugs—I didn't want my mental images to get any fuzzier than they already were or I'd have trouble painting them. Every feeling I had was odd enough by itself without being artificially enhanced, and reality made my art complex enough. I even had my appetite for chocolate mostly under control. So all the indications of my disgustingly normal behavior that I had found so counterfeit in high school and college were now saving me from surrender to addictions, deep depression and sloth. My normalness was my best friend at last. I saw that as the good news and the bad news, since being so normal was still not attractive to me.

But I kept painting. It was a true addiction, but of the soul to the art. Could be a whole lot worse, I thought. Still I doubted my full potential as an artist—could I make the leap to painting on a steady basis? It seemed pretty steady to me already, so given a little more focus and time, perhaps there was no telling what I might be able to do with it. Still I had no idea how to begin to jump into the serious world of art. What to paint, who to show it to and how to ask for real money for it all seemed daunting to me.

During this time, an instructor in a continuing education course I attended (several years after college was past me) asked, in our second class session as we were all painting along, what I was doing in her class. *Oh my God*—I am a failure, I thought. I am actually correct about myself—in spite of my degree, I am no good. I was momentarily emotionally destroyed, quietly in my mind, until she further explained that I should be painting with the serious intention to sell—and that I should be teaching her class instead of her. She told me that she already knew I was born to paint by watching me, because it came so intuitively. I was stunned by her remark, and amazed at her frankness and generosity in giving me that encouraging compliment. But on that particular day, as I left her class, I was disgusted with myself. Why hadn't I arrived at this conclusion on my own? Why was I so lacking in self-esteem?

I pulled into the parking space near the door to the art shop and stopped in a split second, yanked on the hand break and jumped out of the car. Music form *The Big Chill* soundtrack that had been blaring stopped instantly. I was mad at myself for being such a self-doubting, chicken-shit fool. All grown up and no place to go in the career department; sick and tired of being directionless. In the three or so minutes it took to get a tube of titanium white paint and walk to the line at the checkout stand I knew that something in me had snapped like a big fat rubber-band. In one glorious firecracker explosion of truth I decided I would rather take my chances at being alone and broke, with the wise dog-guru and a highly accessorized tent if necessary, than stay in my bad mind place wondering what might have been if I could not ever take the risk.

There was a lapel pin that I had noticed many times before in a display at the art supply store counter that said "Potential Bag Lady" (every artist's worst fear, thus a sure sale to the insecure and impulsive). I grabbed it up and pinned it proudly to the black ball cap that I was wearing. I must have uttered an audible growl of determination because four people in line looked at me as if I were a danger to society, stepping back and away, looking right and left at each other for comfort.

I smiled broadly and stared them all down with a wild, blue-eyed look that seemed to say, "Don't mess with me! I am a woman with a mission." My face, flushed with exhilaration and surrounded by springy curls made wilder by my sudden rise in temperature, looked demented, I was sure. I straightened the ball cap, paid for the paint and the pin and practically dove for the door. Additional innocent bystanders quickly cleared a path for me. Mothers clutched their children close. The clerk looked like he was trying to remember the number for 911 while checking the height measurements along the side of the door. She is DANGEROUSLY NUTS they all must have feared—she might have a problem with drugs or booze, everyone told me in their expressions. But then I was gone, like Zorro art-girl in the night.

My God. What a natural high you can get on just rough sandpaper emotion I thought to myself as I started the car and headed for home. Adrenaline kicks butt. *I knew I had had an epiphany of the best kind.* In so brief a time span that it made my head crackle with excitement, I had pushed into that narrow window of time, of drastic action, that is critical to the process of success. I finally knew undeniably that the perfect cosmic moment had come to dam the torpedoes, jump off the proverbial cliff, take the big bite, and make the no-guts-no-glory move. The wise dog-woman guru and I and the art thing were on a course as of that instant. There would be no turning back. Throw the spaghetti directly into the fan and let someone else scrape it off the ceiling for a change.

I allowed the activity of painting to sweep me away. I felt used by the power of it. I seemed to be a rider on a head-strong horse, feeling the muscular motion underneath me and getting where I wanted to go but not feeling in total control of the journey. It felt large and it felt energizing. It gave me life. The process of painting became my ritual and my solace. After a few more months of warm-up time I gradually began to sell the art faster than I could paint it. I wrapped myself in a warm, creative energy that had a life of its own and in my quiet and busy surprise, I just followed the odyssey.

You build up a head of steam. If you're four days out of the studio, on the fifth day you really crash in there. You will kill anybody who disturbs you on that fifth day, when you desperately need it. Susan Rothenberg

My instructor helped me to more clearly define my style, re-introduced me to the technique of mixed media collage and my paintings began to sell in local summer festivals and exhibits. Soon the artwork was enjoying high recognition from local critics along with an unexpected sort of popularity with yuppies purchasing Parade of Homes type residences.

It made a strong and confident statement in the Denver gallery scene. But the art world was a fickle one, I knew, and I had to ride my success along as far as I could. The journey was mildly intoxicating, and it kept me on the best creative edge I had ever been able to sustain. Nothing like success to stoke the artistic fire in my soul, I thought. After all, timing is everything, and it came just when I needed it most.

For about seven or eight years, maybe ten, I was a passenger on the train to success, looking out the window at things rushing by in a blur. I was enjoying one of those brief windows of time in life when your stars are all aligned and you are doing what you love and the money does begin to follow. Galleries called, art was placed, shows were scheduled and things took off. At one point I was in twelve galleries in four states and every once in a while in that frenzy I had a moment when I could not have told you which of my paintings was where, even while keeping good records. One of my affiliations was with a chain of galleries and they could transfer pieces from place to place, even across state lines, without my knowledge or approval. They also had auctions from time to time and any of my inventory that had become lost in the shuffle could and would be sold to the highest bidder on some sleazy auction circuit that I had no way of knowing about or getting paid for. I had lost my grip, which was easy to do when people were not being honest with me about what had sold and when it had sold. Art of my style was hot and the gallery owners were playing it fast and loose; not paying me on time and living off the fat of the land which was my borrowed money. In the ski resort towns the gallery owners were the worst offenders, living the high life. I heard stories from the locals about expensive dinners out every night, champagne flowing, wine-ing and dining local big-wigs and limousines just to go across town and pick up other artists flying into the airport. When I had difficulty getting paid for winter ski season sales and it dragged into the summer months until my checks arrived I knew I was being used.

I learned that if you are successful as an artist and you or a trusted manager can maintain creative and financial control, enjoy those times and stay on top of the situation. If you are completely on your own, and the joyful job of painting is crowded out by tracking down inventory and scrambling to get paid on time, then watch out. Periods of wild success are often fleeting. It is a very difficult task to maintain a consistent level of success as an artist over an entire lifetime. In addition to the problems already mentioned the art world is a fickle and trendy universe in which to time travel. You can be out as fast as you got in. Circumstances change and politics influences people's choices and if there is one thing that is a sure thing, it is that the economy will eventually change. Everything in life fluctuates. In my situation, Ronald Reagan showed the world that he enjoyed realistic western art and the Kuwait War happened. Those two undeniable facts were all it took for my art to be out of favor. Galleries that had been selling contemporary abstract art began to close or morph into Western galleries and because of the war, the economy took a dive (art and other luxury items are the first things to reflect that kind of change) so the ball started rolling downhill for many of us in the art world.

As the shift happened, I moved on to other more dependable positions in teaching interior design and marketing. My window of opportunity had slowed and then nearly closed completely. The train to success became more of a traveling bus. But I am forever grateful that I had the experience of crazy success and chaotic opportunity. It was exhilarating and fun and I learned a lot. Since that time I have continued to paint and show my art, but not as frantically.

Circumstances changed. Have I changed? No—how I do what I do has been altered but I have not changed. I have showed my art in fewer galleries and at visiting shows and in private invitation-only situations. Experiences have influenced me and carried me in new, wider directions. Travel is the best inspiration for me—it offers me instant desire to pick up the paintbrush. I have slipped slowly into a different, more ethnic style of painting that combines well with some African art and artifacts that a friend of mine and I were importing. Oddly I find myself doing figurative art—demonstrating my fascination for a face etched with character or the wisdom of a person's eyes or a woman in colorful native dress. I like a primitive theme; I enjoy tribal colors and pattern and the raw beauty of an abstract composition with a hint of Africa implied. This love of Africa came decades before the African import business—but exactly where it originated is a mystery to me. Is it from a life before? Perhaps there have been other volumes in the book of my life. Because life itself is the fuel for my creativity.

I admit that I have become less driven as I have gotten older; or perhaps just driven in other directions. What has been substituted for the chaos of fleeting success is a more quiet intensity to do better work and keep growing as an artist. Landscapes do not grab me much anymore as a subject for my art; in real life, however, they are my constant drug of choice. I need to see vistas and far horizons. But now, more than mountains, it is the ocean that pulls me.

Making art is very much like making love; it *is* making love in a sense. It transports you. It has the potential to take you out of the moment and into bliss. The exercise is tactile and sensuous. The ritual begins as always but you are never sure where it will take you. It could be delicate; it could be strong. You are leaving on a journey. It comes over you like the ebb and flow of powerful waves on a beach you have visited somewhere before in time. You are one with the rhythm of the moon tide. You are traveling on a light breeze whistling through tall lavender-tipped grass on a distant seaside meadow and then you are following a procession of some ancient people winding high to a mountaintop. You have left the confining time of your life and are in a moving sphere where ages and universes overlap and you see the space of time stretching back to the beginning and then coming forward to now and beyond to the never. You hear nothing but you hear everything. You understand the perfection of life and why snow falling softly on evergreen trees in deep December can make you weep. You understood the loneliness of the sea, why men are still drawn to it and why the aching moan of the wind can move you to unutterable emotion. You sit on warm buffalo robes while natives chant and their images dance in the firelight reflected on the fabric of your tent. In one afternoon you can be gone to everywhere and back to here again, all rosy-cheeked and out of breath with exhilaration.

As with affairs of the heart involving lovers and marital partners, it is priceless to find one particular passionate pursuit that will carry you through all the decades of your life; one that consistently remains the "bottom-line passion" to all of your other activities and interests. The attraction must be strong enough, it must be intriguing enough, it must be changeable and mysterious and challenging enough to keep you fully engaged, with a tight hold on your heart and soul. When you have a love for a creative pursuit to that high degree, it is not dependent upon whether or not it is earning you money or fame—it is beyond that. If the money comes with it, that is certainly a great bonus, but in the times when it does not, you are no less the dedicated lover of that passion than you were before. You are no less gifted at it than before. You must not allow your estimation of your talent in that passion to change...you are the same gifted person you were before circumstances changed.

When you ask yourself questions, as do I, about where you are heading and what your destiny is, try this. Think of your life as an artistic creation born of love and gratitude for the good fortune of just being alive—a blank canvas upon which combinations of color, pattern and texture are recorded as your life's experiences unfold—as in a fine work of art. This piece of art reveals deep, complicated areas in the composition where the most intense portions of your life story are told, light areas where the inspiration and love has come to you, faded areas where the worn and weathered past has been lovingly recorded over the years. This painting is your diary, your journal, your memoir of every decade you have lived. You can see it in your mind as though it were a mural spread out before you on a large wall. You can see parts of it that offer comfort and warmth against the cold and become a soft place to look at when you are tired. You can see other stories in the mural that explain how you became who you are and perhaps even where you are headed next. This life-mural has everything you ever need to know woven into the composition in a simple recording of your truth. If you are unsure, or troubled by some problem, look deep into your life's art for the answers. And when you hear your inner voice speaking to you—when your personal mission statement is clearly and confidently stated again and again at the very center of all the activity in the painting, in the moments when you most need to hear it, you have had an epiphany. Your mastery of your creativity is revealed in how you incorporate this message of epiphany into your life. It is a wise and gifted person who knows his reason for being; it is a creative person who can sustain that purpose through many incarnations over an entire lifetime.

BIOGRAPHY

JO ANN BROWN-SCOTT

I grew up in Ohio on eight acres of green rolling hillside, until we moved to Dayton View when I was thirteen or so. I attended the University of Colorado in Boulder, chosen for its art department and its location in the West, and never returned, knowing I had found my favorite part of the world. I graduated with a BFA, having developed a passion for contemporary painting and sculpture in addition to studies in English literature and psychology.

I married, had two wonderful children; and then eventually moved to Evergreen, Colorado in 1976 where we raised our family for a number of years. It was there I began to sell my artwork professionally.

In 1984 I was commissioned by the Evergreen Chamber of Commerce to create an original painting—a snowy winter scene, reminiscent of the mountain area around Evergreen at Christmas time—from which the very first *Christmas in Evergreen Limited Edition Posters and Christmas Cards* were printed and sold. That endeavor was a huge success for our lovely mountain community and the following year began a tradition of the Evergreen Christmas Poster Contest which was then opened to all local artists.

1988-1991 I taught a three-credit class of my own development for the Interior Design Department at Arapahoe Community College in Littleton, Colorado, instructing designers in accessorizing interior spaces using art, antiques, collections and found objects.

I have held various interior design related positions with home furnishing establishments in the Denver area and I have also managed an exclusive interior design fabric shop.

1996-2001 I was employed by a prominent financial advisory firm in Greenwood Village, Colorado where I was Client Manager, responsible for new business development and marketing. I also assisted in editing a non-fiction financial book authored by my employer and was then appointed Director of Marketing for that book.

Concurrently with the various professional positions I have held, I have continued to paint and show my art, represented through the years by galleries in the mountain resort areas of Colorado and the West. For many years I was one of the few local Denver artists represented by a prominent chain of galleries based in Denver, which represented internationally known contemporary and old world artists with locations throughout Colorado and the West.

More recently I was a partner in an import business called UBUNTU with my friend and colleague Christine Mahree Fowler, importing African art and artifacts. During this time my art took on an ethnic, tribal theme which has remained a strong influence.

Recently I have shown my art in the Cherry Creek area of Denver, but in 2006 I relocated to northern California and I am currently showing at private shows by invitation only.

My paintings are most often mixed-media collage on canvas—using acrylic paint, inks and exotic papers and often Indonesian fabrics. Themes include an African Series, a Tapestry Series, an Italian Series and a 3-Dimensional Paper Construction Series called The Rituals, using scrolled papers embellished with beads and tokens.

For my complete art resume and bio please visit www.tenspeedstudio.com and read Chapter Eighteen in my first book, *Epiphany and Her Friends—Intuitive Realizations That have Changed Women's Lives.*

CHAPTER NINETEEN

DIAMONDS, KIDS AND KARMA
Laura Susskind

I'm not one of those naturally creative types. I can't draw, paint, sculpt, or even sew. For that matter, I don't iron, either, but that's because, after spending half an hour "perfecting" that special garment, it doesn't look any better. Growing up in Iowa City in the 1960's, though, I was fortunate to have a full range of art and music classes offered at Lincoln Elementary School.

My friend's parents proudly displayed their kid's art work in the kitchen, for all to see. These masterpieces were plastered on walls and refrigerators with glow-in-the-dark Caspar the friendly ghost magnets, and reminders about Girl Scout meetings and grocery lists. My mom, however, hung her favorite school art projects way downstairs, in our dark and dank laundry room. This was not a huge issue for me personally, as (who's counting) my older sister Diane had eleven projects pinned onto the cedar wood above the Frigidaire chest freezer, and my brothers together contributed another sixteen pieces. My count was only three, and that's if you included my bright green and yellow pinch pot that mom stuck behind the towels in the downstairs laundry room. That pot was really my first attempt at a jewelry box.

I forgot to mention that I can't sing or dance either. My mom and I share way too many things, but our favorite saying, one that our family is sick and tired of hearing, is that in our next life I'll come back as a singer, and she'll come back as a dancer and we'll both have flat stomachs. (She, unlike me, can carry a tune, and was even in glee club.) The truth is that regardless of my singing inability, I did sing to my three boys when they were young. Loudly. Payback is a bitch. Two of the three inherited my lack of a singing gene, and now I have to listen to them sing at the top of their lungs! But, thank goodness, all three have flat stomachs, like their dad.

What I do well is have an undeniable love for jewelry. Any kind of rings, bracelets, or earrings will be fine, thank you very much. I don't go for anklets, or multiple piercings, which is probably tied to my conservative Iowa upbringing. This selective conservatism is illustrated well by a chat I had with my college son Matt. He couldn't understand why I wouldn't fork over two thousand dollars for some fancy "rims" for my car. First of all, I explained, I'm from Iowa and your daddy is from West Virginia. You grew up in California, where flashy rims are as common as plastic surgery. Not where we come from, I told him. And besides, if I had an extra two thousand dollars, I'd buy diamonds. Any diamonds. "You already look like a disco ball," he said.

Yes, I do love diamonds! Unfortunately, they don't come cheaply; think of the price difference between ribbons by the yard and diamonds by the yard. Since the jewelry I make doesn't contain diamonds, I sell the pieces I've created with semi-precious stones and fresh water pearls to enable me to fund my addiction. I work with the "a through z" collection of materials—from azurite to zebra jasper. "D" in my inventory, is for druzy quartz, not diamond. Once in a while I splurge and buy sapphire or ruby beads. But these pieces undeniably end up being 'pour moi'. Because, after all, diamonds look great with all colors, and red blue are especially nice.

I have been happily making jewelry for four years now. All I really do is string beads. I once took a four hour wire-wrapping course at the local bead shop. They promised I'd make a pair of professional looking earrings and a matching bracelet to take home. After eight hours, I had one sorry looking earring finished. The instructor was very sweet. "Wire wrapping isn't for everyone," she said. And in two seconds flat she had twisted and mashed out a matching earring for me. "You should stick with stringing," were her final words.

My beads sell in fancy places like the Napa Valley, Maui, Hawaii, San Francisco, and Benicia, California (at a world renowned glass blower's studio). I even had some things in a nice store in my hometown of Iowa City. But mostly I do local art shows and have lovely parties at friend's homes where we drink wine and talk about the latest trends in jewelry and fashion. I go on field trips to Neiman Marcus, Sac's Fifth Avenue and Nordstrom to see what's hot. And I actually have to "read" magazines like *In Style* and *Lucky* and *Vogue* to stay on top of the latest trends. It's a tough job, but someone has to do it.

Let me say, right now, that I do believe in karma, that things happen for a reason, that the good guy wins, and that diamonds are forever. If those things weren't true, how could a jewelry-loving girl from Iowa meet her prince and the love of her life whose family happens to OWN A JEWELRY STORE? And a "fine jewelry" store, one that deals in diamonds, rubies, sapphires, emeralds, and gold—not sterling silver or lucite. (That they weren't an authorized Rolex dealer didn't matter back then. It would take me another twenty-four years and several Omega watches to appreciate the thick, beautiful Rolex face.)

My husband, Mark, and I met as if it'd been scripted. We were both on spring break in Palm Springs, California. I, who was soon to be a Boston University graduate, stayed with my grandparents (my grandpa called it "Palm's gotta Springs). Mark, taking a break from Duke University Medical School, visited his grandmother (who founded the afore mentioned jewelry store in Fairmont, West Virginia).

Our grandparents didn't know each other. Rather, in a throwback to our heritage, we were victims of a yenta. A matchmaker. You know the story: "Nice Jewish girl needs to meet nice Jewish boy," and vice versa. It was the grandparents' dessert mantra. Mark was just plain naïve. But, I'd been subjected to this scheme on several other occasions while visiting my grandparents. One spring break, my cousin and I had to play hostesses to two sons of my grandparent's friends. I got the short, pimply, curly-haired boy who wore one of those black skeleton shirts where the neck bones stop and your head completes the picture. Yuck! He was as creepy as his t-shirt.

I didn't have high hopes for the latest match. My brother Jeff was also visiting. The "Palms Gotta Springs" yenta stories by now were legendary in my family, and I instructed my brother rigorously. "No matter how nice I am to my date (it will all be an act) your brotherly duty is to get rid of him. No exceptions!" Luckily, Jeff failed in ridding me of Mark, although he did receive an academy award for trying!

In all honesty, I don't think I knew right away Mark's family was in the jewelry business. We spent a dreamy week together with perfect chemistry, swimming, shopping, playing racquetball, and even driving in to Santa Monica Beach one day. It didn't hurt that he was graduating medical school. The details aren't important, but two years later I was wearing my very own marquis diamond engagement ring, straight out of my new family's very own fancy jewelry store! (Of course now that lovely diamond has been transformed into a handsome pendant, because, after all, we've been married over twenty years, and that calls for something very special—and large!) Three years later we were married.

Once when I was young, we were driving home from a family reunion in Omaha. My dad saw a white Cadillac on the side of the rode. Believing it was my grandparent's car, we stopped to assist the stranded vehicle. It turned out it wasn't my grandparents at all, but the driver was a nice man who happened to be a candy salesman. In appreciation of our help, we were showered with a myriad of candy samples. My parents and siblings were thrilled. We all got sick stuffing our faces with candy on the four hour drive home. "We couldn't have chosen anyone better to rescue," my sister Diane said of our candy salesman's occupation. "Just think if he'd have sold jewelry," I said.

My remark came as no surprise to my sister. We were like night and day. I was a priss, she was athletic. I was gregarious, she was a loner. She was intellectual, I was average. I lived for the day, she thought about tomorrow. (Maybe that was part of her being intellectual?) We had lots of time to dwell on our differences, as we shared a very small room. The house we grew up in is all glass and cedar planks, and although it's still a show piece, when it was being built, mom and dad had to scale it down, and the two kids' bedrooms were given the partial ax. Even now, over forty years later, the house is a contemporary beauty, one that cars are forever slowing down to see.

One difference between us that was to my advantage was that Diane didn't like jewelry. Score! It's not like we had tons of expensive pieces, but we were both Bat Mitzvahed. Score! To this day she blames me for losing her pink star sapphire and diamond ring. But how could I be at fault? I loved that ring! I also had her add-a-pearl necklace, never fully completed, from Aunt Liz, who religiously sent us another pearl for every birthday and Hanukkah. Do they even make them any more?

The ironic thing is that I now have three boys, who, at least for now—until they're married?—could also not care less about jewels. (At least there's no one to borrow my things?!) Diane has a boy and a girl, and eventually I had to cough up all the trinkets she'd "loaned me" over the years.

It's a little far-fetched, but my fantasy of coming to the rescue of a jewelry salesman—not a candy salesman—did (kind of) come true... Sure, Mark is the only son of a family of jewelers. And, although I like to think I've rescued him from living in the small town of Fairmont, West Virginia (population thirty thousand), I don't for a minute think he would have settled there. But, fate and karma combined to attach me, forever, to an aspiring doctor whose parents owned, gasp! a jewelry store. Not bad for a girl from Iowa.

One thing I will forever thank my in-laws for, besides producing their darling son, is turning me on to the world's largest gem and jewelry show, held every February in Tucson, Arizona. It's amazing! The entire town transforms into an international bazaar featuring—jewelry! Every ornamental material known to mankind is there. They even sell moon rocks and pieces of asteroids that fell to earth, to wear in rings and pendants!

Imagine seeing table after table with cereal size bowls filled with rubies, emeralds, and sapphires. And huge tents filled with strands of other gem stones like topaz, amethyst and aqua marine. There are literally fresh water pearls by the sea full. Every size, shape and color of stones I hadn't even known existed surrounded me: rhodalite, appatite, hessanite and demantoid garnets. It was this endless collection of gems which fueled my pre-existing fascination with jewelry, which got me to thinking. If I truly loved all these things, why couldn't I learn to string my own pieces? How hard could it be?

I started off slowly, purchasing only a few strands. By this time, my three boys were teenagers. I was pushing forty-five, and still teased that I didn't know what I wanted to be when I grew up. I'd kept myself involved in their earlier lives by substitute teaching at their school, even in their classrooms. As they matured, we all realized high school wasn't for me. This was their journey. But I still wanted to be part of their lives.

The idea of not rushing out the door in the morning to teach thrilled me. I loved my art-filled house, and was anxious to spend time there enjoying the ambiance we'd created. Mark and I had spent years collecting art we loved; two Leroy Neimans, and several sculptures by a local artist are my favorite pieces. But who ever had time to enjoy them or the house? My life at home, while teaching, had been cooking, cleaning, cooking, sleeping and cooking. Teenage boys live to eat.

So I set up my jewelry supplies in the middle of the kitchen...And there it was! My own private epiphany! I'd combined my love of jewelry with my love of family! Here I could be so engrossed in creating, that, of course, I couldn't hear about the weekend parties or the skipping school plans of my children and their various friends! I became such a permanent fixture that the kids didn't realize my "mom antennae" were always on red alert. I spent long hours connecting with my kids' girlfriends while beading. And it was Matt's girlfriend Brittany who introduced me to her friend Sarah who managed "the" local gallery in town. I was in business!

On a final note—it's one thing to buy beads. It's truly something else to string them in such a way that someone actually wants to buy them. As I said before, I am not a creative person...But within these walls is a creative karma I can't deny. The woman responsible for building our house, and its first owner, is an artist in the real sense of the word. She put her heart and soul into creating this house. Her attachment to it is best illustrated by her inviting my entire family—including my three small boys—over so she could "give us some specifics regarding the house." She showed us where she hung her canvases, and how she drew inspiration from the clear oval duck pond below. I marveled at the details she had included in the house: four tall, cream colored pillars in the entry way, a great room large enough for a full-size pool table (a necessity for three growing boys and their friends), and a master bathroom to die for. With pink and grey marble and a sunken Jacuzzi tub, it's the perfect retreat. Her beautiful canvases hung everywhere. They were colorful, traditional acrylic paintings that gave this French country-style home a feeling of old world charm. She even toured us through the non-descript garage. My pre-school son Jacob saw her brand new grey Porsche Carrera. "Wow, does that car come with the house?" he asked.

No, neither the Porsche nor any of her paintings remain. She took them all when she moved out. We tried to buy one of her works, but couldn't afford the five zero price tag. She did leave behind several murals she painted on the walls and she also left her philosophy of life.

The words that spoke to her soul are painted above the kitchen sinks in lilac calligraphy and say:

"Food, Art, Reality, Hope, Life, Literature, Liberte."

Although her unique words to live by aren't necessarily my own personal philosophy, nor do they mention anything about family, karma or beaded jewelry, or even diamonds—they are still meaningful to me. And I know if I ever move out of this special home, I, too, will be leaving something inspirational for the next owner: hundreds of tiny beads that have found their way into the woodwork of this very creative, very beloved house!

BIOGRAPHY

LAURA SUSSKIND

Laura Susskind has been peddling her jewelry around the San Francisco Bay area for the past four years. Prior to that, she was a self proclaimed "mother at home" who was also a teacher. Laura taught elementary students the dangers of using tobacco, in a unique, county-wide program. She also substituted at her children's school, which enabled her to be well acquainted with her sons' friends. "I still go to the mall or the grocery store and am often greeted by kids I've taught over the years." she says.

"I don't have a long list of accomplishments to my name. I am most proud of the three young men we raised," Laura says. Her sons, Matthew, Andrew, and Joel Jacob all presently attend college. Laura enjoys cooking with husband Mark, traveling together, exercising and gardening. They all also adore their klutzy Springer Spaniel puppy "Lily."

AUTHOR'S ACKNOWLEDGMENTS

Compiling and editing a book such as this is a solitary pursuit, in spite of the constant contact with people—a contradiction, I realize. I begin by networking and searching for contributing writers. This is a project made possible by the internet; I put out the word to people across the map, so that everyone will scour their brains for the "raw material" that I need for the theme of the book. During this period of inquiry, there is a tremendous amount of time spent on the phone and the internet, dispensing information to people who are potential writers and who are for the most part, strangers to me—sent in my direction by my "scouts." So first of all, I want to thank my scouts—without them I would have no network! You all know who you are. You seem to know everyone in the world or how to get to everyone—proving the "six degrees of separation theory" to me again and again. Specific categories of people that I needed for this book (artists, musicians, writers, adventurers, etc. and those people who are just champions at living a creative life in general) were practically hand delivered to me.

Then I start introducing myself to my candidates, explaining the mission and the scope and the requirements of the project to each and every prospective writer in an ongoing process, requiring months. Interviewing, gathering information, questioning, evaluating, sorting, persuading and editing and encouraging; it requires more effort to explain to people what I am doing and obtain their commitment to writing a chapter than it does to just get down to the process of doing it. If it were possible to see people's eyes glaze over by email or phone, I would have seen that reaction dozens of times. ("You are *Who?*" "You are doing WHAT?" "How did you get my name?" is usually their initial reaction. Sometimes followed by a click as the phone goes dead…I am often placed in the same category as the unsolicited telemarketer, in email communication I am seen as the dreaded Spam.) But I have learned to *hear* the "glazed-over-eyes reaction" in a voice, or a cough, or a sigh or even an audible gulp; and that is my first red-flag clue that I will probably have to move on to the next possibility, and the next, and then perhaps the next, searching for the brave and the willing. The ones with a great story of epiphany to tell and the eagerness to get it down on paper. The ones who begin to sizzle with excitement as we talk on the phone. The ones who light up the wire with a palpable energy.

Those kinds of risk-taking, positive action people are rare. People do not exactly line up and take a number in wanting to write for a book; it surprises me how few accept the challenge. I have learned not to dwell on the less than enthusiastic ones who cannot decide—who straddle the fence—because they are generally the ones who drop out of the project mid-stream. Scrambling to fill places in the Table of Contents and then maintain them with extraordinary people and fascinating stories is my constant struggle.

After just so much of that routine, the tendency is to not say much to special friends and family who are "outside" of the project about how things are going because I am simply talked out. I thank all of you who remained sincerely interested in how things were going with my second book, and were brave enough to ask, and keep asking; and willing to sit down and stop what you were doing and truly listen to my reply and offer support. That was a gift to me.

I thank the writers of the first book for *being* the writers of the first book—you were my "learning curve" and the example to be followed in so many ways for this second book. You constantly reminded me what *dedication* was with your determination to write, and therefore I knew what to look for in my search for writers for this book—I knew what it would take to get me where I needed to go by the standards that you and I set together in the very beginning. You were the first; you will always be the first, and I thank you for the courage required for you to write your stories. When I heard that a psychologist was recommending our first book to some of his patients who were experiencing various difficulties, I knew that was reason enough to have told your stories. I am proud and thankful for you.

I thank my highly gifted and creative children for their constant support and encouragement. My artistically talented daughter Kelly has designed both of my book covers (as well as writing a splendid chapter in the first book) and she has been, once again, my balance and my voice of sanity in compiling and editing this book as well. She and I are usually on the same page in life as well as in creativity, and yet every once in awhile when I have lapsed into a momentary stupor and wandered off the project's path, she will point out the obvious to me and reel me back in, and I value that very much. She is the only other person who would be close enough to my own vision for the book project to be able to do that. She has great instincts. My son, Thomas C. Brown, a most talented writer, is currently publishing a non-fiction book of his own which will be available on Amazon.com. It is an accounting of his hair-raising, global adventures in search of oil as well as a bold statement on the oil crisis told from inside the industry looking out. We have discussed his book for years and I am pleased and proud for him to finally be published, and the timing could not be more perfect. To have these common literary interests with my grown children is indeed rare and wonderful, and it would also be a great source of pride to my mother, their Grandma R. She was a fine English teacher and the oldest child of Arthur Evans, a professor at Miami University in Ohio, who wrote a book on Botany so many years ago.

My sister Vicki has more than risen to the occasion in her help to me; not just with her wise "scouting" suggestions but with her constant crazy humor and supportive calls and emails. She understands the creative force; being highly creative herself, and living in a family of lovable eccentrics. She understands the artistic mind; she knows creativity when she sees it in a child or an adult—having raised two extraordinary sons and been a legendary teacher—and her nurturing of the artistic temperament usually brings support to any wild plan or off the wall idea I might have. And I have had a few.

Once again I thank my husband Ed, who has finally stopped speculating about the possibility that I just might write a book someday, and acknowledged that it might even be happening for the second time. His suggestions to calmly step away from the computer come less frequently now. He has learned to make a great homemade salsa and has mastered other delicious recipes for his basic survival during book deadline times. He remains tolerant and supportive of my humble efforts to be a published writer, and his expressions of quiet amazement and pride do not go unnoticed.

Last but not least...

When the first book was published, I felt that the world as I knew it had lost its mind—and now I feel that it is certifiably insane. It seems things have escalated from bad to worse. Inside of this chaos however, I continue to find solace and hope in creativity, as do many others. The common challenge for creative people is to communicate what is in our hearts, souls and minds in order to leave a positive mark on the world, and to still be able to do that in stressful and unstable times. What could be a more noble purpose?

Therefore I thank the amazingly gifted and creative people who have written their stories for this book. The book offers you a glimpse into their thought processes, struggles, frustrations and intuitive breakthroughs which we term "epiphanies;" they are relatively few people but they are fine representatives speaking for all creative creatures. Their stories carry universal messages—their teachings are life lessons. These contributing writers are simply hoping to be remembered as being sincerely dedicated to the greater good in a world gone mad. I am so appreciative for the eloquence, honesty, wisdom and beauty of expression of these men and women—they have all become my friends and compatriots in the life-long scramble for expression. They range in age from about twenty-seven to a proud seventy-eight. They do not lack energy or enthusiasm in any of those decades—never failing to provide me with text when I needed it and conversation after conversation for the purpose of editing and polishing their stories so that they would be told gracefully and powerfully. I thank them from the bottom of my artistic soul.

Creativity is what gets us up in the morning and it is what we dream about at night. Take away our brushes, our canvases, our tablets, our computers, our gardens, our kitchens, our Sunday afternoons at the movies, our theatre, our travel, our music, our poetry, our voices, our wood, clay and stone, our adventurous spirit and our other creative activities and you might as well just kill us now. We live in the world of ideas; the neon "OPEN" sign constantly blinking in our windows; our eyes. Give us something intriguing to think about and we will run with it. Let us imagine; let us dream; let us create. Without this we would shrivel up. I cannot thank you enough—you—who wrote your hearts out and told stories of your life-changing epiphanies within your challenging lives. You are the humble but iridescent souls I needed to find for this book. Perhaps it is you who found me...and I am grateful that you did.